Christiane Lütge, Mark Stein (Eds.)

Crossovers

Fremdsprachendidaktik in globaler Perspektive

herausgegeben von

Prof. Dr. Christiane Lütge
(Ludwig-Maximilians-Universität München)

Band 6

LIT

CROSSOVERS

Postcolonial Studies
and Transcultural Learning

edited by

Christiane Lütge and Mark Stein

LIT

This book is printed on acid-free paper.

Bibliographic information published by the Deutsche Nationalbibliothek
The Deutsche Nationalbibliothek lists this publication in the Deutsche Nationalbibliografie; detailed bibliographic data are available on the Internet at http://dnb.d-nb.de.

ISBN 978-3-643-90878-0

A catalogue record for this book is available from the British Library

Klosbachstr. 107
CH-8032 Zürich
Tel. +41 (0) 44-251 75 05
E-Mail: zuerich@lit-verlag.ch http://www.lit-verlag.ch
Distribution:
In the UK: Global Book Marketing, e-mail: mo@centralbooks.com
In North America: International Specialized Book Services, e-mail: orders@isbs.com
In Germany: LIT Verlag Fresnostr. 2, D-48159 Münster
Tel. +49 (0) 2 51-620 32 22, Fax +49 (0) 2 51-922 60 99, e-mail: vertrieb@lit-verlag.de
In Austria: Medienlogistik Pichler-ÖBZ, e-mail: mlo@medien-logistik.at
e-books are available at www.litwebshop.de

Acknowledgements

The editors would like to thank all contributors for their lecture at the University of Münster and for contributing their work to this volume. We'd also like to acknowledge Caroline Kögler's artwork on the front cover. And the staff at LIT for their professional handling of the project. A big thank you to Ina Batzke for her professional technical editorship of the present volume.

Christiane Lütge would like to thank Michele Stannard for reading her chapter.

Mark Stein would like to thank Caroline Kögler for her welcome suggestions on the draft version of his chapter.

Contents

CHRISTIANE LÜTGE & MARK STEIN

Postcolonial Studies and Transcultural Learning

The intersections between Postcolonial Studies and Teaching English as a Foreign Language (TEFL) are not only manifold but also highly significant and it is these intersections and crossovers, which this volume seeks to explore. The postcolonial field can be conceived of as a critical discourse which examines, addresses and critiques colonialism – including its current incarnations. TEFL not only theorizes the practice of teaching English, one of its key concerns is to enable teachers and learners to reflect critically not only on the cultural implications of teaching and learning a dominant language; the implications of using a 'foreign' language, of negotiating overlapping and yet distinct cultural spaces; and of intervening, culturally, linguistically, both in source and target languages also requires reflection. It is such inter- and transdisciplinary questions which are being addressed in the present collection. This volume, then, brings together papers that explore, perform and theorize various kinds of crossovers, be they disciplinary, thematic or intermedial ones. It seeks to contribute to the growing body of work on disciplinary crossovers between Postcolonial Studies and TEFL with respect to various aspects of teaching in the broadest sense (both, at university or school level). Contributors address the revised literary canons of our postcolonial and globalized world; the new diversity and emphatic pluralism in many English-speaking countries; and aspects of 'decolonizing the mind' in their impact on transcultural learning. The book also contributes to thematic crossovers – referring to transcultural discourses, fictions of migration and ecodidactics, fields that invite students and learners of all ages to engage with and intervene in global, cultural, political and social debates and contexts. Finally, the area of intermedial crossovers are addressed, those across different media such as texts, films, photography etc., scaling the divide between scribal, visual and cultural literacy. These perspectives bring into play multi-faceted representations of cultural encounters in a variety of locations and contexts, especially in terms of imagining otherness and the dynamic re-negotiations of cultural meaning.

Edward Said has underscored the centrality of 'the figure of crossing over' to his work: "The fact of migration is extraordinarily impressive to me: that movement from the precision and concreteness of one form of life transmuted or imported into the other." He continues,

> there is this tradition which you are required to understand and learn and so on, but you cannot really be of it [...] Then you get the crossings over [...] and then of course the whole problematic of exile and immigration enters into it, the people who simply don't belong in any culture; that is the great modern, or if you like, post-modern fact, the standing outside of cultures.[1]

In this conversation with Raymond Williams, Said questions the notion of *belonging* and conceives of cultures as *man-made*, as constructed, rather than given. Whilst he celebrates the cultural outsider, who belongs nowhere, Said is fascinated by crossing over, by changing sides, by belonging first to one culture and then another.

The way we use this term in the present volume, *crossover* not only refers to the subject in an intercultural situation; it also references the transdisciplinary energies released on the questions formulated above. The transgression of boundaries, disciplinary, national, cultural, has the potential to question, to abrogate, and also to re-inscribe boundaries.

Crossing boundaries is one of the key issues for EFL teaching. It is an objective not only for the foreign language classroom in schools that are facing increasingly global influences both in terms of more heterogeneous societies – and hence classrooms –, but also with a view to the reflection of this growing heterogeneity in the literature, media and material used in these classrooms.

The teaching of literature and culture always addresses questions of belonging and is closely connected with the question of identity, part of which is the discourse of 'us' and 'them'. Overcoming these binary oppositions is one of the main goals in inter- and transcultural learning. Closely connected with this concept is the notion of 'changing perspectives', one of the dominant principles in literature didactics. Still, the question remains whether the experience of otherness in various contexts – not necessarily restricted to notions of cultural otherness – should be discarded as an experience quickly to be overcome or rather be made productive. It seems that the impact of postcolonial literature with its versatile topics and multi-faceted backgrounds has not yet been exploited well enough – both with a view to text selection and also regarding methodological questions of classroom application beyond simplistic and essentialist approaches. This volume, then, addresses these processes with a view to exploring and understanding their critical potential, in the classroom and beyond.

In the first article, Miriam Mayrhofer and Susanne Reichl attempt to emphasize the potential of visual narratives for the EFL classroom. *The Lost Thing*, by the Australian artist Shaun Tan, serves as an example to demonstrate how these

---

[1] Taken from "Media, Margins and Modernity", a Conversation between Raymond Williams and Edward Said, Appendix to Raymond Williams, *The Politics of Modernism: Against The New Conformists*, page 196.

narratives combine visual complexity with inter- and transcultural concepts and thus invite the 'reader' to gradually unfold the different layers of meaning. After an introduction into visual literacy and the ideas of inter- and transcultural learning, Mayrhofer and Reichl discuss the use of visual narratives in the classroom and provide a detailed analysis of the most important visual and content-related aspects of *The Lost Thing*.

Looking at three overall topics in the light of postcolonial environmentalism, Kylie Crane takes a double-focused approach dovetailing postcolonial and eco-critical perspectives into a politically charged patterning of textual analysis. Under the headings of 'waste', 'wilderness' and 'whales', Crane discusses environmental issues evoked by human behaviour and cultural concepts, topics of human habitation as well as the relationship between human and non-human agents across cultures, while proposing primary literature for the EFL classroom and critically assessing the material's potential.

Inspired by a recent postcolonial perspective on trauma fiction, Grit Alter considers the residential school experiences of First Nations, Inuit and Métis peoples in Canada, captured in picturebooks for children. A close reading of Nicola I. Campbell's *Shi-shi-etko* (2005) and *Shin-chi's Canoe* (2008) attempts to demonstrate how writing and publishing processes can be used as a form of working through traumatic experiences. Alter parallels the ideas of trauma fiction with the concept of developing Intercultural Communicative Competence (ICC) for intercultural learning scenarios, both in the EFL classroom and at university level.

Arguing that contemporary problems such as overcoming binary oppositions can only be understood in relation to the past, Peter Freese's article presents verbal, visual and auditory material on the history of the U.S. national anthem and its recent Spanish version as suitable means for introducing the controversial relationship between one's identity and one's language into the EFL-classroom. The article not only sketches the gradual development of an 'American' identity by defining unconditional assimilation, Americanization, Anglo-Saxon racialism, cultural pluralism, and multiculturalism as the basic attitudes in the course of U.S. history, but also discusses how different historical and contemporary American approaches to making immigrants learn English have a high transfer value for German EFL-learners and can increase their intercultural competence.

In the following article, Werner Delanoy focuses on postcolonial thinking and its translation into the EFL context. Working with two of the children's books of Mexican-American writer Gloria Anzaldúa as examples, he elaborates on the concept of postcoloniality, emphasizing the notion of cultural hybridity and the trans-modernity of her approach, before presenting a concrete translation project, carried out in an ELT context and also incorporating a plurilingual dimension.

Mark Stein addresses the idea of crossovers with an essayistic chapter on modes of translocal representation and the circulation of narratives of porosity. Despite its brevity, the chapter roams widely, connecting 'twitter litter' to novels by Teju Cole and Mohsin Hamid, and Judith Butler's concept of "grievable lives" to textual translocations. The concept of porosity is deployed here in order to account for spatial and textual connections which these 'cultural products' fashion, exploit, and transform at the same time. Porosity has the potential to render borders – despite their evident and frequently harmful function of division and separation – as connectors, as membranes, which foster and modulate connection, traffic, cross-fertilisation, and allogamy.

Finally, Christiane Lütge points out some trodden paths and pitfalls in the discourse on inter- and transcultural learning with postcolonial literature. In her article, she reflects the educational dilemma that lies at the heart of the dichotomy of 'self' and 'other', a dichotomy which is usually sought to be overcome and which yet serves ever so often as a starting-point for inter- and transcultural learning. She points out the potential of postcolonial literature in this process of overcoming binaries through awareness raising.

The connections between postcolonial theory and inter- and transcultural learning are manifold. Not only do they offer thematic inspirations and methodological innovations based on questions of text selection for university students or pupils in the literature classroom. More than that, they provide a chance for mutual disciplinary crossovers. Coming to terms with the sometimes fuzzy borders of changing or travelling concepts may be one of the major challenges both for postcolonial studies and TEFL contexts. Their constant and ongoing academic dialogue seems vital, though, in order to provide critical readings of literary and pedagogic approaches.

Miriam Mayrhofer & Susanne Reichl

Shaun Tan's *The Lost Thing*: An Exercise in Looking

The importance of visual input and its multifarious levels of meaning in our daily learning processes has been universally accepted and consequently been incorporated into the scope of interdisciplinary learning aims like visual literacy and transcultural learning. In this paper, we argue that visual narratives like Shaun Tan's The Lost Thing *involve a multitude of both visually complex and culturally rich layers of meaning that merit further analysis and attention, especially in the context of teaching visual literacy, abstract thinking skills and transcultural learning in the English language classroom.*

1. Introduction

In the course of the last century, images have inarguably conquered plenty of territory in our public and private spheres, and have thus altered the way we as recipients encounter visual media today. Images have largely been responsible for shaping and constructing views about other cultures and ways of living. But what is it that makes the nature of images appear so emotionally immediate, allegedly credible and ultimately ambiguous, and in how far do visual narratives differ from verbal ones? Furthermore, how can these traits be exploited for educational purposes, and which concrete multimodal media could be used in order to focus on the inclusion of visual literacy and critical thinking skills in classrooms? And how can we combine two important learning aims, visual literacy and intercultural learning, into a productive approach that is adoptable in the English language classroom?

The following article suggests different ways of handling some of the major challenges set by today's abounding media landscape and a communicative language curriculum. By engaging in an 'exercise in looking', an analysis of the picture book *The Lost Thing* by Australian artist Shaun Tan should invite the promotion of visual literacy as a starting point for both visual and cultural thinking skills. We will first introduce the concept of visual literacy, then move on to ideas of inter- and transcultural learning and a discussion of visual narratives in the classroom, before we actually offer an analysis of the various textual and visual layers of *The Lost Thing*, from close visual analysis to an investigation of its political subtext. It is our aim to demonstrate its potential for classroom use rather than to suggest concrete activities for teaching it in an EFL context. In our experience, it is up to the individual practitioner to adapt promising material such as this one to his or her own pedagogic and didactic purposes.

2. The Power of Images and Learning to Look

Among the abundance of different media in 21st century Western societies, images prevail with remarkable supremacy (see Black 2009: 690), and vision is one, if not the most significant sense among the spectrum of human perception. Therefore, it is little wonder that we perceive two-dimensional pictures, in other words representations or "illusion[s]" (Gombrich 1960: 5) of the real world, much as we perceive our 'actual' visual surroundings (Bang 2000: 81). This is essentially what links images to the "affective domain" of experience (Avgerinou 2001a, 2001b, 2003, quoted in Avgerinou 2009: 29), or more precisely, this is what makes images so emotionally powerful in our everyday lives.

This unique asset of the visual becomes especially obvious when we look at the value of images in learning. The neurological processing of images is neither located in nor limited to only one area of our cognitive system: Rather, the perceptual processing of visual content draws on a whole range of brain areas, involving neurological, psychological and aesthetic aspects, forming thus an integral part of learning processes altogether (LeDoux 1998: 16, quoted in Barry 2005: 57). However, even though we might be 'naturals' in seeing, does this automatically make us experts in looking?

Being so immediate in their mental processing, the most basic visual skills do not require explicit training but are mostly acquired by natural exposure to visual stimuli (Smith et al. 2005: ix; Messaris 1994: 9; Barry 2005: 45). Therefore, the way in which we process visual information is deeply rooted in our past experiences and dependent on the extent to which we have been exposed to reading socially agreed codes in our visual surroundings (see Messaris 1994: 133; Gombrich 1960: 16; Bang 2000: 29).

With ceaselessly increasing possibilities to share and perceive images through media and social networks, there is no doubt that today's percipients need to adapt to the more and more sophisticated visual content they encounter on a daily basis. Quite obviously, this entails more than just distinguishing the simplest or most obvious layer of meaning in images: the various contexts, the origin(s) and production history of images contribute to the overall significance of visual content, especially if we consider the manifold appearances of "visual manipulation" in Western media (Messaris 1994: 10). Enabling a young generation of students to take on a critical and therefore empowering approach to visual input, therefore, requires some degree of formation beyond the mere exposure to visual media over time (see Messaris 1994: 133).

3. Teaching Visual Literacy

Even before today's media landscape had evolved in its highly complex forms, a rising number of scholars from a variety of disciplines focused on the pedagogical questions arising in the wake of the upcoming information age and digital paradigm shift of the last decades before the millennium. On average, their research circled around two main questions: How can one possibly prepare a new generation for the challenges and possibilities posed by visually dominated media, and which capacities would recipients and users of media have to acquire in order to face visual stimuli with adequate competence, healthy criticism and appreciative attention (see Black 2009: 689)?

As a result, a new term, visual literacy, emerged and has continued to describe essential visual and critical thinking skills required from a new generation of 'viewers' in order to remain self-governed and empowered in a world of sensory overload (among others, see Cope / Kalantzis 2000). The concept of visual literacy itself, though resisting hard-and-fast definitions owing to its versatility in all kinds of scientific areas, can be broadly defined as "the ability to understand and use images, including the ability to think, learn and express oneself in terms of images" (Braden / Hortin 1982: 38, quoted in Seglem / Witte 2009: 217)[1]. Hence, this term comprises a number of both receptive and productive skills, which makes visual literacy a complex and overarching set of skills (see Hallet 2008: 221, also see Mayrhofer 2014).

Today it is commonly accepted that a certain degree of visual literacy is needed in order to ensure our learners' cognitive and cultural development (see Messaris 1994: 125; Seglem / Witte 2009: 217). Especially the years after the millennium have shown a growing awareness of the importance of raising visual literacy in students (see Black 2009: 689). As a result, most current theory on visual literacy training appears to have shifted from the question of why to how to include visual literacy in educational settings (see Cazden et al. 1996; Mayrhofer 2014: 67ff). As far as the actual inclusion of visual literacy in school subjects is concerned, we are convinced that one of the main potential inclusion areas of visual literacy (apart from obvious choices like art or art history classes) is located in language classrooms, for two main reasons.

[1] For an extensive overview on the many aspects and the historical development of the concept of visual literacy, see Avgerinou 2001a, 2001b, 2003, quoted in Avgerinou 2009: 29.

On the one hand, images have the potential to evoke strong and immediate emotional response in their onlookers through their use of colour, perspective and composition (Kress / Van Leeuwen 1996: 165ff; Seidl 2007: 5), which makes them valuable triggers for meaningful, communicative tasks (see Messaris 1994: 175; Seglem / Witte 2009: 217f; Richards / Rodgers 2001: 223). On the other hand, images might convey some layers of meaning immediately, while the full range of their various aspects of meaning can barely be decoded instantaneously, nor by each percipient alike (see Seidl 2007: 4; Mayrhofer 2014: 9ff). Therefore, the effect of visual content on a group of viewers, or on a group of learners, can create a natural urge or simply an opportunity to communicate, discuss or question the different meaning(s) of images (see Snyder 2014).

If we take into account the previously mentioned natural acquisition of a basic degree of visual literacy (see Smith et al. 2005: ix; Messaris 1994: 9; Barry 2005: 45), obviously, teaching visual literacy does not rely so much on teaching and learning things 'from scratch', but rather on the further development, refinement and active critical reflection of what learners have already acquired through prior exposure to visual media. However, regardless of the concrete setting of visual literacy teaching, enhancing this set of skills in learners would obviously involve a non-prescriptive, learner-centred approach to teaching, in which instructors and learners would need to confront each other's perspectives on a regular basis (see Hallet 2008: 212; Höpel 2008: 64). In this way, visual literacy teaching does not only further critical thinking skills, but also promotes general communicative and social skills.

Nevertheless, the way in which visual literacy is incorporated into a language teaching syllabus remains, of course, open to the pedagogic practitioners in charge. In general, though, the structural assets of visual texts and their effect on recipients push for two broad ideological directions. Any inclusion of visual literacy in language learning would first and foremost require a communicative approach to language teaching, in the scope of which language is used in authentic, meaningful contexts (see Richards / Rodgers 2001: 223). Secondly, both teachers and students would need to remain open towards learning through new and unfamiliar visual input, to engage in the discovery of its meaning(s) via language and to uphold a collaborative working atmosphere (see Seidl 2007: 6; Seglem / Witte 2009: 217; Black 2009: 696).

Apart from the general cognitive, communicative and social abilities that show us the broad scope of visual literacy, which skills does a basic degree of visual literacy entail, after all? Although there can hardly ever be just one answer to this question, we argue that there are certain components that are undoubtedly a basic prerequisite for the perception of any visual content and thus, constitute the 'technical' basis of the term visual literacy (Kress / Van Leeuwen

1996: 154). As various different researchers claim, this basic 'kit' of visual literacy skills comprises, among others, an understanding of perspective and angle, of colour, and of the effects of composition and framing (see Bang 2000: 7ff, Kress / Van Leeuwen 1996: 135ff, 165, 181). Having said that, we argue that visual literacy is at no point limited to these skills, but, as a set of social and cognitive abilities, extends and shifts its scope permanently in conjunction with the visual media landscape. On top of that, a learner's visual literacy also relies on their sheer capacity to 'look closely', or in other words, to dedicate time and energy to the perception of (and possibly even research about) the unfamiliar or unknown contents they encounter in their surroundings.

Our analysis in the second part of this article is intended to show how both of these aspects, the visual and the cultural layers of images, complement each other to create a lasting impact on readers who engage in looking closely at complex, thought-provoking visual narratives.

4. Learning with and about Cultures

Working with images and their complex structures, meanings and effects on their percipients cannot only open up ways to fulfil visual literacy teaching aims, but is also a viable tool for teaching and learning about cultures. In foreign language classrooms across Europe and beyond, language teaching has long transcended its immediate function of catering for basic communicative needs and has developed a concern with cultural learning, in a variety of guises and terms. Most curricula feature a learning aim that is commonly known as 'intercultural learning', or 'intercultural education' (IE) in the terms of the Council of Europe, and focuses on the dynamics in the relationship of self and other, both represented through diverse cultural practices, and both challenged in their potential for understanding and communication by exactly those divergent practices.

While curricula seem to provide well enough for the aims of intercultural education, a survey conducted for the Council of Europe in 2012 comes to the conclusion that in practice we must still speak of IE as the "poor relation" (Beacco 2011: 1), and that intercultural learning is rarely seen as an aim in itself but rather as serving the more functional purposes of learning the structures and lexis of a language. IE, according to this study, needs to be a much more integral part of language learning, and not so much in a comparative sense, as the 'inter' of the term often seems to be understood. Beacco comes to the conclusion that intercultural competence is often tied to a simplistic vision of a culture as a nation represented by a language, and that the knowledge that teachers try to construct in such a situation is simplified as well, equating as it does one culture with one world view, and ignoring any internal division within the "other" society or indeed students' own (Beacco 2011: 1-2; Byram 2009: 5).

In cultural theory[2] and postcolonial studies[3] alike, the transcultural paradigm has long been acknowledged to make up for these reductions and simplifications, which result from a monolithic view of culture as a kind of contained entity with clearly marked boundaries, or a set of essential characteristics that people are basically stuck with. Originating in the aim to account for the kind of cultural networks that necessarily come into existence in a globally linked society that is marked by a multiplicity of cultural connections and ways of synthesising or syncretising them, transculturality points to the impossibility of allocating the self and the other to any clearly defined cultural space. Rather, transculturality dispenses with the spatial metaphor, evoking instead a network of relations that intersect and continuously call into question the legitimacy of perceived boundaries between so-called 'cultures'. In a recent contribution to the teaching of the New Literatures in English, Sabine Doff and Frank Schulze-Engler provide a rationale for a transcultural approach to replace the intercultural paradigm. In their plea to go "[b]eyond 'Other Cultures'", which is also part of the title of their collection and its introductory article, they suggest the following scenario:

> If a more or less absolute cultural difference is posited as the starting point for processes of 'intercultural learning', and essentialist binary oppositions between one's own culture and 'strange', 'alien' or 'other cultures' are set up, the well-meant pedagogical objective of 'intercultural understanding' actually reproduces stereotyped notions of cultural difference that are hard to reconcile with the social and cultural realities that teachers and learners are faced with in an increasingly globalised world. (Doff / Schulze-Engler 2011: 1)

This moving away from the simplistic assumption that individuals are bound by the respective cultures they belong to or inhabit (again, a spatial metaphor) suggests a variety of alternative cultural practices that grant individuals more agency in the handling of their multifarious cultural influences and resources. Concepts such as hybridity, creolisation, appropriation and a view of culture as a social practice, as 'doing'[4], rather than as something that individuals are subjected to, have steered the debate away from the notion of radical alterity that is often the result of comparative approaches of "cultures" (Doff / Schulze-Engler 2011: 2f). Such a view lends more agency to the individuals 'doing' culture, which is especially productive in a pedagogical context, since it grants learners

---

[2] See, for instance, Hannerz 1992, Geertz 1973 and Welsch 1999.

[3] See, for instance, Schulze-Engler 2002 and 2006, or Ashcroft 2011.

[4] See the contributions on transdifference studies and on 'doing' culture by Allolio-Näcke / Kalscheuer 2003 and Breinig / Lösch 2002.

more agency, too, with respect to the way they deal with their cultural processes as well.

While Beacco paints a bleak image of the presence of intercultural learning in European classrooms, we would claim that in pedagogical and didactic theory, intercultural learning is a thriving scene, and if the ideas have not quite arrived in all the schools concerned, it is not due to a lack of thinking or writing that has been done on the topic, but rather a problem of transferring the theory to the field. It would go beyond the scope of this paper to elaborate on the various models of inter- and transcultural learning, and the related suggestions (in the context of global citizenship learning, peace education and sustainability learning) that have been made, but we would like to point to a vivid scene, especially productive in but not restricted to German-speaking countries. Those are partly represented by individuals working in the area of postcolonial literatures and basing their views on recent cultural theory (such as Antor 2006, Doff / Schulze-Engler 2011, Volkmann 2011), partly by those working with models of intercultural learning that started out as 'Fremdverstehen' at the University of Gießen and have since been developed further (such as Bredella 2002, Burwitz-Melzer 2002, Freitag-Hild 2010, Hallet 2002) and partly by those suggesting dialogic approaches to language learning that include but do not prioritise the notion of 'culture' (such as Delanoy 2008a, 2008b). A good portion of the work done by teacher educators or pedagogic practitioners in this area is based on Michael Byram's notions of intercultural communicative competence (1997) or Claire Kramsch's view of culture being intrinsically connected with language (1998).

What all these approaches have in common is the aim to promote respect and understanding between people from a diversity of backgrounds in the context of a foreign language, and the way in which they differ is in the degree to which a dissolution of borders is granted to the notion of culture and to the centrality of the concept of alterity. Whereas Byram (1997 or 2009) and Bredella (2002) seem to regard cultures as relatively stable containers and the individual as innately able to distinguish between his/her own culture and the 'other' culture, Doff and Schulze-Engler stress that such distinctions cannot easily be made in a globalised world, and that a clear identification of self and other has become impossible (2011). The "cultural otherness" that, according to Byram (2009: 6), is one of the aims of experiencing interculturality, is as problematic in its theoretical position as it is unproductive for a concrete pedagogical setting in which many participants already come equipped with a network of diverse cultural connections, which they will not be able to locate with either their 'own' culture or an entirely foreign one. Similarly problematic is the way in which most work on the topic deals with the notion of understanding, raising the expectations that humans are or should be capable of understanding others. In cognitive psychology, socio-constructivist learning theory and sociolinguistics, there has long been full agreement that even conversational understanding is only partially possible and that any kind of learning is constructed and not reproduced in its completeness (see Reichl 2009: 24-26, or 2013). How, then, can we expect learners to have the power of understanding the cultural practices of someone they are learning to accept as their extreme other?[5]

While both inter- and transcultural approaches have undergone criticism (see, for instance, Auernheimer 2006), we would like to side with Delanoy's view that maybe the term itself does not matter quite as much as the practice implied in it (2008a: 96-7). And while we go with the editors of this volume and use the term 'transcultural' on the basis of recent cultural theory, as outlined above, we would also like to stress that many models of intercultural learning would be compatible with our views.

5. Visual Narratives for Transcultural Learning in Language Teaching

Having established a basis for teaching both visual literacy skills and transcultural learning, we come back to the medium of the image itself. The type of visual input with which students in language classes are provided depends on both the content and the aesthetic structures of visual media. While the applicability of visual input is dependent on a variety of factors (see Griffith 2010), among which we also find highly subjective aspects such as personal likes or dislikes of readers, there are general aesthetic characteristics in visual texts that cause certain responses in percipients in general. Even more so, such visual features can be enhanced when combined into a sequential narrative, that is, into a graphic narrative or picture book. As with verbal texts, which also evoke a variety of subjective responses as well as giving rise to intersubjective meaning-making, the reading of multimodal narratives also depends on how far conventionalised the meaning-making processes connected to the medium are.

Most references to teaching about and around culture/s draw on verbal texts from non-dominant national or ethnic backgrounds that enable empathy on the basis of an internal perspective, an individual who is concerned with racism, migration, refuge, and other identity-threatening issues. Our example, Shaun Tan's *The Lost Thing*, is a multimodal text that refers, as the title suggests, to a

[5] Burwitz-Melzer is an exception here: she acknowledges already in the title of her book, *Allmähliche Annäherungen*, that we cannot expect any kind of full understanding (2003).

thing rather than a human being, and the story is narrated from an external perspective. This story is not only exceptional in its way of addressing some of the previously mentioned issues about culture and identity through multimodal ways of expression, but it also shows how multimodal texts could help include both of the two aforementioned learning aims, visual literacy and transcultural learning, in language classes. We would claim that transcultural learning works extremely well with images and with the skills promoted by visual literacy education, and that visual narratives make interesting material for teaching these aspects in the English language classroom. The reasons for this assumption lie in the structural assets of the medium.

Although visual narratives were born as a medium "in the marketplace" (Wolk 2007: 22), they have slowly entered public awareness as a viable form of literary expression (McCloud 1993: 45), especially in Europe and the US, where comic book sales have been steadily increasing in the last decade (see Griffith 2010: 182). One of the main reasons for this development is that visual narratives or 'comics' have ever since delighted their readers by giving them the simple but inherently pleasant experience of "being caught up in a story" (Wolk 2007: 23). The art form of comics achieves this, as Scott McCloud explains, because it is more than a "mere hybrid" of images and words (1993: 92). By building tensions between different modes of expression, the medium explicitly demands the reader's active participation in the process of reading visual and verbal texts, and as such, involves them in the process of meaning making (ibid., also Eisner 2008: 57). As McCloud rightly states, it is exactly this demanding process of "observing the parts and perceiving the whole [or] mentally completing [...] [by drawing from] past experience" in which deep reader involvement originates (1993: 63, 92). In order for the narrative to be decoded, understood and, ultimately, enjoyed by the reader, the structural assets depicted are required to ignite an identification process aided by emotive responses, which in turn, is caused by the reader's real-world associations with the visual content (McCloud 1993: 33). What is widely known as a typically 'comic-like', simplified iconic artistic style is intended to cause exactly this reaction; to enable the reader to amplify the given structures with meaning and thus, to make meaning of the narrative from a highly subjective point of view (McCloud 1993: 30; Wolk 2007: 23).

Therefore, it can well be said that the iconic depiction of visual content is "a metaphor for the subjectivity of perception" (Wolk 2007: 23), which means that the structural assets of a visual narrative make it a highly involving and visually stimulating medium. Apart from this aspect of visual narratives, the past of comic or picture book publishing also shows that this medium is not limited to any genre or degree of complexity[6], and open to any balance in relation to the visual and verbal mode (McCloud 1993: 45, 89f, Nikolajeva / Scott 2001: 12). Through the subjectivity and the openness of the meaning of images, and consequently, also of visual narratives, stories presented in this medium are bound to confront their readers with a certain degree of ambiguity. Instead of seeing this as a lack in specificity, the openness of the medium should be appreciated as a viable asset that has the power to initiate active discussions about the various potential meanings of a narrative.

In the case of *The Lost Thing*, its 'potential meanings' embrace such topics as the constant negotiation of self and other, the intersecting networks of local and global cultures, the alienation of the self in postmodern society, questions of belonging and home, the transcending of borders and categories, and many more. It is a consequence of the wide meaning potential of visual narratives as such and of this particular example that we suggest reading *The Lost Thing* on a variety of textual and visual levels.

6. *The Lost Thing* and Its Various Levels of Meaning

We are not the only or the first ones to suggest that Shaun Tan's work makes for excellent teaching material: Evelyn Arizpe et al. recently published the result of an empirical study with children on Shaun Tan's wordless narrative *The Arrival*, entitled *Visual Journeys through Word-less Narratives* (2014), in which they applied a reader response methodology to children who themselves had an immigrant background. Arizpe et al. refer to *The Arrival* as a "visual invitation" (2014: 159) that students respond to, and this, we would argue, characterises *The Lost Thing* as well. Other than *The Arrival*, *The Lost Thing* employs verbal language as well as pictures, and while Arizpe et al. claim that "Tan employs a variety of complex artistic techniques and aspects of sequential art narrative to provide a network of wordless cues for readers to make meaning and put together a coherent story" (2014: 159), we would claim that with more mature readers, the aim is not simply to put together a coherent narrative, but to detect and analyse a variety of levels of meaning that can be explored in quite some depth. Therefore, we would not classify *The Lost Thing* as a picture book for children in the first place, but as a picture book for all ages. For whatever readership and audience, *The Lost Thing* is, as Ommundsen describes it, "a many-layered, visually and verbally inventive text which cannot be pinned down to a

[6] See, for example, the graphic memoirs *Maus* (by Art Spiegelman) and *Persepolis* (by Marjane Satrapi).

single reading" (2009: 223). Or, as the artist himself puts it, his picture books are simply aimed at

> anyone who reads and looks. That is, anyone who is curious, who enjoys strangeness, mystery and oddity, who likes asking questions and using their imagination, and is prepared to devote time and attention accordingly. (Tan 2002: Picture Books)

Although Tan refers specifically to his own works here, he actually describes vital assets that apply to picture books and other sequential art in general. Being so open in its structural outset, the medium of visual narrative could appeal to a potentially unlimited number of target groups. However, recent developments on the market show that visual narratives are especially popular with today's generation of teen-aged students (see Griffith 2010: 182). A visual narrative like *The Lost Thing*, thus, deploying the highly involving but also ambiguous structural assets of a multimodal narrative and the transcultural scope of its story, presents itself as a rich tool for both visual literacy teaching and transcultural learning in a language classroom.

As Stephens points out, *The Lost Thing* "proliferate[s] meanings" and employs an "excessive use of signs" (2008: 94), and we would suggest that these characteristics turn it into an invitation to look, an encouragement to see, and represents perfect material to train visual literacy with. The picture book provides a variety of angles from which to approach looking and seeing, and our structure in the following analyses is based on a recognition of various levels of interpretation. While the obvious structure of picture books would suggest an analysis on the verbal and on the visual level (and a comparative analysis of the two), we have found a number of other textual layers in the book that are worth investigating. If this seems too lofty a proceeding for the language classroom, it is nothing that learners need to be made aware of; it merely enables a relatively structured approach to the analysis and an insight into the density of the book's meaning potential.

On the verbal level, *The Lost Thing* is about a boy, a first-person narrator, who one day finds a thing on the beach that does not seem to belong anywhere. He tries to find a place for it, and after some unsuccessful attempts he is directed to a place for lost things, says goodbye, and returns to his normal life. This is what the verbal text suggests. The visual text, the material subtexts, the metatexts, intertexts and paratexts, however, tell a different and decidedly more complex story. To classify the lost creature as a 'thing' is clearly the result of an inability on the narrator's side to categorise it as a living creature. Visually, it is presented as a bright red living being of a gigantic teapot-like shape with tentacles, which can communicate to some extent, needs nourishment and some kind of housing, is able to establish contact with human beings and displays very human emotions. It definitely does not fit into the narrator's overregulated world.

Looking at the various verbal and visual levels gives us a chance to move from the general schematic story to a more concrete referential setting. To get from the one to the other takes an exercise in looking. This way our learners' visual literacy and, by extension, their critical thinking skills can be developed.

7. The Visual Text

What do the images of *The Lost Thing* suggest, then? First of all, we need to be clear what we are referring to when we write about the images. There are various layers of images on each page, and the words and the images tend to blend into one another. The main illustrations that accompany and drive forward the verbal text are mounted, together with the verbal text, on reproductions of collages, in which snippets from mechanics textbooks and other sources are visibly glued together. Many of those shreds are formulae, equations, illustrations of mechanics phenomena, but some of those seem to have at least a double meaning. Some of the fragments read 'Meaning', 'Valid for one entry only', 'Testing an Indeterminate Hypothesis', which can be read as alluding to the topic of belonging or questioning the notion of meaning and rational thinking. While some of the mechanics details in the background echo the style of the foregrounded images, the words resonate with the story's leitmotif of someone searching for their place in society. Some of the mounted snippets come from passport applications, entry tickets and other documents that regulate social belonging or public identity and, together with the equations and illustrations, create a material subtext that is worth looking at and scrutinising in detail (which we will do below).

Although *The Lost Thing* might appear surreal and unusual in the visual content it presents its readers, Tan employs a number of canonical aesthetic structures that function independently of individual preference and are thus likely to create specific responses in readers (see Kress / Van Leeuwen 1996: 119ff; Hungerland 1952: 226f).

As mentioned earlier, images can have considerable emotional impact on their percipients, which also applies to negative feelings: if we cannot approach, if we do not take an interest (in the broadest sense of the word) in or cannot understand what we see, we normally withdraw from the act of looking (see Eisner 2008: 51). However, there is a level of meaning at which the aesthetic workings of images function which is actually regardless of our "definitions of beauty" (Hungerland 1952: 230) or personal "evaluation[s]" (ibid.: 231), which makes their perception almost an act of objective "interpretation" (ibid.). Of course, personal preferences will always influence the percipients' reaction to an image (ibid.); however, an understanding and visual literacy of basic aesthetic structures can open our eyes to 'understanding' visual content, especially beyond the question of 'liking' or 'disliking' what and how something is depicted (see ibid.: 234).

Looking at the more objective aesthetic make-up of *The Lost Thing* reveals structures that are strikingly similar to those of the picture book's verbal text and its cultural meta-, inter-, para-, co- and contexts. The main components of the picture book's aesthetic structures, namely image perspective, panel composition, page layout and the use of a certain colour scheme convey a sense of detachment and involvement, of familiarity and estrangement, of self and other. Of all the striking visual assets that *The Lost Thing* offers, the three major areas colour, composition and perspective strike us by far as the most influential aesthetic aspects causing the readers' response to the narrative. Therefore, these basic or 'technical' components of visual literacy analysis merit further analysis.

Perspective

To start with, the reader of *The Lost Thing* is presented with highly expressive and contrasting points of view and perspectives throughout the course of the story. When first encountered, the lost thing appears in miniature size and is looked down upon from the elevated and thus powerful angle of the protagonist, evoking a feeling of natural supremacy in the onlooker, who inevitably identifies with the boy due to the use of back view and over shoulder angle (see Kress / Van Leeuwen 1996: 143-49). After this discovery, the readers are immediately led closer when the protagonist inspects the curious parts and limbs of the lost thing from various sides, before finally marking the beginning of their friendship with both the line "It was quite friendly though, once I started talking to it" and a full-page panel in which the slightly diminished boy looks up to his new companion,

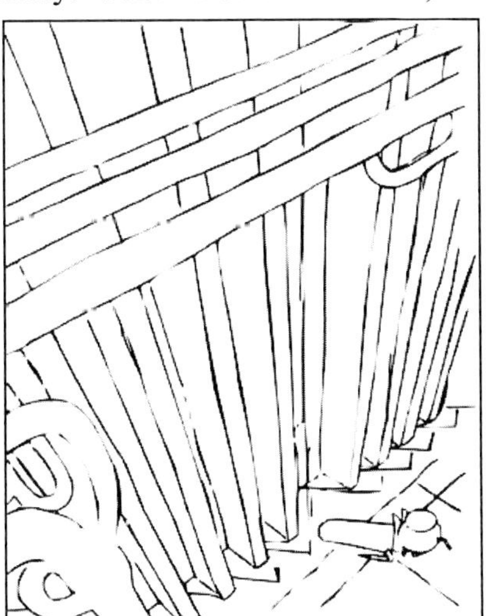

Fig. 1: The boy protagonist and the lost thing in front of the Department of Odds and Ends (vector graphic traced from original by M.M.)

conceding a large amount of picture space and, with that, power and significance to it. Throughout the whole narrative, the fact of the thing being initially lost is most tangible in the frames in which the reader is looking at the thing and its much smaller friend from a very high position and an oblique angle, which both have a strongly distancing and literally belittling effect on the two characters (see Kress / Van Leeuwen 1996: 140ff). Apart from the introduction of the character of *The Lost Thing* on the beach, this applies especially to the long panel of the lifeguard on his high seat making an announcement, to the full-page panel of the thing and the boy standing in front of the "Department of Odds and Ends" (fig. 1), and also to the scene in the "anonymous little street" right before the narrator finds the entrance to the place of "lost things". A highly daunting atmosphere, which alludes to the uncertainty of the lost thing's final fate, marks all of these views.

Opposed to these extreme top-down perspectives, many instances in the narrative shift the reader's point of view to a more and more personal and intimate close-up of the two characters. Not only is the lost thing taking up an increasing amount of space in the sequence of panels showing its search for a place to be, but the readers also find themselves on roughly the same horizontal level, which leads to a high level of identification with the lost creature on the side of the reader (Kress / Van Leeuwen 1996: 149). This is best illustrated by the panel showing the two characters on the street before arriving at the boy's home, by the highly intimate feeding scene in the shelter of the parents' back shed, by the panels showing the boy and the lost thing inside the rather bleak "Department of Odds and Ends" and by the scene of the lost thing rushing towards its designated 'place' in the end. These scenes enable us to identify and feel with the big red protagonist that simply does not belong (ibid.: 149).

Fig. 2: The boy searching for the thing's origin or place (vector graphic traced from original by M.M.)

Composition and Framing

This effect is aided by the composition of panels and page layout, which both go hand in hand with the use of perspective. As mentioned earlier, *The Lost Thing* does not fit in anywhere (until, of course, we adapt our view with a turn of the page and discover that there actually is a place for it, too). Its 'ill-fitting' existence is reflected by the thing's visual appearance: the creature is, after it has been introduced, notoriously extending its body and limbs beyond the margin of the narrative's single frames, which is especially visible when the boy starts its search for the thing's owners or origin (fig. 2), when *The Lost Thing* is squeezed into the living room in the boy's home and back shed (where at least one tentacle sticks out of the door), and in the scenes inside the "Department of Odds and Ends". Obviously, it can hardly ever be contained within the given frames of the story, and in this way, neither in the margins of the reader's perception: its presence literally extends our view beyond the visual boundaries of the narrative. This can easily be read as a metaphor for cultural belonging as well: the container metaphor (see above) does not work here, the identity of the lost thing simply cannot be contained.

Since we do not know about the thing's actual propensity to work its various extremities, and therefore can hardly ever presume with certainty what it is about to do or where it is actually heading in the single frames (apart from the panel showing the lost thing's escape to its designated destination), its position in the various instances of the narrative may cause a somewhat uncanny effect on readers. In addition, the aforementioned partial views on the lost thing and its physical shape make it barely graspable as a character in the story, which in turn, makes its presence elusive and even mysterious: We can neither anticipate its physical movements nor know which of its parts are currently showing and which are not; in short, we perceive it as a downright strange, and maybe even intimidating object within the composition of the single panels (see Kress / Van Leeuwen 1996: 143; also Sammartino / Palmer 2012: 877).

Colour

Together with the use of certain kinds of colour, the presence of the lost thing in the composition of the visual narrative results, however, in a strong identification with the strange creature. Throughout the whole narrative, abundant picture space is taken up by the lost thing, a fact that, as mentioned earlier, grants considerable importance and significance to this extraordinary character. In some instances of the narrative, though, one might even go as far as to say that the lost thing 'fills up' uninhabited space, bridging a 'gap' between the visual components of the panel. This applies, for example, to the cover panel showing an adapted version of Jeffrey Smart's "Cahill Expressway" (on which we will comment in more detail below), but also to many other frames that depict empty streets and monotonous concrete landscapes, in which occasional other human

Fig. 3: The two protagonists on their way to the Department of Odds and Ends, inspired by John Brack's "Collins St., 5 p.m." (vector graphic traced from original by M.M.)

characters, or rather ciphers, merge mostly with their unidentifiable urban backdrop. This impression of an interchangeable and unrealistic 'dystopian' visual frame of the narrative is achieved by the large-scale use of a relatively monotonous, yellowish, brown and grey-toned colour scheme that creates not only a rather bleak, sinister atmosphere, but also makes the visual content inevitably more abstract and generic, and hence, less "true [or] real" to the reader (Kress / Van Leeuwen 1996: 176). The distance that is thus created, however, contrasts the indistinguishable background and the unique character of the thing, which undoubtedly forms the main point of visual interest in the story (see ibid.: 165). Apart from its warm signal red colour and bizarre shape, *The Lost Thing* also draws the reader's attention and makes us 'look' for it with each turn of the page by inhabiting a position that often frames and thus, 'stages' the thing by dividing its respective background in the golden ratio (fig. 3) (see Sammartino / Palmer 2012: 878).

As this analysis of *The Lost Thing*'s aesthetic characteristics already suggests, one could continue this list with a number of other aspects of the narrative's visual texts. However, our intention is to introduce some of the most outstanding assets of this visual narrative rather than to give an exhaustive, let alone complete analysis of its aesthetic structures.

The Paratexts

The topic of belonging and finding one's place in society is already firmly embedded in the book's paratext, especially the endpapers. The endpapers are a photograph of a bottle top collection (presumably one belonging to the boy protagonist of the story, who is shown to collect bottle-tops and owns a handbook for bottle-top classification), and this collection, too, is mounted on a collage of fragments of drawing and snippets, similar to the one in the book's pages. The neatly ordered bottle tops display all kinds of illustrations, equations, arrows and words, and while they echo the story's obsession with overregulation and order, they also allude to the notion of identity with text bites containing words such as "like", "dissimilar" and "visibly unlike". More surprisingly, the bottle-tops, in all their neat order, allow subversion, chaos and doubt, as some of the words written on the bottle-tops suggest: "Entropy", "But", "If". The paratext, as we shall demonstrate below, is a place for searching for the unexpected, too, and the detail with which they have been assembled invites some detailed looking.

The Transcultural Intertext

The Lost Thing is a book that is full of references to other texts, but most obviously to other images. Shaun Tan himself, on the last page of *The Lost Thing*, draws our attention to the work of Australian and US-American artists that he borrows from in order to locate his lost thing and the dystopian cityscape that surrounds it in a tradition of Australian or American painting, to make a home for the lost thing in an artistic landscape, national and international. The cover design, displaying the boy and the lost thing in a grey concrete cityscape, is an unmistakable reference to Jeffrey Smart's "Cahill Expressway" from 1962, a painting of Sydney's first freeway, a passionately hated landmark of the city, with a man as a marginal figure next to the massive concrete structure. Smart's painting is usually interpreted as symbolising the alienation of human beings from their environment and homes, and in Tan's version, we do not only have an alienated human being there, we also have a creature labelled as a "lost thing". In the Smart painting, the man is roughly in the position that the boy is in, whereas the lost thing takes up some of the space that is left blank in the original painting. Because of its size and colour, the lost thing stands out clearly against the grey concrete, and looks very much at home there (this might also be an effect of the little smoke clouds coming out of one of its tentacles).

Similarly, Tan makes use of John Brack's "Collins St., 5 p.m.", an equally well-known Australian painting from 1955, depicting a busy street in Melbourne. This painting, kept in shades of grey, is also an iconic piece of Australian art to portray the anonymity of the city and the lack of social cohesion among city workers (see "Collins St., 5 p.m."). In Tan's version, again, the lost thing stands out with its striking colour and organic round shape against the muted colours of the people in Collins Street and the regularity and almost grid-like structure of the cityscape. The strategy seems to be to give the lost thing its place in art history and in the streets of Australian cities. By drawing attention to the way it is noticeable as something alive and colourful against the dead colours of those that populate those cities, Tan achieves an othering effect as well as a familiarisation effect at the same time. The art historical intertext, then, contributes to the play of sameness and difference, of belonging and alienation that the book engages in.

While the references to Australian painting would point to a national referential concern[7] at the bottom of Tan's use of intermediality, he goes further and adds an image based on Edward Hopper's "Early Sunday Morning" (1930). The regularity of the architecture and the shadows are striking and comparable to the other two reference paintings, but on top of this, this American classic can easily be identified as US-American, owing to the characteristic barber pole and to the international popularity of Hopper in general. Tan (re-)peoples the painting with the boy and the lost thing and by doing so, extends his strategy to find lost things a home in art history to US paintings as well. This seems to be comparable to what Tan does in *The Arrival*: the arrival scene can be identified simultaneously as a reference to Sydney Harbour and to New York harbour – and although the subsequent images in *The Arrival* point more to New York than to Sydney, both books seem to insist on being multireferential. For transcultural learning this is crucial: rather than pin down the experience of not belonging and finding a place in society, of migration and of the exclusion of "objects without names", to a national setting such as the USA or Australia, the book clearly points at a universal or at least transnational experience. In the same way, the fact that the paintings were produced between 1930 and 1962, spanning from the American prohibition to Australian urbanisation, also indicates that alienation from one's environment and the need to belong is nothing new and certainly not a phenomenon of our time alone. By choosing a variety of temporal and geographical settings, Tan turns the whole experience of not having and looking for a place in society into a time- and placeless experience. This, too, is crucial for its potential to promote transcultural learning.

---

[7] See Stephens, who claims that the boy's language rhythms and the title of his book, *What Bottle Top Is That?*, both also point to an Australian setting (2008: 95, 97).

The Metatext

The Lost Thing is a book about looking for unusual things, for "objects without names", and this is enacted on a variety of levels. On the verbal story level, the boy's search for a home for the lost thing goes virtually unnoticed by any of the adults involved ("Too busy doing beach stuff, I guess"; "Too busy discussing current events, I guess"). On the image level, this is supported by a number of people taking no notice of the lost thing, despite its impressive size, shape and colour. Some of these have intricate devices for looking or elaborate (sun-?) glasses, a technique that Tan already made use of in his illustrations for *The Rabbits* (with John Marsden, 1998) in order to draw attention to the alienation that human beings (or rabbits) can develop towards the things they should be studying or observing. Significantly, the character in the book who sees the most, the boy's friend Pete, is shown taking off his glasses and cleaning them while talking about the lost thing.

The story is told within a frame narrative that stresses the power of story-telling in a rather off-handish way – "[s]o I'll just tell you about the time I found that lost thing." We can conclude that the story is told retrospectively, and that when the boy tells us "I still think about the lost thing from time to time", he has become a grown-up, too, and has stopped seeing things that do not fit his perceptual schemata any longer. He realises that he "see[s] that sort of thing less and less these days though" and explains it with a familiar formula: "Too busy doing other stuff, I guess." This echoes the subtitle of the book (for which you also have to look closely so as not to miss it): "A tale for those who have more important things to pay attention to" and the text on the inside flap which parodies flap texts and blurbs by stating "Already this cover flap is proving to be quite useless, uninformative and a waste of time." The not so subtle message is: take time to read the story, take time for and choose to see unusual objects and creatures that cannot be easily explained or categorised.

If this appears to be a banal message transported via very obvious channels, there is more to make the invitation to look not merely cognitive but experiential, such as the material subtext, the collage we refer to above, which consists of snippets from textbooks but also several other cut-offs from documents, forms and other official and private documents. Each turned page, then, is in itself an invitation to look, not just for the details of the clouds, the smoke clouds and the cityscape, not just for intertextual hints such as "More" and "Utopia" (either of which can be read as a polysemic sign), not just for intermedial art references and echoes, but also for hidden traces of the author (or is it a coincidence that there should be a number of equations including a tangent, abbreviated as "tan"?), for references to state domination and regulation ("control", "Surveillance", "valid for one entry only"), for terms that seem to make sense from both a mechanics and a philosophical or anthropological perspective ("a sense of proportion", "moment of inertia", "the nature of light", "harmonical progression", "displacement"), and for little bits of ironic fun or the big questions of life that cannot be suppressed even in an environment of overregulation ("result-mental", "Tick Tock", "reality", "love", "without malice". "What's in a name?"). On closer inspection one can detect stamps and forms from all over the world, Chinese signs, a lightbulb, and what seems to be the right eye of a Shakespeare head peeps through the collage on one of the first pages. We are handsomely rewarded for looking closely, even if there is no unambiguous denotative meaning to be constructed from what we see.

Looking and seeing is the topic on every level of the text, but never more so than with the main centrefold. Unusually for a picture book, three doublespreads from the end, the reader is forced to turn the book vertically to be able to see the full image properly. What Tan constructs here is the 'space' which he takes the lost thing to. While the verbal narrative gives us reason to believe that it is a confined space that these fantastic creatures are put into, on closer investigation it becomes obvious that we are looking out from a confined space into the freedom of wide open spaces, where 'objects without names' can move freely and enjoy their apparently undisturbed existence. Tan forces us to change our perspective, physically, by turning the book around, and rewards us with what John Stephens has called "a strange heterotopia" (2008: 96): a marvellous view of creatures that are neither animals nor humans nor machines but, just like the lost thing, hybrids. In many ways, they function as an antithesis to the dystopian city setting: the frame this time is not a collage but a black frame, and we are made to believe that the boy and we as observers are standing "in the dark", as it were, in the shadow of a doorframe, looking out into a space of absurd freedom. Hardly any of the lines we can see here are straight, all the objects have a round, organic shape to it, none of them are identical or have a discernible structure or function. There is a bottle on legs with glasses reading a book called "The Idiot"; there are mushroom-headed lizards on long legs; there are bloated flying eyeballs with tiny arms and legs and a tail attached; there is a self-playing accordeon with a cat's head drawn on top. There are blue wide skies and there is no sign of regulation and order. It is an entirely fantastical world that alludes to M.C. Escher, to Salvador Dalí and Hieronymus Bosch, and that harbours promises of a creative freedom that is unheard of, not just in the dystopian setting of the book, but also in our world.

If we look closely, we can even detect an explicit reference to the utopia that we are presented with in this doublespread. On the walls of this fantastic world we can spot the word "utopia" in white chalk letters (written in individual, upper or lower case letters, with the 'o' being embellished) and in connection with various earlier occurrences of "MORE" in the cityscape this can be read either as capitalist propaganda or as a reference to Sir Thomas More, Renaissance chancellor and philosopher, and author of *Utopia* from 1516. The shape of "utopia" is in subversive contrast to the straight and unmistakable form of the word "more" earlier on – which, despite its formal clarity ironically conveys semantic and referential ambiguity, and points once more to the irregularity of life, art and individuals.

After this metareferential intervention, this material changing of perspectives, we are expected to turn the book back the same way it came from, and continue reading the boy's story, in the same way that he goes back to his ordinary life of increasingly not noticing things.

The Political Subtext

Dystopias are always concerned with the present state of the world, or even a nation, and clearly, *The Lost Thing* works hard, on a variety of levels, to bring this concern about not seeing and thus excluding people from society across as a transnational, a global concern. And yet, we are invited to also look for more national references, in addition to the two Australian paintings discussed above. There are snippets that refer to Australia in the material subtext, such as the bottom third of an Australian postage stamp, an employee's pass from Melbourne's Metropolitan Tramway Board, the letters AUS, a fragment from what seems to be a visa application in French, which includes the word "Australie", a cut-off from a declaration form which reads "I am an Australian citizen", a bit of a map with Australia on it (and an arrow pointing to Perth). The most striking political reference, though, and one that leaves less leeway in terms of its interpretation, is a little handwritten note under the bottle-top collection in the endpaper which reads "comfortable & relaxed". It is hard, in an Australian context, not to read this as a reference to John Howard's take on multiculturalism and immigration. In an interview in 1996, when asked how he wanted to see Australians in the year 2000, Howard said this: "by the Year 2000 I would like to see an Australian nation that feels comfortable and relaxed about three things: I would like to see them comfortable and relaxed about their history; I would like to see them comfortable and relaxed about the present and I'd also like to see them comfortable and relaxed about the future" (Howard quoted in Jackson 1996). This has often been quoted against Howard as an attempt to deflect attention from Australia's problematic historical past and from Australia's increasingly tightening migration policies (see e.g. Clark 2010). This one subtle political reference, which we do not only have to detect but which we also need to research, enables us to read this book as a comment on Australian history and migration policies, too.

8. Conclusion

While Tan points to a national frame for his story about a lost thing and his friend, he also very clearly wants his book to be understood as portraying a universal, global concern. This meandering between local and global, between universal and specific, is the stuff of transcultural learning. *The Lost Thing* is so apt as material for teaching transculturality and promoting visual literacy because it plays with the dynamics of the global and the local, of self and other: The boy and the lost thing are in a position in which it is impossible to say who is at home and who is lost, or who is same and who is other. At the same time, the aesthetic structures of the visual texts of *The Lost Thing* and the general assets of the medium of visual narrative show a somewhat "low modality" and highly "interpersonal" layers of meaning (Kress / Van Leeuwen 1996: 160), which invite and enable the reader to participate in the narration. In this way, *The Lost Thing*, as the visual narrative that it is, has the potential to make its readers want to communicate and share their experience of 'looking' at the picture book's various layers of meaning with others. *The Lost Thing* not only conveys a significant story with aesthetically stimulating visual means, and constitutes thus an estimable example of the medium of visual narrative. It also employs a cornucopia of visual 'treats' that reward any reader who decides to engage in an exercise in looking at the multitude of meaningful or simply entertaining textual and visual details that the story holds. And while the book is busy conveying an impasse between all its various layers of meaning, it keeps reminding us to keep looking for more, for More, and for Utopia.

Bibliography

Allolio-Näcke, L. / Kalscheuer, B. (2003). Doing Identity – Von Transdifferenz und dem alltäglichen Skeptizismus. In: Fitzek, Herbert / Ley, Michael (Eds.). *Alltag im Aufbruch. Ein psychologisches Profil der Gegenwartskultur.* Gießen: Psychosozial-Verlag, 152-62.

Antor, Heinz (2006). Inter- und transkulturelle Studien in Theorie und Praxis: Eine Einführung. In: Antor, Heinz (Ed.). *Inter- und transkulturelle Studien. Theoretische Grundlagen und interdisziplinäre Praxis.* Heidelberg: Winter, 25-40.

Arizpe, Evelyn / Colomer, Teresa / Martínez-Roldán, Carmen (2014). *Visual Journeys through Wordless Narratives. An International Inquiry with Immigrant Children and* The Arrival. London: Bloomsbury.

Ashcroft, Bill (2011). Reading the Other. Constitutive Transculturality in a Hong Kong Classroom. In: Doff, Sabine / Schulze-Engler, Frank (Eds.). *Beyond 'Other Cultures': Transcultural Perspectives on Teaching the New Literatures in English.* Trier: WVT, 17-30.

Auernheimer, Georg (2006). Kulturwissen ist zu wenig. Plädoyer für ein erweitertes Verständnis von interkultureller Kompetenz. In: Antor, Heinz (Ed.). *Inter- und transkulturelle Studien. Theoretische Grundlagen und interdisziplinäre Praxis.* Heidelberg: Winter, 145-158.

Avgerinou, Maria D. (2009). Re-Viewing Visual Literacy in the "Bain d'Images" Era. *TechTrends* 53(2), 28-34.

Avgerinou, Maria D. (2003). A Mad-tea Party No More: Revisiting the Visual Literacy Definition Problem. In: Griffin, Robert E. / Williams, Vicki S. / Jung, Lee (Eds.). *Turning Trees.* Loretto, PA: IVLA, 29-41.

Avgerinou, Maria D. (2001a). *Visual Literacy: Anatomy and Diagnosis.* (Diss.) Bath: University of Bath.

Avgerinou, Maria D. (2001b). Towards a Visual Literacy Index. In: Griffin, Robert E. / Williams, Vicki S. / Jung, Lee (Eds.). *Exploring the Visual Future: Art Design, Science & Technology.* Loretto, PA: IVLA, 17-26.

Bang, Molly (2000). *Picture This: How Pictures Work.* San Francisco, CA: Chronicle Books LLC.

Barry, Ann Marie (2005). Perception Theory. In: Smith, Ken / Moriarty, Sandra / Barbatsis, Gretchen / Kenney, Keith (Eds.). *Handbook of Visual Communication: Theory, Methods, and Media.* Mahwah, NJ: Erlbaum, 45-62.

Beacco, Jean-Claude (2011). The Cultural and Intercultural Dimensions of Language Teaching: Current Practice and Prospects. Text presented at the Seminar on "Curriculum Convergences for Plurilingual and Intercultural Education". Strasbourg, 29-30 November 2011. http://www.coe.int/t/dg4/linguistic/ (15/01/15).

Black, Rebecca W. (2009). English-Language Learners, Fan Communities, and 21st-Century Skills. *Journal of Adolescent & Adult Literacy* 52(8), 688-697.

Brack, John (1955). *Collins St., 5p.m.* National Gallery of Victoria, Melbourne. http://www.ngv.vic.gov.au/col/work/3161 (10/03/15).

Braden, Roberts / Hortin, John (1982). Identifying the Theoretical Foundations of Visual Literacy. *Journal of Visual/Verbal Languaging* 2(2), 37-42.

Bredella, Lothar (2002). *Literarisches und Interkulturelles Verstehen.* Tübingen: Narr.

Breinig, H. / Lösch, K. (2002). Introduction: Difference and Transdifference. In: Breinig, Helmbrecht / Gebhardt, Jürgen / Lösch, Klaus (Eds.). *Multiculturalism in Contemporary Societies: Perspectives on Difference and Transdifference.* Erlangen: Universitätsbund, 11-36.

Burwitz-Melzer, Eva (2003). *Allmähliche Annäherungen: Fiktionale Texte im interkulturellen Fremdsprachenunterricht der Sekundarstufe 1.* Tübingen: Narr.

Byram, Michael (2009). Multicultural Societies, Pluricultural People and the Project of Intercultural Education. *Council of Europe. Language Policy Division.* www.coe.int/lang. (15/01/2015).

Byram, Michael (1997). *Teaching and Assessing Intercultural Communicative Competence*. Clevedon: Multilingual Matters.

Cazden, Courtney / Cope, Bill / Fairclough, Norman / Gee, Jim / Kalantzis, Mary / Kress, Gunther / Luke, Allan / Luke, Carmen / Michaels, Sarah / Nakata, Martin / Cook, James (1996). A Pedagogy of Multiliteracies: Designing Social Futures. *Harvard Educational Review* 66(1), 60-92. Reprint. in: Wodak, Ruth (Ed.) (2013). *Critical Discourse Analysis: Volume II – Methodologies*. London: Sage, 61-95.

Clark, Anna (2010). Politicians Using History. *Australian Journal of Politics & History* 56(1), 120-131.

Cope, Bill / Kalantzis, Mary (Eds.) (2000). *Multiliteracies: Literacy Learning and the Design of Social Futures*. New York: Routledge.

Delanoy, Werner (2008a). Transkulturalität und Literatur im Englischunterricht. *FLuL* 37, 95-108.

Delanoy, Werner (2008b). Dialogic Communicative Competence and Language Learning. In: Delanoy, Werner / Volkmann, Laurenz (Eds.). *Future Perspectives for Language Teaching.* Heidelberg: Winter, 173-188.

Doff, Sabine / Schulze-Engler, Frank (2011). Beyond 'Other Cultures': An Introduction. In: Doff, Sabine / Schulze-Engler, Frank (Eds.). *Beyond 'Other Cultures': Transcultural Perspectives on Teaching the New Literatures in English.* Trier: WVT, 1-14.

Eisner, Will (2008). *Graphic Storytelling and Visual Narrative: Principles and Practices from the Legendary Cartoonist*. New York: Norton.

Freitag-Hild, Britta (2010). *Theorie, Aufgabentypologie und Unterrichtspraxis inter- und transkultureller Literaturdidaktik. British Fictions of Migration im Fremdsprachenunterricht*. Trier: WVT.

Geertz, Clifford (1973). *The Interpretation of Cultures. Selected Essays*. New York: Basic.

Gombrich, Ernst H. (1960). *Art and Illusion: A Study in the Psychology of Pictorial Representation*. Princeton: Princeton University Press.

Griffith, Paula E. (2010). Graphic Novels in the Secondary Classroom and School Libraries. *Journal of Adolescent & Adult Literacy* 54(3), 181-189.

Hallet, Wolfgang (2002). *Fremdsprachenunterricht als Spiel der Texte und Kulturen. Intertextualität als Paradigma einer kulturwissenschaftlichen Didaktik*. Trier: WVT.

Hallet, Wolfgang (2008). Die Visualisierung des Fremdsprachenlernens: Funktionen von Bildern und *visual literacy* im Fremdsprachenunterricht. In: Lieber, Gabriele (Ed.). *Lehren und Lernen mit Bildern: ein Handbuch zur Bilddidaktik*. Baltmannsweiler: Schneider Verlag Hohengehren, 212-222.

Hannerz, Ulf (1992). *Cultural Complexity. Studies in the Social Organization of Meaning*. New York: Columbia University Press.

Höpel, Ingrid (2008). Bildkompetenz als pädagogische Schlüsselkompetenz: Forschungsstand und Perspektiven einer interdisziplinären Bilddidaktik. In: Lieber, Gabriele (Ed.). *Lehren und Lernen mit Bildern: ein Handbuch zur Bilddidaktik*. Baltmannsweiler: Schneider Verlag. Hohengehren, 60-71.

Hopper, Edward (1930). *Early Sunday Morning. Whitney Museum of American Art*, New York. http://collection.whitney.org/object/46345 (11/03/15).

Hungerland, Helmut (1952). Perception, Interpretation and Evaluation. *The Journal of Aesthetics and Art Criticism* 10(3), 223-241.

Jackson, Liz (1996). An Average Australian Bloke. Interview with John Howard. Four Corners Programme. *ABC* 19 February 1996. Edited transcript. http://www.abc.net.au/4corners/content/2004/s1212701.htm (01/03/15).

Kramsch, Claire (1998). The Privilege of the Intercultural Speaker. In: Byram, Michael / Fleming, Michael (Eds.). *Language Learning in Intercultural Perspective.* Cambridge: Cambridge University Press.

Kress, Gunther / Van Leeuwen, Theo (1996). *Reading Images: The Grammar of Visual Design.* London: Routledge.

LeDoux, Joseph (1998). *The Emotional Brain.* New York: Simon & Schuster.

Marsden, John / Tan, Shaun (1998). *The Rabbits.* Sydney: Lothian.

Mayrhofer, Miriam (2014). *English Language Teaching with Shaun Tan's* The Arrival*: A Case for Visual Literacy.* (MA thesis). Vienna: University of Vienna.

Messaris, Paul (1994). *Visual Literacy: Image, Mind, and Reality.* Boulder, CO: Westview Pr.

McCloud, Scott (1993). *Understanding Comics: The Invisible Art.* New York: HarperCollins.

Nikolajeva, Maria / Scott, Carole (2001). *How Picturebooks Work.* Oxon and New York: Routledge.

Ommundsen, Wenche (2009). Brave New World: Myth and Migration in Recent Asian-Australian Picture Books. *Coolabah* 3, 220-226. http://www.ub.edu/dpfilsa/coola3ommundsen.pdf (15/01/15).

Reichl, Susanne (2009). *Cognitive Principles, Critical Practice: Reading Literature at University.* Göttingen: Vienna University Press.

Reichl, Susanne (2013). Doing Identity, Doing Culture: Transcultural Learning through Young Adult Fiction. In: Bland, Janice / Lütge, Christiane (Eds.). *Children's Literature in Second Language Education.* London: Bloomsbury, 107-117.

Richards, Jack C. / Rodgers, Theordore S. (2001). *Approaches and Methods in Language Teaching.* Cambridge: Cambridge University Press.

Sammartino, Jonathan / Palmer, Stephen E. (2012). Aesthetic Issues in Spatial Composition: Effects of Vertical Position and Perspective on Framing Single Objects. *Journal of Experimental Psychology: Human Perception and Performance* 38(4), 865–879.

Satrapi, Marjane (2003). *Persepolis.* New York: Pantheon Books.

Schulze-Engler, Frank (2002). Transnationale Kultur als Herausforderung für die Literaturwissenschaft. *Zeitschrift für Anglistik und Amerikanistik* 50(1), 65-79.

Schulze-Engler, Frank (2006). Von 'Inter' zu 'Trans': Gesellschaftliche, kulturelle und literarische Übergänge. In: Antor, Heinz (Ed.). *Inter- und Transkulturelle Studien: Theoretische Grundlagen und interdisziplinäre Praxis.* Heidelberg: Winter, 41-53.

Seglem, Robyn / Shelbie Witte (2009). You Gotta See It to Believe It: Teaching Visual Literacy in the English Classroom. *Journal of Adolescent & Adult Literacy* 53(3), 216-226.

Seidl, Monika (2007). Visual Culture: Bilder lesen lernen, Medienkompetenz erwerben. *Der Fremdsprachliche Unterricht Englisch* 87, 2-7.

Smart, Jeffrey (1962). *Cahill Expressway. National Gallery of Victoria*, Melbourne. http://www.ngv.vic.gov.au/explore/collection/work/3000/ (11/03/15)

Smith, Ken / Moriarty, Sandra / Barbatsis, Gretchen / Kenney, Keith (Eds.) (2005). *Handbook of Visual Communication: Theory, Methods, and Media.* Mahwah, NJ: Erlbaum.

Snyder, Jaime (2014). Visual Representation of Information as Communicative Practice. *Journal of the Association for Information Science and Technology* 65(11), 2233-2247.

Spiegelman, Art (1986; 1991). *Maus: A Survivor's Tale* (2003). London: Penguin.

Stephens, John (2008). "They are Always Surprised at What People Throw Away." Glocal Postmodernism in Australian Picturebooks. In: Sipes, Lawrence / Pantaleo, Sylvia (Eds.). *Postmodern Picturebooks. Play, Parody, and Self-Referentiality.* New York: Routledge, 89-102.

Tan, Shaun (2006). *The Arrival.* Melbourne: Lothian.

Tan, Shaun (2002). *Picture Books: Who Are They For?* 30 March 2014 http://www.shauntan.net/images/whypicbooks.pdf. (02/01/15)

Tan, Shaun (2000). *The Lost Thing.* Sydney: Lothian.

Volkmann, Laurenz (2011). The 'Transcultural Moment' in English as a Foreign Language. In: Doff, Sabine / Schulze-Engler, Frank (Eds.). *Beyond 'Other Cultures': Transcultural Perspectives on Teaching the New Literatures in English.* Trier: WVT, 113-128.

Welsch, Wolfgang (1999). Transculturality. The Puzzling Form of Cultures Today. In: Featherston, Mike / Lash, Scott (Eds.). *Spaces of Culture. City, Nation, World.* London: Sage, 194-213.

Wolk, Douglas (2007). *Reading Comics: How Graphic Novels Work and What They Mean.* Cambridge, MA: Da Capo.

KYLIE CRANE

Whales, Waste and Wilderness: Postcolonial Environmentalism in the Classroom

This contribution provides an introduction to issues and approaches of postcolonial environmentalism and how these might be broached in secondary or tertiary classrooms. The three themes of waste, wilderness and whales take up familiar issues (pollution, space and animals) to engage theoretical and cultural texts (specifically literature and film). Practices of position-taking are foregrounded to stress the role of teacher and students alike within matrices of (post)colonial power and with respect to human-nonhuman entanglements. By engendering an atmosphere of discussion and of self-reflexive critique, analyses of stories from across the globe are brought in conversation with 'home', stressing the mediating role of both teacher and students in a globalized and globalizing world of multiple agencies.

1. Introduction

Postcolonial environmentalism draws on two fields of literary and textual analysis to critique how we think about the world in which we find ourselves. First and foremost, these two approaches are therefore dedicated to critiquing constructions of place, drawing on a general concern for the politics of place, and concomitant issues of belonging, stewardship, care. It foregrounds an undoubtedly *global* component to the environmental issues we face today, at the same time as refusing to neglect *local* specificities, thus augmenting ecocritical themes with postcolonial impulses (see also Nixon 2005). The double focus also, conversely, brings the focus of environmental humanities – a broadening of entities to whom agency can be attributed, for instance – to postcolonial critique. In this manner, Elizabeth Deloughrey and George B. Handley suggest that the "central common ground between ecocritical and postcolonial critique" is marked by "[d]emanding an imagination of a totality and an otherness that nevertheless cannot be possessed" (Deloughrey / Handley 2011: 8). It is, in this piece and elsewhere, a politically charged patterning of textual analysis. As Graham Huggan and Helen Tiffin suggest, such an approach "preserves the aesthetic function of the literary text while drawing attention to its social and political usefulness" (Huggan / Tiffin 2010: 14). Postcolonial environmentalism might lead to a critique of discourses of 'development', and, in the analysis and discussion of literary and artistic texts, questions pertaining to voice (who speaks for whom, when, why?), amongst numerous other lines of enquiry, three of which I will outline in what follows.

Although the context of this piece in a volume about postcolonial studies and transcultural learning suggests that the reader may already (or at least by now) be familiar with some of the approaches and goals of postcolonial studies as well as what is meant by the phrase transcultural learning, I find it useful, even necessary, to position this contribution. I think it is an integral part of what these concepts entail – for daily behaviours, teaching and scholarly work alike – to elucidate the particular positions one adopts or performs in conjunction with the material one wishes to address. Otherwise, the impact of these positions on the ensuing interpretations is glossed over or ignored outright, suggesting a universalising interpretative position, and, further, the assumption that the audience has a particular kind of knowledge presupposes that such a thing as a normative audience exists.

Accordingly, I wish to briefly outline the terms 'postcolonial' and 'ecocritical' (which is the literary analysis upon which the 'environmentalism' of my title rests) as they influence this piece. Both fields have an abundance of materials, and all manner of introductions to these materials: The short definitional work here is by no means conclusive, but rather a path into the field as I see it. In a definition I find myself returning to time and again, Stephen Slemon sees postcolonialism

> as a way of ordering a critique of totalizing forms of Western historicism; as a portmanteau term for a retooled notion of 'class', as a subset of both postmodernism and post-structuralism (and conversely, as the condition from which those two structures of cultural logic and cultural critique themselves are seen to emerge); as the name for a condition of nativist longing in post-independence national groupings; as a cultural marker of non-residency for a Third World intellectual cadre; as the inevitable underside of a fractured and ambivalent discourse of colonialist power; as an oppositional form of 'reading practice'; and [...] as the name for a category of 'literary' activity which sprang from a new and welcome political energy going on within what used to be called 'Commonwealth' literary studies. (Slemon 1994: 16-17)

It is quickly apparent, then, that the work being done under the banner of postcolonialism is broad. For the purposes of this piece, I want to stress that postcolonial thought reminds us to pay particular attention to power dynamics. These dynamics might be at force between text and reader, in the case of literary or cultural studies, or within the cultural frameworks depicted in or acting as frames to the particular texts at hand. At the same time that postcolonial thought reminds us that this 'us' is, at best, a tenuous construct, it cautions us against taking particular positions for granted.

Ecocriticism, to turn to the second field of literary and cultural inquiry, as Cheryll Glotfelty's by now rather famous definition has it,

> is the study of the relationship between literature and the physical environment. Just as feminist criticism examines language and literature from a gender-conscious perspective, and Marxist criticism brings an awareness of modes of production and economic class to its reading of texts, ecocriticism takes an earth-centred approach to literary studies. (Glotfelty 1996: xix)

In the way I employ it here, and in doing so, draw as much on the field of 'environmental humanities' as on ecocriticism "proper", this 'earth-centred' approach might be more adequately envisioned as 'environmentally-centred'. Ecocriticism, the form that much analysis of the environment in literary texts takes, thus draws attention to the material aspects of the world that surrounds us, the environment, and its effects and affects. Note: environment derives, etymologically, from the roots 'en' (in) + 'viron' (circuit) from 'virer' (to turn, veer). As such, the term itself stipulates a position from which to perceive, an idea perhaps quite familiar to postcolonialists. Like postcolonial approaches, the political impetus of the convictions that drive environmental thought forward are often inseparable from the analyses that result from critique thus labelled: Convictions, for instance, that historical imbalances of power continue to have very material impacts on current day lives; that our lives, and our ways of thinking about and thinking through our lives, are impacted by the way we treat the world that surrounds us (both human and non-human). This is not to reduce either postcolonialism or environmentalism to politically motivated forms of critique, but I do feel that acknowledging this impetus – in scholarly work as well as in the classroom – will lead to a more honest and more productive analysis, and, possibly, more heart-felt action.

In what follows, I switch around the themes in the title in order to draw not so much a trajectory of complexity, but to draw in further theoretical and philosophical considerations, postulating as the audience of the teachers of this contribution upper secondary and BA students at German(-language) institutions. This level of education suggests a sound command of written English and a certain level of awareness of themes of political and social importance.

By starting with 'waste', themes of quotidian behaviours can be evoked, themes very likely familiar to students through exposure to other media and, possibly, from other classroom contexts or seminar frameworks. 'Waste' can act as a placeholder for the production of waste, for wasteful behaviours, as well as point to the sites of waste and the global repercussions that these materials and behaviours might have.[1] In the context of this contribution, 'waste' evokes

[1] Accounts such as *Die Essensvernichter* and the tie-in recipe book *Taste the Waste* can function as placeholders for this phenomenon in the German-speaking world.

further environmental issues, pointing to the extent to which cultural concepts are complicit in their production. Pollution, like waste, implies a distinction of desirability, and thus a value framework from which such distinctions are made. Energy production is a theme that will be familiar to many – carbon-based technologies, nuclear power and waste (which is an evergreen issue in Germany), renewable energy sources – and also the disparate exposure to the waste products thus produced. Food production and consumption – disparity of production and consumption sites, ecological damage through monocultures, morally laden issues of genetically modified plants, the monopolisation of genetic material (key word 'Monsanto') and, obviously, disparity of hunger, these are all issues with which students will be familiar that pick up on environmental themes and can be addressed through a postcolonial lens. Other resources are similarly unevenly spread. All of these issues have local and global reaches: Whilst a postcolonially informed approach may appear to privilege the global component, it does so by stressing the placed-ness of the perspective, insisting on a connectivity that rests rather well with the ecological idea of 'interconnectivity'.[2]

The second section turns to 'wilderness' in a direction that draws strongly on cultural geography. 'Wilderness' alludes to topics of human habitation. In the secondary classroom, cross-over with geography lessons might produce interesting insights here into population density and spread, as well as migration. A historical dimension, with a critical glance towards practices of cartography, may also emerge here, with a focus on migration, migration history and topics pertaining to (colonial) exploration and settling. Tropes of writing, such as the pastoral, but also city-based writing and film, are themes encompassed here, as well as a critical gaze towards the phenomena of urbanisation and suburbanisation. The latter, in turn, might develop into a perspective that examines segregation of living: gentrification, gated communities, apartheid, all themes that can develop awareness of uneven development and uneven distribution of wealth (and, of course, uneven consumption, linking back to the themes of the previous section). Further issues include habitat protection and conservation (which lead back to a framework that considers values and their cultural specificity: what kinds of habitat are considered worthy of protection or even conservation? which specific (animal or plant) species are deemed similarly worthy?). This theme highlights the overlap between habitation – human living – and the world around us.

---

[2] Although, please note, that the comprehension of ecology as 'everything it connected with everything else' has come under critique for being simplistic and, well, not true (see i.e. Morton or Phillipps).

The third section takes 'whales' as a placeholder for the relationships between humans and non-human animals – which may be extended, in light of more recent ecocritical trends, to also encompass plant species and other actants in the world (to the extent that these are given agency[3]). In a classroom that brings postcolonial and environmental humanities approaches together, dealing with the issues subsumed by this subsection, suggests looking across at other cultures and the way these accord specific non-human things agency; the ways in which non-humans are understood as agents exerting influence on day-to-day life and considerations of the world around us; and the different ways in which these relationships are created or performed (specifically in written, visual or audio-visual media). The choice of 'whales' is one motivated, of course, by the alliteration of the title to this piece, but it also points to the issues surrounding this particular species, which has received a lot of (media) attention and continues to spark debate – as for instance in the relations as practiced by Inuit peoples.

In each of the sections, I outline the specific concerns that comprise the postcolonial and ecocritical implications of the themes, alluding to numerous texts for further reading. These texts are both background reading (what is often called 'theory' in literary and cultural studies) as well as a number of primary texts that teachers may examine together with their students and discuss in class. In each thematic section, I outline briefly the issues at stake with a specific English-language texts, or corpus of shorter texts that might be considered in the classroom. The respective analyses are to be considered as thought-provoking rather than 'final words': For a piece such as this, I imagine my audience, as teachers, as being quite capable of coming to their own analytical conclusions – and believe this indeed to be more productive as the ideas are transposed into the classroom.

2. Waste

Several accounts of ecocriticism, including Greg Garrard's contribution to Routledge's *New Critical Idiom* series entitled simply *Ecocriticism*, take the work of Rachel Carson as a starting point, and thus highlight the importance of waste's close cognate 'pollution' for work done in environmental humanities. Where pollution can be invisible, even odourless, beyond all of our senses, 'waste' foregrounds the physical manifestation of environmentally unsound

[3] I am not entirely convinced that 'agency' is the best kind of term for what I want to cover here, but it is one that has some reach. It is a shorthand for the ways in which things (here: non-human actants) might affect us. See Jane Bennett *Vibrant Matter* for more).

behaviours.[4] This is not to argue that waste is more important than pollution, it is just more easily accessible to our senses. 'Waste' therefore foregrounds the disparate dispersion of unwanted materials and the risks this entails.[5] As a material, it can be stored and transported in ways that pollution cannot always be dispersed. Of course, pollution may arise from waste – decomposition might produce rather disgusting and hazardous gasses, for instance – but similarly, waste may arise from pollution – as pollutants enter the atmosphere, ultimately causing deaths (of plant and animal, including human, life).

The rubric of 'waste' thus covers issues that are clearly identifiable as environmental issues. The way in which such issues are portrayed and presented is key to understanding the impact they have on daily behaviours, and also on how we might react to them: A sense of urgency, even of apocalyptic demise, accompanies many accounts of environmental change and/or damage, fictional or non-fictional, even film.[6] Understanding the way texts encode the issues at hand, and fostering an understanding that leads to the recognition of them as well as teaching the necessary skills for decoding the way such issues are presented in all forms of media (from newspapers and television news through to advertisements and pop videos), is an essential part of the kind of postcolonial environmentalism I put forward here – and an essential part of media literacy. Being able to identify the particular tropes employed to present specific issues is an integral part of language and foreign language education.

When Robert Young writes of postcolonialism as "a general name for these insurgent knowledges [with reference to anti-colonial movements and 'other perspectives'] that come from the subaltern, the dispossessed" he claims that said knowledges "seek to change the terms and values under which we all live. You can learn it anywhere if you want to. The only qualification you need to start is to make sure that you are looking at the world not from above, but from below" (Young 2003: 20). This is a humbling gesture, and an important aspect of the perspective adopted by Animal in Indra Sinha's novel *Animal's People*. The protagonist Animal (or Janvaar, as the locals call him) was not only left orphaned by an environmental disaster, his spine was twisted so badly that he is unable to move upright, instead crawling on all fours.

---

[4] See also the documentary *Waste Land* (2010) that follows artist Vik Muniz to the Jardim Gramacho landfill on the outskirts of Rio de Janeiro.

[5] For a sustained account of risk and how this ties in with the local and global (and indeed cosmopolitanism), see Ursula K. Heise's *Sense of Place and Sense of Planet.*

[6] Margaret Atwood's *Oryx and Crake* trilogy, Bill McKibben's *The World Without Us*, Cormac McCarthy's *The Road*, T.C. Boyle's *A Friend of the Earth*, to name just a few written texts – interestingly, a strong North American contingent, echoed through many crisis films, such as *Waterworld*, to name one prominent example.

It is a relatively recent novel that is easily accessible, narratologically interesting, and well-liked by students in my experience. First published in 2007, Sinha takes the Bhopal disaster of December 1984 as the historical backdrop to the novel. The pollutants released by the leak cause widespread waste in the environment of the fictional setting of Khaufpur, affecting deaths and effecting all manner of life. Set in the aftermath, the novel is preoccupied not so much with the disaster itself, but rather with the ongoing effects that follow the gas leak of the pesticide factory located in the city (and thus the waste and wastefulness of the disaster): "Our wells are full of poison. It's in the soil, water, in our blood, it's in our milk. Everything here is poisoned. If you stay here long enough, you will be too" (107-8). In this sense, it traces what Rob Nixon has called 'slow violence', which he notes for the novel is a "violence that has yet to run its course" (Nixon 2013: 44):

> *Animal's People* can be read as a novel of risk relocation, not just in [...] [a] spatial sense but across time as well, for the transnational off-loading of risk from a privileged community to an impoverished one changes the temporal topography of fear in the long term. (Nixon 2013: 46)

As a favourite of postcolonial ecocriticists, there are a number of articles and book chapters on this novel, with various ways of reading the conflicts that emerge in the novel. Some of these accounts focus on the apocalyptic component (see i.e. Bartosch), others suggest a reading framework that foregrounds risk (see i.e. Levihn).

Above, I suggest that *Animal's People* is 'narratologically interesting'. This component of the text is an important aspect of how the text encodes the waste discourses – and thus discussions of this are an important step towards transferrable skills. Here, I refer to two aspects of the way that the story is told: The explicit naming of the addressee (the 'Eyes'), and the particular position in the community the protagonist adopts and repeatedly dwells upon. To the first: In her article on the humour of the novel, Heather Snell notes the "uneven relations of power" implied in the novel through the construction of the "Eyes". "By constructing the journalist he [Animal] encounters" she argues,

> and, by extension, his implied readers as vultures out to salvage the pitiable remains of the disaster, Animal points to the negative effects of transnational capital on nations consigned to the periphery and the economies of reading and interpretation that might translate him into an exotic object to be consumed. (Snell 2008: 1)

The interpolation implied by the use of the second person pronoun 'you' in addressing the implied reader, the 'Eyes', is therefore an integral part of the novel. By foregrounding this component of the text, discussions about the positions readers take up can emerge, working towards discussions that critically analyse the investments we have as readers in texts, and the way such texts work to position us.

Secondly: Subaltern theory meets Critical Animal Studies in the character of Animal. In the classroom – be it at secondary or tertiary level – Animal's position in the community portrayed in the novel is a point of discussion, and the teacher, I suggest, should take care to push the discussion beyond the simplistic question of whether Animal is indeed an animal, or whether he is human. The yes/no responses such a line of questioning evokes, even if it leads to a lively discussion, harbours too much potential to 'shut down' responses, avoiding the more interesting – to me at least – questions of what it means to occupy a position, to wish to occupy a position, on the boundary between human and non-human. In particular the agency Animal refuses, the responsibility for his actions he wishes to avoid. By just thinking through these two components of *Animal's People*, it is possible to engage in a wide discussion of environmental issues – and not just at the level of them *being* issues, but the very specific ways they are constructed, that is, aesthetically encoded. 'Waste' does not remain an issue 'out there' (or 'over there', i.e. in India), but is intrinsically languaged, aestheticized.

3. Wilderness

As outlined in the introduction, I evoke the category of 'wilderness' to draw attention to the spatial dimensions of the overlaps between postcolonial and environmental thought. Spatial concerns are present in three of the four schisms Rob Nixon identifies in his article "Postcolonialism and Environmentalism" (alluded to above), and is at the foreground of one of them, in particular, where he contrasts the former's concern with displacement and the latter's tendency to "give priority to the literature of place" (2005: 235).[7] Patterns of colonial domination are patterns of spatial domination; and patterns of environmental domination are also patterns of spatial domination, often enough.

Specific aesthetic tropes can be addressed in this rubric, for instance, the 'translatability' of the pastoral into non-European contexts.[8] In a different direc-

[7] The contrast in the first of the four, between highlighting hybridity and cross-culturation with discourses of purity, is demonstrated with nothing less than ecocriticism's (initial) preoccupation with wilderness; and, in the 'third schism', Nixon points to the cosmopolitan and transnational in contradistinction to the national (even nationalist), which is also, at the end of the day, a spatial concern.

[8] See my interpretation of Andrew McGahan's *The White Earth* and J.M. Coetzee's *Life and Times of Michael K* in Crane 2014a. The former is a book that deserves more attention in the classroom, particularly for the way it introduces readers to the complexities of land right's issues

tion, and providing for productive overlaps with the themes touched on through the rubric of 'waste' above, the postcolonial ecocritical classroom might look at slums.[9] There are many texts that address the issues that 'wilderness' picks up on (see Crane 2012). Margaret Atwood's *Oryx and Crake* trilogy, for instance, does not explicitly address wilderness in its explorations of 'post-natural' nature, but the tension between purity and hybridity (as put forward by Nixon) and how this is spatially manifested remains a crucial component to how the discourse of nature works in the text. Sean Penn's adaptation of Jon Krakauer's *Into the Wild* to the screen offers another text which might provide for interesting discussions in the classroom. Notions of spatialised wilderness and the environmental and postcolonial repercussions this concept has are also present in one of the first novels written in English – Daniel Defoe's *Robinson Crusoe* – and echo through many texts that 'write back' to this novel. What I will focus on here in this context is the way in which wilderness itself might be considered a European (or American-European) import to other regions of the world, and the specific effects this transposition might have.

In the classroom, it is possible to trace the impact of US American definitions of wilderness by drawing on a number of essays and documents included in J. Baird Callicott and Michael P. Nelson's collection *The Great New Wilderness Debate*. The 'touchstone' document in this respect is the Wilderness Act of the United States government dating to 1964, included in the collection, which outlines the following definition, quoted here at length:

> (c) A wilderness, in contrast with those areas where man and his own works dominate the landscape, is hereby recognized as an area where the earth and its community of life are *untrammeled by man*, where man himself is a *visitor* who does not remain. An area of wilderness is further defined to mean in this Act an area of undeveloped Federal land retaining its *primeval character* and influence, *without permanent improvements or human habitation*, which is protected and managed so as to preserve its natural conditions and which (1) generally appears to have been affected primarily by the forces of nature, with the imprint of man's work substantially unnoticeable; (2) has outstanding opportunities for solitude or a primitive and unconfined type of recreation; (3) has at least five thousand acres of land or is of sufficient size as to make practicable its preservation and use in an unimpaired condition; and (4) may also contain ecological, geological, or other features of scientific, educational, scenic, or historical value. ("The Wilderness Act of 1964" in Callicott / Nelson 1998: 121, my emphases)

---

in Australia from the post-settler perspective, the latter for the vivid contrasts between war imagery / apartheid in South Africa and the bucolic associations of gardening.

[9] For a very readable account of the issues involved, see Mike Davis' *Planet of Slums*. Aatish Taseer's *The Temple Goers* (also set in India!) is a good example a novel one could read in this respect.

Ramachandra Guha's concern regarding the translatability of certain ideas of wilderness, included in the same volume, foregrounds issues of (colonial and imperial) historical difference as follows:

> Because India is a long settled and densely populated country in which agrarian populations have a finely balanced relationship with nature, the setting aside of wilderness areas has resulted in a direct transfer of resources from the poor to the rich. Thus, Project Tiger, a network of paths hailed by the international conservation community as an out- standing success, sharply posits the interests of the tiger against those of poor peasants living in and around the reserve. (Guha 1998: 235)

By tracing the debate through such essays, students gain an awareness for the work that specific concepts do: Familiarisation with the particular readings of 'wilderness' provided by postcolonial and ecocritical accounts as well as for the permutations of such a concept when its historical, cultural or geographical frameworks are shifted will elicit a deeper understanding of the contingency of these concepts, as well as evoke comprehension for the powerful effects they produce on stages of political importance (i.e. through the UN, the WWF, etc).[10] Thus, the transposition of a US American concept (here: of wilderness) to a context which will be strange for most students (India) might also be traced to a much less 'strange' environment – the Bavarian or Swabian Black forests, for instance. Global considerations also become local concerns; local concerns lead into global considerations – with a heightened sensitivity for the differences afforded by the specific historio-socio-economic frameworks.

There is, of course, a vast body of texts that this kind of approach can draw on. The United Nations, World Monetary Fund, and more interest-motivated governmental agencies and non-governmental organisations (here: Greenpeace, Friends of the Earth, various non-profit organisations, indeed even "Reclaim the Streets" and anti-globalisation networks) publish numerous texts in English that can serve as basis for close reading and discussion, here, for tracing the impact the idea of 'wilderness' has had on environmental policy. Reading policy documents and laws in the classroom provides discussion with a 'real world' component: Competencies integral to the humanities classroom, and specifically, the language-learning classroom – be it at secondary or tertiary level – are essential beyond the reaches of the classroom itself.

The crossover to informed interpretations of media of all different kinds should be, at the risk of sounding prescriptive, a cornerstone of teaching. Querying the particular rhetorics of written and audio-visual texts – speeches, newspaper articles, advertising, to just name a few – draw on the skills honed with respect

---

[10] Part Two of Callicott and Baird's collection, entitled "Third and Fourth World Views of the Wilderness Idea" provides nine further assessments of the problems of transposing wilderness.

to those texts which are more familiar to teachers and students of (foreign) language learning, that is, fiction, film, poetry, and drama. Such readings can be compounded through the analysis of specific films and novels. A particularly evident and nice explication of the problems of such a transposition as the one alluded to by Guha is explored in Amitav Ghosh's *The Hungry Tide*, which I will address in more detail in the following section (taking the 'whales' of the section title with a certain amount of flexibility).

4. Whales

In their book *Postcolonial Ecocriticism*, Graham Huggan and Helen Tiffin allocate the issue of animals a starring role in the subtitle — which reads *Literature, Animals, Environment* — elevating it to the same level as the keywords of literature and the environment, a privileging that continues within the covers of the book, as the second of the two parts of the novel is called "Zoocriticism and the postcolonial". "Throughout western intellectual history", Huggan and Tiffin write in the introduction to this part, "civilisation has consistently been constructed by or against the wild, savage and animalistic, and has consequently been haunted or 'dogged' by it" (Huggan / Tiffin 2010: 134). As alluded to in the reading of Indra Sinha's *Animal's People* above, the relations between humans and non-human animals imply power relations that map well from both postcolonial and environmental concerns. A comprehension of postcolonial studies that pays particular attention to the dualistic constructions underlying the power constructs of civilisation maps rather well onto and over particular patterns of environmental thought that critique similarly functioning dualisms that uphold divisions such as that between the human and the non-human, or culture and nature.[11]

With regard to some texts, the issues that arise from Critical Animal Studies might provide a productive overlap with Food Studies. As I have argued elsewhere, specific negotiations of human / non-human animal difference also take place at the 'dinner table', so to speak (see Crane 2014b). The overlap with issues of food and waste might be emphasised here. Alternatively, work done with postcolonial theories might push issues of representation and colonial power to the fore, as Graham Huggan and Helen Tiffin stress in the introduction to the second section of *Postcolonial Ecocriticism*:

---

[11] For further reading about this overlap, I must recommend Val Plumwood's *Feminism and the Mastery of Nature*. Her insights into dualistic thought have been influential in the formation of my own thoughts on postcolonial environmentalism.

> This fiction of irreducibility [of the border between human and non-human animals] is reproduced through the language we use in spite of our knowledge that some peoples considered 'human' by some have been dubbed 'animal' by others; and in spite of our awareness that the species boundary is not fixed at all, but always temporally and politically contingent, continually constructed and policed by the processes of representation itself. (Huggan / Tiffin 2010: 135)

Adventurous teachers might then foray into the 'otherising' that has taken place through discourses of (presumed) cannibalism.[12]

Like Sinha's *Animal's People*, the novel I want to address here, Amitav Ghosh's *The Hungry Tide*, is set against historical events on the Indian subcontinent. The conflict in *The Hungry Tide* is a conflict exacerbated by wilderness thought. Indeed, it is with reference to the historical circumstances surrounding the mass relocation of the humans of the Sundarbans (code word: Project Tiger) that Ramachandra Guha asserts the shortcomings of a US-American centred conceptualisation of nature-as-wilderness – the events that form the historical backdrop to Ghosh's novel. *The Hungry Tide*, like Sinha's novel, has been popular with postcolonial ecocritics.[13] Two animal species figure predominantly in such analyses, the Bengal tiger (Panthera tigris tigris) and the Irrawady dolphin (*Orcaella brevirostris).* Conflicts between the global and the local, and between humans and animals, form the cornerstone of such analyses, played out through these animals.

In *The Hungry Tide*, the tiger is a complex symbol. As the text tells us, indeed *teaches* us, the tiger is considered a demon by the villagers – a conception that stands diametrically opposed to its metonymic function as a symbol for Western environmentalist notions. When the tiger is caged and tormented by villagers in the Sundarbans, Piya's protests can only be subdued by her removal from the scene. It is Kanai, the interpreter, the translator, whom she turns to for support in her protest, but Kanai's final response is to say "'He [Fokir, a local] says, when a tiger comes into a human settlement, it's because it wants to die" (295). Piya, a US American biologist with Indian roots, has a sentimental attitude towards the animals of the Sundarbans that is epitomised in her statement that she would die for the dolphins she is researching: "'If I thought giving up my life might make the rivers safe again for the Irrawaddy dolphin, the answer

---

[12] Certainly a contentious field of inquiry upon itself. Sherryl Vint notes: "As both Foucault and Agamben make clear, the human-animal division is both external and *internal* to human being, and thus the anthropological machine's work of including and excluding can – and has – put some *Homo sapiens* in the category 'animal'; that is, the category of those who can be killed but not murdered because their lives and deaths are not included within the scope of our ethical discourse" (Vint 2010: 20).

[13] Both books figure prominently in Upamanyu Pablo Mukherjee's *Postcolonial Environments*, for instance.

is yes, I would'" (301-302). Sacrifice (of tiger or of human) is figured here as a means of exploring different environmental sensitivities.

As Graham Huggan and Helen Tiffin suggest "the real clash of interests is displaced[.] [...] In recent decades, the strongest international pressure on the Indian government has been for tiger, not river dolphin, conservation" (Huggan / Tiffin 2010: 188). The emphasis on the two mammalian species of the Sundarbans in the critiques of the novel works to shadow over the presence of other species: In particular, the crabs of the dunes, without whom, it is suggested in the novel, the ecosystem and its constant state of ebb and flood would collapse. This observation might give rise to discussion of privilege amongst species, and of a careful questioning of the kind of species we think of when we think of 'animal'. It further draws attention to crucial questions of uneven power, already implicit in the (allegorical) roles afforded to the other two animal species: To subalterns and animals who do not 'speak' or are not 'heard'.

On a different level: The layering of different stories within the novel – the narration that follows Piya, the level that focusses on Kanai, the inclusion of Kanai's uncle's journal – suggest a multiplicity of stories at the same time as they do *not* represent stories written by the traditional inhabitants of the region (be these human or non-human). These stories remain external to the events portrayed in *The Hungry Tide*; as readers of a novel *in English* we are not privy to the meanings such perspectives might attribute to the events portrayed – or even if the events portrayed would warrant the telling of a story. In this sense, the borders of communication are integral to the narrative structure of the text. Kanai's position in the story as a translator/interpreter and mediator between (globalized) Piya and (localized) Fokir might give rise to discussions about intercultural communication and for reflections on what it means to be learning a foreign language.[14] Beyond observing the status of English as a language in India, the key role afforded to interpreters and mediators in texts such as these foregrounds the important work done in the foreign-language learning classroom.

5. Conclusions

Reading postcolonial literature, at the risk of sounding prescriptive, need not result in the exoticisation of positions taken and stories told. When combined with environmental issues, this would run the double risk of the compartmentalisation of the earth's fragility and our (collective) behaviours to far-away plac-

[14] Note that translation also figures as a key theme for the frame narrative of *Animal's People*.

es, ultimately deflecting responsibility and exporting consequences. Further, caution must be taken to resist any urge to interpret texts from other places in an allegorical sense, where the one particular 'story' comes to act as a placeholder for all possible stories from this other location – not only writing over the top of other stories, but also smoothing over the particular tensions and sensitivities within the text at hand.

Interpretative practices within a postcolonial environmentalist frame must, instead, foreground the interrelations between the global and the local, even if (possibly *because*) they are difficult to trace. The connectedness of flows of capital through multinational companies, the unevenness of risk as it spreads over the globe from local sites, the roles of borders (national, as pertaining to exchange of goods and flows of humans, but also between human and non-human), the impact of concepts as they mis-translate in their transpositions, the list of possible questions goes on. There are many 'real-world' repercussions for these kinds of questions. Some classroom environments might lend themselves to a rather *Landeskunde*-like approach, tracing the historical events and seeing these influencing fictional (or otherwise 'artistic') re-configurations. These can be valuable questions leading to rich insights on their own, but do not, in my opinion, reach the full extent of their capacity to affect change unless accompanied by more critical interpretative habits. The question, therefore, of 'to what extent does Ghosh/Sinha/whoever represent the historical events of the Sundarbans-Project Tiger/Bhopal/whatever affair?' stops well short of the kind of questions that avail themselves to transfer and to developing critical interpretative habits.

The language-learning classroom is an important site for learning such critical habits. The specific terminology we use to refer to the issues at hand is a language issue, and hence one that is clearly 'at home' in the language-learning classroom. Consider the difference between 'global warming' and 'climate change', where the first might evoke warm summer holidays rather than a disaster leading to ice-caps melting and widespread flooding (or indeed hurricanes or drought) and is rhetorically disarmed as soon as it is 'not warm'. 'Climate change' avoids this problem, but, as Ursula K. Heise suggests, is "a far more neutral term, [which] might not only convey no sense of but also concede territory to political [and other kinds of] parties interested in minimalizing its importance" (Heise 2008: 205). A language issue. The foreign-language classroom augments such insights: By engendering an atmosphere of careful and caring critique and fostering an awareness of the language-learner as 'culture-learner' and future mediator, students are not just seen as receptacles for facts, but learn, and learn to appreciate, the full extent of their agency (as mediators) in a globalized and globalizing world.

Bibliography

Atwood, Margaret (2013). *MaddAddam.* New York: Nan A. Talese.

Atwood, Margaret (2009). *The Year of the Flood.* New York: Nan A. Talese.

Atwood, Margaret (2003). *Oryx and Crake.* New York: Nan A. Talese.

Bartosch, Roman (2012). The Postcolonial Picaro in Indra Sinha's Animal's People – Becoming Posthuman through Animal's Eyes. *Ecozon@: European Journal of Literature, Culture and Environment* 3(1), 10-19.

Bennett, Jane (2010). *Vibrant Matter: A Political Ecology of Things.* Durham and London: Duke University Press.

Boyle, T.C. (2001). *A Friend of the Earth.* London: Bloomsbury.

Callicott, J. Baird / Nelson, Michael P. (1998) (Eds.). *The Great New Wilderness Debate.* Athens & London: The University of Georgia Press.

Crane, Kylie (2014a). Vellum, Visions and Postcolonial Transformations. *The Journal of Ecocriticism* 6(1), 1-12. http://ojs.unbc.ca/index.php/joe/article/view/464/481 (08/12/2015).

Crane, Kylie (2014b). When Pigs Cry: Teaching the Gaze, Materialities and Environmental Ethics with the Film *Babe.* In: Bartosch, Roman / Grimm, Sieglinde (Eds.). *Teaching the Environment.* Frankfurt am Main: Peter Lang, 97-114.

Crane, Kylie (2012). *Myths of Wilderness in Contemporary Prose Texts: Environmental Postcolonialism in Australia and Canada.* New York: Palgrave Macmillan.

Davis, Mike (2007). *Planet of Slums.* London: Verso.

DeLoughrey, Elizabeth / Handley, George B. (2011). Introduction. In: DeLoughrey, Elizabeth / Handley, George B. (Eds.). *Postcolonial Ecologies: Literatures of the Environment.* Oxford: Oxford University Press, 3-39.

Garrard, Greg (2004). *Ecocriticism.* London: Routledge.

Ghosh, Amitav (2005). *The Hungry Tide.* London: HarperCollins.

Glotfelty, Cheryll (1996). Introduction: Literary Studies in an Age of Environmental Crisis. In: Glotfelty, Cheryll / Fromm, Harold (Eds.). *The Ecocriticism Reader: Landmarks in Literary Ecology.* Athens, GA: University of Georgia Press. xv-xxxvii.

Guha, Ramachandra (1998). Radical American Environmentalism and Wilderness Preservation: A Third World Critique. In: Baird, Callicott, J. / Nelson, Michael P. (Eds.). *The Great New Wilderness Debate.* Athens & London: The University of Georgia Press, 231-245.

Heise, Ursula K. (2008). *Sense of Place and Sense of Planet: The Environmental Imagination of the Global.* Oxford: Oxford University Press.

Huggan, Graham / Tiffin, Helen (2010). *Postcolonial Ecocriticism: Literature, Animals, Environment.* London: Routledge.

Into the Wild (2007). Dir. Sean Penn. Paramount.

Krakauer, John (1997). *Into the Wild.* New York: Anchor Books.

Levihn, Karsten (2015). Toxic Terror and The Cosmopolitanism of Risk in Indra Sinha's Animal's People. In: Buchenau, Barbara / Richter, Virginia. *Post-Empire Imaginaries? Anglophone Literature, History, and the Demise of Empires*. Leiden and Boston: Brill Rodopi, 371-391.

Morton, Timothy (2007). *Ecology without Nature: Rethinking Environmental Aesthetics*. Cambridge, MA and London: Harvard University Press.

Mukherjee, Upamanyu Pablo (2010). *Postcolonial Environments: Nature, Culture and the Contemporary Indian Novel in English*. Houndsmills, Basingstoke: Palgrave Macmillan.

Nixon, Rob (2013). *Slow Violence and the Environmentalism of the Poor*. Cambridge, MA: Harvard University Press.

Nixon, Rob (2005). Environmentalism and Postcolonialism. In: Loomba, Ania et al. (Eds.). *Postcolonial Studies and Beyond*. Durham and London: Duke University Press, 233-251.

Phillips, Dana (2003). *The Truth of Ecology: Nature, Culture and Literature in America*. Oxford & New York: Oxford University Press.

Plumwood, Val (1993). *Feminism and the Mastery of Nature*. London: Routledge.

Sinha, Indra (2009). *Animal's People*. New York: Simon & Shuster.

Slemon, Stephen (1994). The Scramble for Post-Colonialism. In: Tiffin, Chris / Lawson, Alan (Eds). *De-scribing Empire: Post-Colonialism and Textuality*. London: Routledge, 15-32.

Snell, Heather (2008). Assessing the Limitations of Laughter in Indra Sinha's Animal's People. *Postcolonial Text* 4(4), 1-15. http://postcolonial.org/index.php/pct/article/view/990/896 (08/12/2015).

Taseer, Aatish (2011). *The Temple Goers*. London: Penguin.

"The Wilderness Act of 1964" (1998). In: Baird, Callicott, J. / Nelson, Michael P. (Eds.). *The Great New Wilderness Debate*. Athens & London: The University of Georgia Press. 120-130.

Vint, Sherryl (2010). *Animal Alterity: Science Fiction and the Question of the Animal*. Liverpool: Liverpool University Press.

Waste Land (2010). Dir. Lucy Walker, Karen Harley and João Jardim. Arthouse Films.

Waterworld (1995). Dir. Kevin Costner and Kevin Reynolds. Universal Pictures.

Young, Robert J. C. (2003). *Postcolonialism: A Very Short Introduction*. Oxford and New York: Oxford University Press.

Grit Alter

"I want you to remember the ways of our people" – First Nations Trauma Fiction in the EFL Classroom

Trauma fiction and postcolonial studies have recently been in the focus of literary and cultural studies – not least with publications such as Craps' Postcolonial Witnessing *(2013) or Gibbs'* Contemporary American Trauma Narratives *(2014). This essay outlines some of the basic ideas of trauma fiction in a postcolonial perspective and parallels these with a close reading of two picture-books,* Shi-shi-etko *(2005) and* Shin-chi's Canoe *(2008) by Nicola I. Campbell, a children's book author of Interior Salish and Métis ancestry. The overall frame regards intercultural learning scenarios in EFL classrooms and at university. Thus, this essay not only attempts to cross over the fields of trauma studies and postcolonial fiction, but also to transfer these complex field to children's literature and the development of cultural competences.*

1. Introduction

> We want to take back our education and teach our history, our language and our culture. We have begun to tell our story – our history – and we want to tell it in our own words to the world, so that this will never happen to any of the other nations in the world.
> ("100 Years of Loss", Shirley Williams, Survivor)

Although trauma theory has been a field of interest since the 1980s and 90s, it has recently entered a new dimension with Alan Gibbs' (2014) and Stef Craps' (2013) criticism of Cathy Caruth's foundational research. Both perceive of trauma and trauma fiction beyond its Western-based paradigms and parallel the reading of trauma fiction with postcolonial texts and contemporary literature. In their "Introduction: Postcolonial Trauma Novels", Craps and Buelens state that their perspective involves to "examine whether and how trauma studies can break with Eurocentrism through the analysis of novels that bear witness to the suffering engendered by colonial oppression" (2008: 2). As Gibbs and Craps elaborate, so far the academic field of trauma theory which is mainly founded on the scholarship of Caruth and LaCapra has failed "to live up to this promise of cross-cultural ethical engagement […] on at least four counts" (Craps 2013: 2). These components include that the founding texts

- "marginalize[s] or ignore[s] traumatic experiences of non-Western or minority cultures,"
- "tend to take[s] for granted the universal validity of definitions of trauma and recovery that have developed out of the history of Western modernity,
- "often favour[s] or even prescribe[s] a modernist aesthetic of fragmentation and aporia as uniquely suited to the task of bearing witness to trauma,"
- "generally disregard[s] the connections between metropolitan and non-Western or minority traumas" (ibid.).

Yet, it can be questioned in how far traumatic experiences of indigenous people,[1] for example, can be reflected with Western concepts and understandings of trauma, literary aesthetics and ethics, or whether, "the traumas of non-Western or minority populations [need to be acknowledged] for their own sake" (Craps 2013: 19). I very much agree that such approaches are justified, yet, trauma theory should nevertheless include the different social and historical contexts in which trauma narratives develop and should be flexible enough to consider further processes and strategies of narrating trauma and the different functions that could be attached to them? (see 2013: 5).

While I am not able to trace the development of trauma fiction and elaborate on Gibbs' and Craps' detailed critical reading of Caruth's scholarship within the scope of this article, I would like to continue this line of thought and further engage with the currently evolving topic of post-colonial trauma fiction. Using the reflection of the residential school experiences of First Nations, Inuit and Métis peoples in Canada in picturebooks for children as a reference; I will show how indigenous writers in Canada use writing and publishing processes as a form of working through traumatic experiences and enter processes of healing.

These elaborations of trauma fiction for young readers will be paralleled with the concept of developing intercultural communicative competence (ICC)

---

[1] I am aware of the fact that, as Styvendale (2008) describes, the application of the term 'trauma' to Native communities is anything but clear. Reasons for this are manifold, among them a lack of research of Native trauma which "reveals an institutional complicity in larger, nationwide attempt to forget the trauma of Native peoples" (2008: 205). For Styvendale, "paucity of research on Native trauma also reveals a necessary political resistance to the potential revictimization of Native peoples through the nomenclature of trauma [...] through the imposition of yet another Euroamerican framework designed to 'figure out' and 'fix' Native peoples" (ibid.: 206). Yet, I apply this term as I see a need for engaging with Native history in psychological perspective, not in terms of 'fixing' Native peoples, but in terms of reconciliation and negotiations of compensation.

in the English as a foreign language (EFL) classroom. I will focus on the potential of trauma fiction, which is based on historic events and therefore partly non-fiction, to offer incentives for meaningful communication. Furthermore, this context provides a background for fostering cultural knowledge as a means that could initiate understanding otherness. The different stylistic aspects that are chosen as foci for analysing the selected picturebooks can also function as a step-by-step approach for using such picturebooks in EFL classrooms.

While I will draw on the current scholarship of post-colonial trauma fiction, a close reading of two recent picturebooks, *Shi-shi-etko* (2005) and *Shin-chi's Canoe* (2008) by Interior Salish and Métis author Nicola I. Campbell, will take centre stage. My argumentation will furthermore be supported by referring to other children's and young adult narratives on residential school experiences by authors such as Alice Masak French (Ninatakmuit Inuit) and Margaret Pokiak-Fenton (Inuvialuit). In order to contextualize the picturebook examples, also references to historic fiction and discrepancies of Western and indigenous approaches will be important, as well as discrepancies of narrating traumatic experiences for a child audience.

2. Post-colonial Trauma Fiction

In general terms, "post-colonial" refers to "all the culture affected by the imperial process from the moment of colonization to the present day" (Ashcroft et al. 1989: 2). Post-colonialism is, thus, "concerned with the effects of colonization on peoples (colonized and colonizers) and on places formerly subjected to colonial rule" (Bradford 2011: 165). Post-colonial discourse also regards processes in which an indigenous population of a geographical area was put under colonial rule, as was, for example, the case in the U.S., Australia or Canada in respect to Native Americans, Aborigines and First Nations, Inuit and Métis people. Closely related to a post colonial paradigm is the discourse of power, knowledge and language, which is the foundation on which Edward Said builds his argument in *Orientalism* (1978). There he elaborates how Orientalist discourses exercise power over the 'Orient' by "making statements about it, authorizing views of it, describing it, by teaching it, settling it, ruling over it" (Said 1978: 3). This can be extended to other discourses in which a majority seeks to write about other subjects and thus exercises power over those voices and approaches. By having post-colonial authors and scholars publish about discourses themselves, they attempt to regain power over their own voices and history. Thus, they not only add different and differing perspectives to political, social and literary history, but also offer "a corrective to those mainstream texts that [for example] represent Indigenous characters according to habits of thought deeply engrained in post-colonial cultures" (Bradford 2011: 167, also Bradford 2007: 97-119).[2]

In the context of postcolonial trauma fiction, Craps and Buelens come to a similar estimation: postcolonial novels "are seen to offer a corrective to the individualizing, psychologizing, and ultimately depoliticizing tendencies characteristic of Western models of trauma treatment" (2008: 4). This notion is also present in further publications. For example, for Whitehead, trauma fiction "overlaps with postcolonial fiction in its concern with the recovery of memory and the acknowledgement of the denied, the repressed and the forgotten" (2004: 82). Her statement that "[p]ostcolonial novelists seek to rescue previously overlooked histories and to bring hitherto marginalised or silenced stories to public consciousness" (ibid.), agrees to Saunders and Aghaie's function of trauma fiction to "challenge or rework official versions of memory" (Saunders / Aghaie 2005: 21). Their claim that "whenever memory is invoked we should be asking ourselves: by whom, where, in which context, against what?" (ibid.) in turn mirrors Gibbs' call that "there is an urgent political imperative to narrate traumas in order to educate western readers" (Gibbs 2014: 26). Such recent publications not only draw attention to this emerging field, but also to a shift in trauma theory, namely that trauma fiction includes a strong political agenda beyond the personal and psychological processes of narration as means of working-through traumatic experiences and "translating traumatic memory into comprehensive narrative" (Saunders / Aghaie 2005: 26). Yet, as Craps notes, it is important to move beyond a Western perspective and to associate trauma studies with postcolonial discourses. Thus, voices of formerly marginalized experiences can be heard as well. This is essential because

> [t]hough widely considered a single, uniform, timeless, and universal phenomenon, the concept of psychological trauma is a Western artefact determined by its origins in a variety of late-nineteenth- and early-twentieth-century medical and psychological discourses dealing with Euro-American experiences of industrialization, gender relations, and modern welfare. (Craps 2013: 4)

And further because "attempts to construct a normative trauma aesthetic create a narrow canon of valued trauma literature, consisting of high-brow, avant-garde works by mostly Western writers" (ibid.: 5). In reference to the criticism of trauma studies and research of trauma fiction, a postcolonial perspective on

---

[2] Writing this essay about First Nations picturebooks in the light of trauma fiction and its potential for developing ICC, I certainly do not intend to appropriate other voices and derive them from the power to speak for themselves.

this scholarship makes it necessary to reconsider the formerly assumed individual understanding of trauma. As Craps and Buelens note,

> [c]olonial trauma [...] is a collective experience, which means that its specificity cannot be recognized unless the object of trauma research shifts from the individual to larger social entities, such as communities or nations. Yet it is hardly self-evident how this transition might be effected. While some theorists assume an unproblematic translation from individual to collective trauma (LaCapra; Erikson; Hutcheon), others warn that a simple metaphorical extension may be reductive and politically irresponsible (Lloyd; Saunders / Aghaie). However, refusing to move from the individual psyche to the social situation is bound to have damaging consequences. (2008: 4)

Craps additionally points to a certain responsibility that comes with our present knowledge of trauma and the different subjects affected by it:

> [B]y narrowly focusing on the level of the individual psyche, one tends to leave unquestioned the conditions that enabled the traumatic abuse, such as political oppression, racism, or economic domination. Problems that are essentially political, social, or economic are medicalized, and the people affected by them are pathologized as victims without agency, sufferers from an illness that can be cured through psychological counselling. The failure to situate these problems in their larger historical context can thus lead to psychological recovery being privileged over the transformation of a wounding political, social, or economic system. (2013: 28)

Saunders and Aghaie supplement this notion and see an "interaction between private and public forms of memory" (2005: 16). With reference to Ron Eyerman, they believe that trauma needs to be distinguished between affecting individuals and cultural processes. "[A]s cultural process, trauma is mediated through various forms of representation and linked to the reformation of collective identity" (Eyerman, quoted in Saunders / Aghaie 2005: 17).

In this essay I would like to apply trauma fiction to narratives of the residential school experience which stands as an example of a cultural trauma that occurs "when members of a collectivity feel they have been subjected to a horrendous event that leaves indelible marks upon their group consciousness, marking their memories forever and changing their future identity in fundamental and irrecoverable ways" (Alexander et al., quoted in Saunders / Aghaie 2005: 17f). Despite the heavy impact the residential school system has had on First Nations policy and current situation, it is only marginally reflected in cultural studies classes. Pulling residential school picturebooks in the context of trauma studies into the centre helps to close this gap.

Using the example of racism, Craps demonstrates that LaCapra's distinction of "loss" and "absence" and "working-through" and "living-with" (see LaCapra 2001) cannot be applied to all experiences of trauma. Craps' references to South

African literature corresponds to First Nations peoples' trauma in North America as it can hardly be understood as a specific event, but rather as a result of multiple political and social decisions and practices inflicted upon the Aboriginal population. First Nations history includes multiple events which contribute to what Brown labelled "insidious trauma" (Brown, quoted in Craps / Buelens 2008: 3). Events such as the westward movement that drew the indigenous population off the land, the residential school system or also the ignorance of treaties and land rights, counter Caruth's event-based definition of trauma.[3] This contention is also mirrored by Schwab who states that "[s]ome lives are hit with catastrophic trauma over and over again; then trauma, with its concomitant strategies of survival, becomes a chronic condition" (2006: 96). Trauma cannot be understood as "sudden, unexpected catastrophic events" (Craps / Buelens 2008: 3), but rather as an ongoing process that has long term effects; in the context of First Nations peoples referred to as intergenerational impact (see below). Craps further argues that origins of trauma need to be perceived of as "tainted", as "for many disempowered groups [...] trauma is a constant presence" (ibid.: 33) and that "there is no pre-traumatized state of being that can be restored in any straightforward manner" (ibid.).

This is an interesting case in point, because although processes of writing can be seen as "working-through" traumatic experiences and be part of "healing", as Alice French notes, writing and publishing rather need to be seen as bits and pieces of a wider and more holistic endeavour (see Watson 2000). In the context of residential schools this is especially relevant as the intergenerational impact counters attempts of distinguishing between past and present. For indigenous people, the "colonial experience [can be seen] as a key marker of insidious trauma" (Gibbs 2014: 16-17) which should not be overlooked.[4] Such a chronic condition can be ascribed to the experiences of the First Nations, Métis and Inuit people in North America, because their contact with the colonizers has largely, but not exclusively, been a struggle for survival.

The attempt of reading and understanding this kind of fiction "constitutes a new mode of reading and of listening that both the language of trauma, and the

---

[3] As Styvendale discusses, Armstrong's novel *Slash* is indicative of the insidious process of Native trauma (2008: 213ff.).

[4] A further extension of trauma terminology is added when Brown draws attention to the pitfall that "traumatic experiences of people of color, women, gays and lesbians, lower-class people, and people with disabilities often fly under the trauma-theoretical radar because of the fact that current definitions of trauma have been constructed from the experiences of dominant groups in Western society. [...] Routinely ignored or dismissed in trauma research, the chronic psychic suffering produced by the structural violence of racial, gender, sexual, class, and other inequities has yet to be fully accounted for" (Craps / Buelens 2008: 3f).

silence of its mute repetition of suffering, profoundly and imperatively demand" (Caruth 1996: 9). What would "allow us to pass out of the isolation imposed on both individuals and cultures by traumatic experience", as Craps and Buelens state (2008: 1f), is not only recognizing processes of perceiving but also of producing and publishing trauma fiction. This is specifically the case, as I state, in the context of trauma fiction for children, as it constitutes specific challenges to the design of picturebooks regarding content and illustration. Surely, the intended audience of picturebooks is children and it is assumed that they should be saved from harsh realities.

Trauma Fiction in ELT

One can certainly ask which role trauma fiction could play in educational contexts, especially ELT. The justification for using trauma fiction in ELT uses Michael Byram's differentiation of five different *savoirs* of ICC (Byram 1997) as a main reference. Until today Byram's conceptualization of ICC remains the foundational idea upon which cultural learning in ELT is designed. Although further concepts have recently gained popularity (transcultural learning, global education), the five *savoirs* can still be seen as the base on which curricula and textbooks are built.

The first dimension of cultural learning is called "*savoir être*" and refers to an emotional level of ICC. Here, learners need to develop "attitudes of curiosity and openness, of readiness to suspend disbelief and judgement with respect to others' meanings, beliefs and behaviors" (1997: 34). Also the "willingness to suspend belief in one's own meanings and behaviors […] an ability to 'decentre'" (ibid.), which entails abandoning ethnocentric attitudes and relativizing the self with regards to the other is included. A second sub-skills is "*savoirs*," which refers to the cognitive level of ICC. It includes "knowledge about social groups and their cultures in one's own country, and similar knowledge of the interlocutor's country […]; knowledge of the processes of interaction at individual and societal levels" (ibid.: 35). This level reminds of former area studies which focused on the characteristics of the other country or culture and certain facts and figures (see Risager 2012: 145). Additionally, Byram defines "*savoir comprendre*," the skills of interpreting and relating documents from another country (see ibid.: 37) for which learners need "specific knowledge and general frames of knowledge which will allow them to discover the allusions and connotations present in the document" (ibid.: 37). "*Savoir apprendre/faire*" refers to actual interaction in real-life encounters (ibid.: 37-38); it is "the ability to recognise significant phenomena in a foreign environment and to elicit their meanings and connotations, and their relationship to other phenomena" (ibid.:

38). Moreover, "the skill of interaction is [...] the ability to manage [...] constrains in particular circumstances with specific interlocutors" (ibid.) which also includes being able to deal with "dysfunctions" (ibid.).

These four levels culminate in "*savoir s'engager*", the "ability to evaluate critically and on the basis of explicit criteria perspectives, practices and products in one's own and other cultures and countries" (ibid.: 53). Here, the ability to change perspectives is essential; learners need to be enabled to critically compare cultures and regard the other and one's own cultural frame of reference. Such processes of "clarifying one's own ideological perspective and engaging with others consciously on the basis of that perspective" may not be free of conflicts that arise from the different perspectives involved (ibid.: 101).

The application of trauma fiction in ELT offers the chance to develop ICC on all of these levels to more or less balanced extents. Reading and reflecting the picturebooks in class, students develop the competence of interpreting an original text according to certain cultural knowledge. When older students are aware of the girl in the red coat (see below), they are able to discover particular connotations and references such a text includes. Reflecting such texts in ELT prepares students for real-life encounters and interactions with people who have (no) knowledge about the residential school system. Through emphatically engaging with this bleak part of Canada's past, they may be prepared to respectfully and reflectively engage with people who may have first or second hand experiences. They become critically aware of the intergenerational impact this system has had on First Nations people. In sum, using picturebooks that deal with traumatic experiences of a certain group can support students in initiating an understanding of such a traumatic past and develop the necessary cognitive, affective and pragmatic competences so that learners could be cultural mediators between groups of different background knowledge.

The (Im)possibility of Representing Trauma

One central question within trauma theory which caused some controversy over the last few years is whether trauma can be represented, and if so, how this could be done stylistically. Earlier scholars such as the psychiatrist Bessel van der Kolk and literary and cultural studies scholar Cathy Caruth assumed that for people who suffer "speechless terror [...] the experience cannot be organized on a linguistic level" and that it thus becomes inaccessible (van der Kolk / van der Hart 1995: 172). In a similar sense, Caruth maintains that "trauma [...] is not fully perceived as it occurs; or [...], that a history can be grasped only in the very inaccessibility of its occurrence" (Caruth 1991: 187; for a similar reading of both, see Leys 2000: 304). Yet, I agree with Robinett and would ask if

> traumatic experience [...] cannot be represented in language, how are we to understand narratives that clearly bear a relationship to the writer's lived experience? Why do trauma survivors continue to tell stories in which experience and narrative, especially in the case of trauma narratives, are, in fact, very closely interwoven, as demonstrated in works like those of Holocaust survivor[s]? (Robinett 2007: 290-291).

Certainly, also a number of children's books have been published dealing with traumatic events, e.g. 9/11, so that Caruth's and van der Kolk's assumption nowadays seems outdated (see Kidd 2005, Connolly 2008). Yet, the discrepancy of speaking the unspeakability of atrocity certainly is a disputed aspect of trauma fiction, as Schwab explains:

> Stories in 'the likeness of ... life' reside in a transitional space between memory and forgetting. They arise from faint memories, memories not to be trusted. Life writings often emerge from a traumatic core, occupying a space between two parallel universes: daily life and trauma. In real life, it is dangerous for these universes to touch. In writing, they must converge. Otherwise, stories remain cut off, their words stranded in the silence they try to cover, orbiting trauma like satellites. Writing from within the core of trauma is a constant struggle between the colonizing power of words and the revolt of what is being rejected, silenced. Trauma kills the pulsing of desire, the embodied self. Trauma attacks and sometimes kills language. In order for trauma to heal, body and self must be reborn and words must be disentangled from the dead bodies they are trying to hide. (2006: 95-96)

Writing about trauma is essential because a "collective or communal silencing of violent histories leads to the trans-generational transmission of trauma and the spectre of an involuntary repetition of cycles of violence" (ibid.: 100). First Nations children have for years witnessed the consequences of the residential school system in the symptoms of the intergenerational impact it left on the communities. Therefore, Schwab's assumption that "victims [and their descendants] have produced an abundance of literature of witnessing, testimonials, and memoirs" in order to "counter-silence"? (ibid.: 102) can be extended by the notion of making sense of those symptoms by educating the younger generation and healing the older generations which may have witnessed residential schools first hand.

As Schwab further notices

> [t]here are forms of violence – holocaust, genocide, torture, and rape – that are considered beyond representation. Yet, also they call for speech, testimony, and witnessing. This is an irresolvable paradox at the core of traumatic writing. How then do we write what resists representation? We know that traumatic amnesia can generate other prohibitions on thought and emotion that are fundamentally opposed to narrative and storytelling. And yet we also know that telling and witnessing are necessary for healing trauma. We need, then, a theory of traumatic narra-

> tive that deals with the paradox of telling what cannot be told and/or has been silenced. (ibid.)

My elaboration below shows that this is particularly challenging within children's literature. Schwab's interesting solution to the problem outlined is Abraham and Torok's theory of the crypt and cryptographic speech, which entails that

> unless it is worked through and integrated, trauma will be passed on to the next generation. If this happens, the next generation will inherit the psychic substance of the previous generation and display symptoms that do not emerge from individual experience but from a parent's, relative's, or community's psychic conflicts, traumata, or secrets (Schwab 2006: 102).

What seems to blur in postcolonial contexts is a differentiation of 'passing on trauma' and 'passing on memory of trauma' because the traumatic experience of the past is closely related to a continuing discrimination and cumulative trauma that reaches the present. While a parent generation may be traumatized by personally experiencing trauma, e.g. racism, in the past, younger generations are traumatized by their ancestors' inability to cope with traumatic experiences, by narrations through which the older generation integrates their trauma into their children's stories, but additionally by witnessing discrimination themselves. In the context of residential school experience, the intergenerational impact makes it difficult to differentiate between 'passing on trauma' and 'passing on memory of trauma'.

As my close reading of the two example texts reveals, both *Shi-shi-etko* and *Shin-chi's Canoe* can be seen as processes of working through (memories of) trauma, as Nicole Campbell has not witnessed such schools herself but through the narrations of family and community members. However, publishing trauma fiction does not necessarily mean that the traumatic experience is overcome and will not be passed on to the next generation.

One of the early memoirs of residential school experience was already published in 1977 (*My Name is Masak* by Alice Masak French). For French, writing the book was a process of personal healing and educating her own children and the general public (see Watson 2000: 33f, 38f). As indicated, such texts are documents that are available for the following generations who on the one hand can read about their ancestors' trauma, but additionally witness its consequences and the intergenerational impact on a daily base in reality. Thus, their grandparents' trauma is also part of their life; the trauma is voiced and remains part of intergenerational continuity. However, "recovery from the traumas of colonialism is basically a matter of the individual witness gaining linguistic control over his or her pain" (Craps / Buelens 2008: 4). In this understanding oral or written stories are one means of gaining such control.

Therefore, survivors and victims of trauma have indeed found "strategies to manage the pain, suffering, and long-term damage caused by past suffering" (Saunders / Aghaie 2005: 20). Just as the publication of "drama and song to overcome grief, alienation, and victimization" (ibid.: 20f), also writing (children's) literature functions as "cultural performance" (ibid.). As Saunders and Aghaie conclude, the transformation of fragmentary trauma "into a structure that allows for at least some degree of closure or critical distance and grant participants a measure of control over their own stories" (ibid.: 21) is essential.

> Moreover, isolated personal grief, in which trauma victims tend to feel cut off from the rest of the world, once it is expressed in songs and stories, is transformed into a communal experience, which provides a sense of shared meaning and acceptance. […] If narrative offers a way to recuperate meaning from trauma, the embodied practices of dance, song, lamentation, and dramatic reenactment [*sic*!] may offer a sense of environmental control, empowerment, or communality unachievable through language alone. (ibid.: 21f)

Authors of trauma children's literature use pictures in order to reveal what language alone may not be able to express. Where language may be too direct, telling pictures take over as will be analysed in a later chapter.

3. Trauma Fiction for Children

Trauma fiction faces certain peculiarities when the audience and readership of the texts are children. In fact, this field is rather new and so far often limited to Holocaust fiction or also picturebooks that were published post 9/11, as for example elaborated by Connolly (2008). When trauma fiction is closely related to historic events, it gets an additional dimension, as apart from the individual or collective trauma that is reflected, the historic level demands a certain level of accuracy. As the two picturebooks that are analysed in a later chapter refer to the residential school system in Canada, the following section not only elaborates on trauma fiction and its challenges within children's literature, but also takes historic fiction into account.

Children's fiction can be divided into several sub-genres, yet, all of them share a similar value. First and foremost this includes enjoyment – children read or listen to a story because it offers them pleasure; they simply like it. Being lost in a narrative triggers the children's imagination and inspiration, they gain knowledge and new insights to other people's experience and thus develop understanding and empathy for each other. Additionally, children learn something about their and others' heritage and cultural identity, develop an understanding of moral reasoning, and also their literary and artistic preferences (see Lynch-Brown / Tomlinson / Short 2011: 5-7).

When reading or listening to historic fiction, those functions are specified as children engage in stories that merge historic facts and fictional packaging: “Historic fiction is realistic fiction set in a time remote enough from the present to be considered history […] The facts are actual historical events, authentic period settings, and real historical figures. An imaginary story is constructed around these facts” (ibid.: 167). Historical fiction can be seen as an umbrella term, as it can cross the lines to “romance, adventure, mystery, humour, and biography” (Nilsen / Donelson 2009: 276) – or to trauma. In this context it is especially important that the narration, although partly fictional, is “historically accurate and steeped in time and place” (ibid.: 244). Due to the young age of their readers – who at the age of 7 to 9 “develop an understanding of past and future time” (Lynch-Brown / Tomlinson / Short 2011: 13) – writers of historical fiction for this age group need to carefully consider that despite the historic accuracy and an “authentic sense of time and place” they should not overwhelm the story (ibid.: 168). However, this is quite a challenge when it comes to trauma fiction, because it refers to events that were or still are overwhelming to the victims or related people.

Apart from questions of accuracy, questions of authenticity pose a certain challenge to writers of historical trauma fiction for children. This concerns, for example, the representation of socially and politically disadvantaged people as this could lead to an implementation of stereotypes about and prejudices toward certain members of society. As a case in point, Donna Norton (2011) interestingly discusses children’s books about slavery and the Civil War and about and by First Nations people juxtaposing the different images of the specific parties involved that are created depending on the authors and their intentions. Frontier-stories and pioneer stories of moving west are often adventure stories emphasizing family bounds and the impact of nature and the environment, but they also often include one-sided accounts of wild Indians who capture white girls (see Norton 2011: 422f). Such stories need to be expanded by accounts of Native American and First Nations writers who, for example, “describe the harmful influence of an expanding white population” (ibid.: 423), e.g. *Sing Down the Moon* by Scott O’Dell (1970) about the Navaho’s forced march from the Canyon de Chelly to Fort Sumner, 300 miles that not only meant the loss of their home but also spirituality or Joseph Bruchac’s *The Winter People* (2004) about fourteen-year-old Saxso, a boy from the Abenaki people who attempts to save his mother and sister who were taken by the English. Reflecting upon a historic time in which people oppressed other people and which may have contributed to a peoples’ trauma, demands a high level of sensitivity when the authors attempt to offer an account that is accurate historically, but still transports cultural values that are taken for granted in present-day societies.

Beyond this important line of thought, it is essential to be aware of the fact that "[i]nvocations of authenticity tend to construct cultures as fixed, stable and homogenous" (Bradford 2011: 163) and that, therefore, no authentic way of describing history, nor speaking of trauma, can be found, because the experiences of residential schools, as in the example texts below, depend on gender, time, the setting of the school, how long children went there, and the personality of the children. Generalizations are hardly possible, as will also be visible in *When I was Eight* (Jordan-Fenton / Pokiak-Fenton 2013) in which the daughter desperately wants to go to the "outsider's school" and in *Shi-shi-etko*, which focusses on the four last days until the daughter has to leave, emphasizing the strong connections to nature and family.

"Dual audience" (May 1995: 37, 55) is one of the key terms in children's literature scholarship, and this is of specific importance to trauma – and in my discussion – to residential school fiction. When publishing for children, the children themselves are the central point of reference, because they are the ones who later read the books. Additionally, adults are to be taken into consideration, as they are the potential buyers of the picturebooks. Yet, I propose that in the context of trauma fiction, the adults may be witnesses of the trauma and may have survived the atrocity of this 'education.' The children, in turn, may be children who witness identity issues, their parents' social and political struggles, and the consequences of the intergenerational impact, maybe without being aware of the origins and symptoms. Therefore, authors need a specific sensitivity when it comes to trauma fiction for children. Moreover, the authors themselves may have experienced the traumatic event either themselves or through their family members. They may see their writing as processes of working-through and have a very personal relationship to the story they tell. Accordingly, it is not surprising that historic trauma fiction for children functions not so much as an invitation to adventurous journeys to the past as in late nineteenth-century historic novels (see Rahn 1991: 9), and neither as time-travel or passing-gates novels such as *The Root Cellar* by Janet Lunn (1981), but rather as a coming to terms with a community's past, as a means to remember and to educate about the past, but also to educate so as to prevent such atrocities in the future.

The question of how to write about the atrocities of the indigenous populations of North America has been answered by an increasing number of First Nations, Métis and Inuit authors. Those include, for example, Jeannette Armstrong (*Slash* (1985), *Whispering in Shadows* (2000), *Enwhisteetkwa (or Walk in Water)* (1982), *Neekna and Chemai* (1983)), Alootook Ipellie (*Artic Dreams and Nightmares* (1993)), Maria Campbell (*Halfbreed* (1973), *Little Badger and the Fire Spirit* (1977)) and Beatrice Mosioner (Culleton) (*In Search of April*

Raintree (1983), *April Raintree* (1984)). They were not only highly influential in Aboriginal writing and publishing, but also wrote children's and young adult fiction reflecting about the experiences of Aboriginal people in the face of an often hostile and threatening society.[5] In writing their stories from their own point of view and giving voice to the experiences of their people, these authors add an important perspective to approaches to literature, culture and politics that were formerly occupied by scholars and writers of European decent. Therefore, such texts can be perceived in a realm of postcolonial studies as they offer perspectives of authors whose people were colonized in their own country. The authors mentioned above were highly influential in re-thinking the history of Aboriginal people in Canada and beyond, and also in processes of working-through, reconciliation, preservation of heritage and processes of cultural identity formation. Armstrong's and Ipellie's, and especially Campbell's and Mosioner's texts are attempts to create meaning and come to terms with traumatic events, which have also been used for educational purposes in school and Canadian literature and social studies classes.

When looking at the genre historic trauma fiction, it appears that such texts make use of different stylistic devices in representing trauma. One way of representation is reflecting on the traumatic experiences as a form of dialogue, e.g. when grandparents tell grandchildren their own or their peoples' story, or memoirs told by survivors. The two young adult novels *Fatty Legs* (2010) and its sequel *A Stranger at Home* (2011) by Christy Jordan-Fenton and Margaret Pokiak-Fenton are examples of this category. With the picturebooks *When I Was Eight* (2013) and the sequel *Not my Girl* (2014) the two authors make their protagonist's experiences at residential school accessible to younger children as well. Interestingly, in *When I Was Eight* it is the main character Olemoun who desperately wants to learn to read the "outsiders' books" (Jordan-Fenton / Pokiak-Fenton 2013: n.p.) herself rather than having her sister read them to her.[6] As it is at the outsider's school where she can learn to do so, she begs her father to send her there. Because "[h]e knew things about the school [she] did not" (ibid.), her father only reluctantly gives in to his daughter's wish. Despite the hardships she endures at school, such as being deprived of her identity by being renamed Margaret, cutting her hair which makes her feel "naked" (Jordan-Fenton / Pokiak-Fenton 2013: n.p.) and giving her clothes to wear that are too

5 Ipellie's cartoons are accessible for young adults as well, although they were not specifically published for this age group (see Alter 2011).

6 Her being drawn to the outsiders' school could be perceived of in terms of Bhabha's colonial ambivalence, a "mix of attraction and repulsion" of the colonizer, or, in Olemoun's case, being "never simply and completely opposed to the colonizer" (Ashcroft / Griffiths / Tiffin 1998: 12).

small and do not keep her warm, and the nuns' continuous attempts to break Margaret's spirit, the girl is determined enough to succeed in learning to read. Yet, Margaret needs to face the consequences of her education when she returns home after spending two years at residential school. In the opening scene of *Not my Girl* Margaret arrives in her community and is devastated when her mother greets her with "Not my girl! [...] in what little English she knew" (ibid.: n.p.). Margaret remembers:

> When I left for Aklavik, I was just eight. Now I was ten. In that time I had learned how to add numbers and how to read books. I had perfect table manners and knew when to say my prayers. I could speak English and French. But I no longer knew the words in my own language to tell my mother that I *was* her girl. 'Not my girl!' rang out again like the slap of a ruler on a desk." (ibid.: n.p., italics in original)

Margaret increasingly becomes aware that the outsiders' school has turned her into an outsider as well: she cannot speak her language anymore, does not remember the stories of her people and neither is she able to process the food that is prepared for her. Her strong wish to be able to read the outsiders' books now turned into a struggle of being part of her family again. From the dedications at the end of *Not my Girl* it becomes obvious that the consequences of attending residential schools must have been much more severe than reflected in those picturebooks. While the illustrations are drawn in vivid colours and the text only indicates hardships, the book is dedicated to "[...] two beautiful souls who have each created safe places for healing" (Jordan-Fenton / Pokiak-Fenton 2014: n.p.) and "[f]or all the children still trying to find their way home. May you each discover a way to step out from the darkness behind you into the light ahead" (ibid.). Both dedications indicate a "darkness" which makes "healing" necessary, yet, specifics of this darkness are omitted in the picturebooks.[7]

As both picturebooks also include photographs of Margaret's family and the school she attended, both also represent multimodal picturebooks.[8] Through their multimodal design, such narratives add a different level of authenticity. When Jordan-Fenton and Pokiak-Fenton open their picturebooks with actual photographs, the child reader is immediately reminded that there is a certain level of truth in the story that is told, that the girl as well as the school actually exist(ed). The two young adult novels *Fatty Legs* (2010) and *A Stranger at Home* make even more use of this when photographs of the girl's childhood are included on almost every page of the book. Additionally, both novels include

[7] For intermediate readers, Alice Masak French's novels *My Name is Masak* and its sequel *The Restless Nomad* are recommended, which tell of her residential school experience and reflect how difficult it was for her to relearn the tasks an Inuk woman needs to be able to perform in order to secure her family's survival after coming back from residential school.

[8] For more information on multimodal narratives refer to Hallet (2008).

maps which show the setting of Margaret's experiences, her home and the region of the school. A similar approach is chosen in Alice French's *My Name is Masak* (1977), the author's autobiographical account of her residential school experience in Aklavik, Northwest Territories, the same town in which Margaret went to school. Multimodal picturebooks, in supplementing the narrative with maps, photographs or also newspaper clippings, add a non-fictional level to the story and, thus, not only insert a more concrete level of authenticity, but also invite readers to look for more material about the time and engage in inquiry-based reading approaches.[9]

Other historical and trauma fiction picturebooks chose a third-person narrator with a child focalizer. *Shi-shi-etko* and *Shin-chi's Canoe* are told by an unknown narrator. Yet, as my later analysis reveals, this neither implies an outside perspective nor a more distanced view on residential school experience. In both, the author draws on her family's experience, and the lyrical free verse supports the innocence of the children who were taken to those schools.

As mentioned earlier, one means of children's literature is to introduce children to the pleasures of reading and to a lifelong appreciation of literature (see Nodelman / Reimer 2002, Bland / Lütge 2013). Therefore, the context of children's literature is often surrounded by a certain optimism and hopefulness regarding plot development and the solutions that are offered at the end of the narratives. However, as described, historical and trauma fiction stand in discrepancy to such attitudes. Such fiction therefore has the potential to broaden the image of cultures that is usually reflected in ELT, as it allows discussing rather bleak episodes of a culture's past and can contribute to understanding a social and cultural dimension of otherness that has its roots in historic events.

The topic that is to be focussed in the remaining part of this essay is one that for a long time has been neglected by politics but also the public. As described in the introduction, it was only through the reports and published memories of survivors that the practices of the residential school system in Canada have entered the public social, political, cultural and also literary discourse. Yet, the seriousness and impact of historic events render the transformation of residential school experience to picturebooks problematic.

---

[9] For more information on inquiry-based reading and learning approaches refer to Wilhelm / Wilhelm (2010), Bell / Urhahne / Schanze / Ploetzer (2010) or http://www.thirteen.org/edonline/concept2class/w6-resources.html (07/01/2016).

Challenges of Transforming Trauma Fiction to Children's Literature

In the following I would, therefore, like to investigate which strategies Nicola Campbell uses to reflect upon the residential school system in Canada in picturebooks and engage in two examples, *Shi-shi-etko* (2005) and *Shin-chi's Canoe* (2008). As described earlier, the residential school system in Canada can be seen as a policy that was devastating for children, families and communities to such an extent that until today, Aboriginal people suffer from the consequences and intergenerational impact. For many years, the Catholic Church, the government, but also the victims and survivors remained silent about this era of Canada's past. Yet, more and more Aboriginal people reach out and speak publically about their own and their parents' experiences, on a political stage or in literature.

When putting such harsh contents into picturebooks, authors face a certain discrepancy of putting into words and pictures the atrocity of reality and a people's past, while at the same time facing the need of matching an optimistic and hopeful tone that is commonly characteristic of children's literature. As Adrienne Kertzer notes on holocaust stories for children: no matter how bleak the subject, children's literature must be hopeful (2002: 13) and present logical reasons for survival and non-survival. Bosmajian's observation that holocaust literature for children does not function as a child's alienation, traumatization of the child or to numb the child, underline the difficulty of making a traumatic past accessible in children's literature and publish trauma fiction for such a young readership (see Lane 2006: 174f). Yet, it would hardly be possible to develop narratives about a traumatic past free from retrospective sentiment, as "sadness is not only allowed; it is a genuine response to the trauma and grief experienced by both children and adults" (Lane 2006: 178). Yet, one demand of teaching English as a foreign language is to offer students meaningful contents which provide incentives for relevant communication. It can be assumed that historical developments and also (mis)treatment of cultural groups mirror such meaningful contexts and are therefore justified for developing ICC.

One of such contexts is the residential school system of North America. In order to "remember and mourn (traumatic) events, and struggle to reconstruct selves and societies" (Saunders / Aghaie 2005: 16), Nicola Campbell and Kim LaFave collaborated in order to make this topic available for children. The specific devices in language, illustration and intertextuality they have chosen to voice the unspeakable and work through the traumatic past of the residential school experience lend themselves as guiding aspects to analyse these picturebooks. The very same aspects also offer a beneficial approach to reflect upon in the ELT classroom (see below).

Yet, I believe that in order to acknowledge the difficulty of writing and understanding the residential school system as reflected in the mentioned picturebooks, it is necessary to offer more information about its past and current relevance before engaging more with its transformation and representation in text and illustrations.

Residential School Trauma and its Current Relevance

The initial quote at the beginning of this essay indicates that writing about First Nations experiences is an act of regaining power and of writing against forgetting. Furthermore, residential school literature functions as a means to help the younger generations understand current political, social, cultural, individual issues members of various First Nations, Inuit and Métis people face and struggle with today. One of the reasons for this struggle is the terror that was inflicted upon whole generations of children, parents and grandparents between the 1830s and 1996 with the residential school system in Canada. With this system the Catholic Church and the government aimed at "killing the Indian to save the child" (Barker 1997) by civilizing – they called it educating – First Nations, Inuit and Métis children in boarding and day schools. The processes, routines and consequences of this system find no comparison in history. Thousands of children endured sexual, physical and mental abuse, hunger, hard labour and oppression on a daily basis which not only left the children themselves devastated, but also their parents and grandparents. Beyond those immediate effects, this system also had severe intergenerational impacts as the children neither experience what it means to be a child, nor how a child is treated in a family, how to raise a child by being raised as a child, how to love by being loved. Therefore, the separation of children and parents not only disrupted the teaching of language and culture, which resulted in cultural loss, but also "impeded the transfer of valuable parenting skills" (100 Years of Loss: n.p.). The routine of abusive behaviour learnt at residential schools, for example, often resulted in a "cycle of abuse and trauma that passes from one generation to the next" (ibid.).

It took ages until survivors were able to communicate this atrocity and authors found a language and form to tell their stories. One of the first books to reveal that dark side of Canada's history was Celia Haig-Brown's *Resistance and Renewal: Surviving the Indian Residential School* (1988). This book includes thirteen interviews with former students of Kamloops Indian Residential School in the interior of British Columbia. As a non-Native, Haig-Brown is highly aware of the criticism she has to face from some First Nations people who see her "work as an unwanted intervention in First Nations business" (1988: 10). Yet, she argues that "it is important to remember that the story of the schools is one in which non-Natives played a central role" (ibid.). In fact, LaCapra states that "[t]here is the possibility of perpetrator trauma that must itself be acknowledged and in some sense worked through if perpetrators are to distance themselves from an earlier implication in deadly ideologies and practices" (2001: 79). The governments' processing of the residential school past resulted in a formal act of contrition when in 2008 Prime Minister Steven Harper apologized on behalf of Canada to the survivors of the residential school system (Legacy of Hope: n.p.). However, First Nations, Inuit and Métis people across Canada still wait for the Canadian Conference of Catholic Bishops to issue an apology on their behalf. Single representatives of the Catholic Church have indeed acknowledged the wrong-doings of the past (see "Statement by the National Meeting on Indian Residential Schools" 1991: 1). Yet, although the representatives "know" about the suffering, abuse and mistreatment and "acknowledge" and "are deeply grieved" by these, they also point out that "[g]ood intentions and genuine love on the part of many of our Sisters for the children in our care were not enough and in fact were often not experienced as such" (Zarowny 2009: n.p.). When looking closer at the intergenerational impact of the residential school system and knowing that most recent numbers reveal that more than 4,000 children died while attending residential schools[10] (see Kennedy 2014), sentences such as "[w]e were the products of the times in which we lived", "some of our members suffered from emotional problems that they took out on the children" and closing with "[e]ach of our involvements, whether educational, political, spiritual or other [...] has resulted in deep and lasting friendships between our Sisters and many First Nations people. We treasure these friendships and look forward to them deepening in the years to come" (Zarowny 2009: n.p.) seem difficult to understand. Yet, it cannot be denied that such partial acknowledgements are the result of intense dialogue between survivors, the government and Church representatives who all needed to come to terms with their mutual past. As Haig-Brown mentioned in the preface of her work, non-native people were also intensely involved in the residential school system and need to negotiate consequences; in retrospective, a certain trauma can also be identified on their side. Different commissions and agencies were established in order to research, educate and make public not only the devastating past but also to pave the path to a balanced future, for example, the Royal Commission on Aboriginal Peoples or the Truth and Reconciliation Commission of Canada.

[10] According to the Legacy of Hope Foundation, "P.H. Bryce reported a death toll among the schools' children ranging from 15%-24% and rising to 42% in Aboriginal homes where sick children were sometimes sent to die" (n.p.).

Although official recognition, acknowledgement and apologies have been issued, the traumatic experience is still difficult to reconcile. At the same time, many First Nations communities have undergone long processes of healing, by finding words to talk about the past, but also by seeking "out knowledge holders to revive traditional spirituality and to reintroduce healing practices" (100 Years of Loss, n.p.). Certainly, publications by survivors themselves, non-fiction and fiction alike, support this struggle and help younger generations understand the importance of and pride in their cultural identities. One of the early autobiographical accounts of the residential school experience was made public by Alice Masak French (1977) and Basil H. Johnston (1988). By now, several of such eye-witness reports and autobiographical voices have contributed to reconstruct the history, development and impact of the residential school system across Canada. As mentioned, the devastating intergenerational consequences and the atrocity inflicted upon children and their families resulted in individual and collective trauma that can be related to current issues First Nations, Inuit and Métis people are dealing with today. This is especially alarming when knowing that abuse and mistreatment of the children in residential school was recorded as early as 1889 (100 Years of Loss: n.p.) – with no visible consequences or changes. When the last residential school closed in 1996, over 150,000 children had attended those schools. Yet, the ongoing reconciliation and apology discussions also contribute to the present-day trauma which still is not settled.

While their parents thought, they receive an education that prepares their children for live,

> [i]n early 1990s, Survivors came forward with disclosures that included sexual abuse; beatings; punishments for speaking Aboriginal languages: forced eating of rotten food; widespread hunger and thirst; bondage and confinement; and forced labour. […] Other experiences reported from Survivors of residential schools include mental abuse, severe punishments, overcrowding, use of students in medical experiments, illness and disease, and, in some cases, death. (100 Years of Loss: n.p.)

4. Close Reading of Residential School Experience: *Shi-shi-etko* and *Shin-chi's Canoe*

The following close reading of two picturebooks about the residential school experience of a girl and her younger brother, offers a step-by-step approach to analysing picturebooks. In the ELT classroom, a similar approach is recommended in order to enable students to focus on the different aspects that create the story (the text as such, the colours and illustrations, stylistic device and intertextuality). It should, however, be noted that these aspects cannot be perceived of as separated but that their interplay and mutual dependency form the main message of the text – one reason why picturebooks is written as one word (see Bland 2013: 1). Therefore, the results of the different aspects need to be seen as a whole so as to initiate an understanding of the picturebooks and the story these tell. Even though the following elaboration may appear rather detailed, even young learners can investigate texts in a similar manner when they receive sufficient scaffolding and small units to focus on.

In *Shi-shi-etko* (2005), which is simultaneously the name of the main protagonist, the reader follows the last four days until the girl has to leave for residential school. Each day she spends with a family member who shows her something different she needs to remember. Her parents' and grandmother's teaching remind her of the value of nature, family and family ties and how important it is that she does not forget these things. On the first morning Shi-shi-etko and her mother go down to the creek to bathe, while her mother reminds her that she needs to remember the songs and dances, the laughter and joy and also the land of their people. On the second day, it is the father who takes his daughter to this land. While paddling their canoe, he points at the landscape, the lake, mountains and trees that Shi-shi-etko should never forget. On the third day, the girl is with Yayah, her grandmother, from whom Shi-shi-etko receives an empty bag for her memories. Yayah takes her to the forest where they collect all kinds of sprigs from different plants. Shi-shi-etko puts those into her bag. When the truck arrives on the forth morning to pick up the children, Shi-shi-etko does not take the bag with memories with her, but leaves it under a tree. She offers the tree some tobacco as well, and asks him to keep her memories and family safe.

As this main storyline is written in rather simple English, young readers should be able to understand it, especially with support of the illustrations (see below). They could put themselves in Shi-shi-etko's position and reflect upon things their own family would like them to remember if they had to go on a longer trip or collect things they would put in a bag of memories. Such an activity allows young learners to engage in one of the leading principles of literary didactics, namely changing perspectives and connecting their own experiences to these of the protagonist.

When the truck leaves, Shi-shi-etko "could not help herself. She looked at everything" (Campbell 2005: n.p.). This phrase is a direct repetition of her reaction to the cultural and natural aspects her family wants her to remember, and could thus be read as a circle which is, however, not closed: Shi-shi-etko leaves family and community behind to go to residential school. As she does not know what will happen there, the story is an open circle in its narrative structure and illustrations – the last picture shows a truck with people in the back driving off into a far distance – but at the same time also a closed circle in its phrasings. While the openness is reflected in a missing saying good-bye scene of child and family, the repetition of this phrase and the different cultural and natural characteristics her family showed her, emphasize memory, cultural identity and the hope for a soon reunion.

Three years after the publication of *Shi-shi-etko*, Campbell published its sequel *Shin-chi's Canoe* (2008). It is set at the beginning of the second school year that the girl has to go to residential school; this year her younger brother Shin-chi has to go as well. The book begins with the good-bye scene (which was missing in the first book) of the children and their parents during which the children make plans for their return: they ask their father for their own canoe because they want to learn to paddle themselves. This sets a hopeful tone for coming home on the first page already, and additionally resembles the children's wish to keep traditions alive and preserve this part of their culture. As Shi-shi-etko has already been to residential school the year before, she tells the reader of her cruel experiences there, e.g. the punishment for speaking her mother tongue or having her hair cut and washed with kerosene at the beginning of the book and thus warns the reader of what may be following. While *Shi-shi-etko* focusses on the last day before leaving for school, *Shin-chi's Canoe* offers more details about daily routines at school and reinforces a much more serious and sad tone.

Compared to the first book and Shi-shi-etko's close observations, the second book starts with a dusty road on which the children travel to school. While Shi-shi-etko tells Shin-chi that he needs to remember the trees, the mountains and the river, his view is blocked because of the dust from the truck on dry road. The children are hardly able to breathe or see. This initial lack of vision indicates a lack of memory, and stands in contrast to Shi-shi-etko's detailed encounters with nature before she had to leave. However, this negative reading is balanced on the next page which shows an open landscape and tells of Shin-chi's perception of nature. Both representations negotiate the difficulty and insecurity of keeping cultural memory alive while facing a harsh and cruel year at school. Interestingly, the brother's observations are not as closely guided as Shi-shi-etko's in the first book, rather, he himself choses what to observe. Thus, he becomes the agent of his own memories. This more active approach is also reflected in his later encounters at school. Again, young learners can engage with the story by paying close attention to what they see when they are on their way to school. Teachers, however, need to be careful with such tasks in order not to trivialize the residential school experience of the children and make students aware of the harsh realities such schools represent.

As soon as the siblings arrive at school, Shi-shi-etko makes sure to explain some basic rules to Shin-chi as to avoid getting into trouble. She emphasizes that from now on their names are Mary and David[11] and that they should not talk to each for the next year. As a token of memory, before the group of children is separated by gender, she hands him a small wooded canoe their father had made. In the course of the book, more details about the daily routine of residential school are reflected, such as having school in the mornings and work in the afternoons, different tasks for boys and girls, but also time for playing outside. It also refers to the different food for the children and teachers, e.g. porridge and burnt toast for breakfast for the children and bacon, eggs and potatoes for the teachers. Children could use the illustrations for such close observations and compare how differently teachers and children are treated at school. Thus, they could try to trace the hardships the children had to suffer and get a feeling for daily life at residential school.

It does not take long until Shin-chi gets lonely and breaks out of school to go down to the river. He places the canoe in the water being sure the canoe will make it home safe. It is when he is by the river and in nature that the phrase "Shin-chi could not help himself. He looked at everything" (Campbell 2008: n.p.) appears again, almost resembling a mantra of memory and hope. His singing of a prayer song that echoes from peak to peak additionally mirrors a connection to the first book where his sister's and father's song echoed from tree to tree. As his sister returned home after her year at school, those repetitions could be read as signs for another safe arrival at home. As Whitehead notes, repetition is one of the "key literary strategies [which] mimics the effect of trauma, for it suggests the insistent return of the event and the disruption of narrative chronology or progression" (2004: 86). Yet, the repetition of this phrase in both picturebooks is rather connected to memorization of cultural and natural images of the community and, therefore, emphasizes a continuity of memory rather than its disruption. When students are provided with well-formed questions they could be guided to see such connections between both books as well.

This story also reflects a circular narration when dust blocks the children's vision when taking off at residential school to go home – this time indicating a

[11] The choice of those names can be interpreted in different directions. What I find most interesting in the context of the politics of residential schools is that the Bible does not offer any details about Mary's descent or youth. As residential schools attempted to kill the Indian to save the child and erase all traces of their indigenous culture, Shi-shi-etko's renaming to Mary reveals that the school was meant to give her life a new start without any connection to where she comes from. The Bible characterizes David as a strong and smart man who sought power and governed his state with authority. In the case of Shin-chi this renaming could refer to his active role in breaking the rules of school (stealing food, escaping to the river).

lack of memory of their residential school experience. However, only partial because a complete loss of memory would not make books such as *Shin-shi-etko* and *Shin-chi's Canoe* possible. As I will analyse in the following section, such partial lack of memory is also reflected in Kim LaFave's illustrations of both books.

When the children arrive at home, they are greeted by their mother and Yayah. They find their father in the woodshed where he is working on the canoe with which the children can explore nature themselves, gather their own experiences and memories of the land.

If it was not for the peritext that Campbell includes in *Shi-shi-etko*, the reader would not know that Shi-shi-etko is going to residential school. Only through the First Nations context and the historic setting does it become clear that this school must be a residential school. However, such educated guess is only possible if the reader already has some knowledge of the system, otherwise readers can connect Shi-shi-etko's sadness and her family's eagerness for her to remember to further experiences of leaving a familiar and beloved place behind. Therefore, initially students could read especially the first book as a saying good-bye story, in which a family expresses deep affection for their child. For young learners, the school context could either be introduced afterwards or with the help of the second story.

Beyond the question of whether and how trauma is representable, a central claim has been that if it is represented, this can be done mainly through experimental writing, e.g. "fragmented narratives characterized by analepses; digression, diversion and prevarications in narrative trajectory; and dispersal or fragmenting of narrative personae" (Gibbs 2014: 17, also in Craps / Buelens 2008: 5). As Gibbs further notes, "to suggest that this is the only model devalues the experience of and the recovery from trauma" (2014: 25). In order to represent trauma, Gibbs emphasizes a "return to a form of realism" (ibid.: 31). This could also be applied to Campbell's picturebooks, because they follow a rather traditional outline. Both books show a linear narration in which text and pictures to a large extent correspond, meaning that they mainly show similar information and that text and picture are synchronized. Thus, the reader would not have to invest too much in decoding the text in order to understand the main content of the picturebooks.[12] However, this clear and linear plot and narration stands in contrast to the harsh atrocity of the historical references. Yet, the colour code and further details in the illustrations that Kim LaFave employs as well as his thought-provoking use of gaps and white pages add important content to the story.

[12] For more information on picture-word dynamics refer to Mourão (2012).

Colours and Illustrations

As the illustrations are very approachable for young learners, they should be able to investigate the following aspects in their ELT classes as well. With focussing their attention on the pictures and colours that are used, they could already engage in in-depth analysis at a fairly early stage of their foreign language reading career. Thus, this approach to the illustrations not only puts a central stylistic device of picturebooks centre stage but also analytical skills of young learners. These are, as described above, essential to Byram's model of ICC.

In *Shi-shi-etko* it is striking that day and night scenes are illustrated with very different colours. When the girl is outside in nature with her family, the drawings show warm brown, red and orange tones while the night scenes are drawn in dark, gloomy blue and cold green colours. This mirrors Shi-shi-etko's comfort, balance and the love she is surrounded with during the day in comparison to her loneliness, fear and insecurity at night when she counts the nights and days until she has to leave. Additionally, on the page of the first night, and as the only page in the whole book, the upper part of the page is not illustrated at all but left blank white. This feature appears even more prominently and intensively in the *Shin-chi's Canoe* and it will be discussed in more detail in the next section. As colours are taught early the language learning process, young students should be able to compare the colours in the target language while a decoding of the function of such colours may be done with mother language support (Butzkamm 1973: 2011)

Space is another detail worth focussing on, namely space that the people who take the girl to school are allowed to occupy. Compared to the space they occupy in Shi-shi-etko's and her family's mind, being ever present and the reason why they spend so much time together memorizing their surroundings, culture and tradition, they only appear at the very top margin of the second last page. In this scene, Shi-shi-etko puts her bag of memories at the foot of a tree while a strict horizontal line cuts of a small upper part of the picture, placing the cattle truck and a few people at the edge of the ground not making them part of the same ground the girl is walking on. Although Shi-shi-etko may have tried to keep them out of her mind, their placement on top of her, although in a distance and therefore really small, reveals that they have been present in a hierarchic higher position. The following page shows a vast landscape again, through which an unpaved road winds its path. The truck with the children on the cargo area drives off into a distance – Shi-shi-etko being part of them as opposed to their marginal inclusion on the page before. Compared to the colour code, such detailed reflection may only be possible with older learners. As section 5 outlines, picturebooks certainly also have potential for more advanced learners and university students as well.

Shin-chi's Canoe is held in a similar style. Yet, as it is to a large extent set at residential school, mainly greenish, greyish and yellow colours are used instead of the warm colours used in the first book. What is striking, though, is that in illustrations in which a couple of children are drawn, it is only Shin-shi-etko's jacket which stands out because it is red, reflecting individuality of one victim in a mass of others. This scene is reminiscent of the movie *Schindler's List* and respectively to Roma Ligocka's autobiographic fiction novel *The Girl in the Red Coat* (2003, original in German *Das Mädchen im roten Mantel*, 2000).[13] Another scene in which such color-coding is employed is the dinner during which the children are served soup and the teachers, all well fed, have steaming vegetables, meat and corn. While the dinner hall and the children are drawn in greenish yellow, their faces almost looking sick, the teachers' room behind a closed glass door is warmly lit, only the food drawn in red, reflecting its heat, but also its importance. As Lim also notes, "[n]one of the children look happy, which contrasts with the adults" (Lim 2008: n.p.). As the text reveals the "children were never given enough food" (Campbell 2008: n.p.).

A feature that is essential, aesthetically, but also for characteristics of postcolonial trauma fiction is the lack of faces when a couple of children are drawn on one page. The missing faces of the family in the scene before Shi-shi-etko and Shin-chi leave for residential school could be attributed to the long-shot from a bird's view perspective, but also the governments' attitude of not recognizing First Nations as people but as 'wild savages' who needed to be 'civilized' in government and church-run schools. However, medium shoulder shot illustrations of groups of children later in the book either show those children from the back or again without detailed facial structures and expressions. In those groups, no individual can be identified but the children are presented as an undistinguished mass. As also observed by Lim (2008: n.p.) "[t]he generic-looking faces of First Nations children, combined with the shadowed, dark tones in some of the text's illustrations, create an impersonal atmosphere that depersonalizes the children as individuals and subtly highlights the cruelty of a residential school system that treats First Nations children as a homogenous group" (Lim 2008: n.p.). As children in residential schools were assigned English names and were not allowed to practice their cultures, the missing faces correspond to a loss of personal and cultural identity as well as the many unnamed victims of this system. Yet, Lim adds that also the adults at school are portrayed in such "generic-looking faces" which "further emphasizes the depersonalizing effects of the residential school and the uncaring attitude of those in

---

[13] As intertextual references are very telling, I will analyze those in more detail in a separate section below.

charge of it" (Lim 2008: n.p.). Additionally, this style of illustration also allows reconsidering common assumptions of trauma theory, which mainly referred to trauma as individual and personal. Yet, this western concept of trauma is here contested as a collective and cultural trauma. Through the interplay of showing close-ups of Shin-shi-etko's and Shin-chi's faces and the collective unidentified children, LaFave conveys personal and collective trauma.

Fragmentation and Leaving Gaps

As mentioned, among other devices, trauma literature makes use of fragmentation (see Gibbs 2014: 27). In the selected picturebooks, this is also used regarding the illustrations rather than the text as such. This is particularly visible in *Shin-chi's Canoe* in which the night scene and also the scene of the daily routine and chores are drawn as coloured patches on white pages. Such an almost white page of a night scene also appears in *Shi-shi-etko*. As Schwab notes with reference to Durras "'Pain needs space,' [...] But sometimes pain cannot tolerate space because space, especially empty space, invites the ghosts of the past and holds the terror of a self that has been evacuated" (Schwab 2006: 118). Certainly, the white spaces in those picturebooks could indicate parts of the past that are withdrawn from memory, yet, further interpretations are possible. On the one hand, this could resemble the siblings' isolation and their unhappiness, as they are really close but now not allowed to talk to each other. When the text reveals that boys and girls were separated, also the episodes of Shi-shi-etko and Shin-chi are not connected, both children are by themselves and do not know how the other is coping with the situation – a disconnection that is also transferred to the illustrations: Shi-shi-etko on one page and Shin-chi in a coloured patch on white ground on the other. On the other hand, this fragmentation and leaving gaps in the visual representation of the text could also indicate a refusal to display and reflect upon the trauma that was survived. As Campbell stated in an interview, she based both books on what she learnt from family and community, yet, as many survivors revealed, they have for long been lacking the language to describe their experiences and their traumatic childhoods. Those gaps could therefore also reflect all the experiences that could not be remembered for their cruelty and stand for "involuntary flashbacks, nightmares, [...], without having access to memories of the originating cause" (Gibbs 2014: 25). Where language fails to make meaning, so do the drawings and illustrations. This idea carries a transcultural notion as well, because the unspeakability of trauma cannot be limited to a certain culture and trauma but can be transferred to other contexts as well – hence the concept of post-colonial trauma fiction.

Additionally, also the child audience should be kept in mind with this interpretation, as some of the memories may just not be accessible and understandable for them. For example, the book tells how Shin-chi and his friend John steal food without being caught, while other sources prove that punishments for this included eating rotten food for a longer period of time or only the food that was stolen. Malnutrition was a central part of the government run nutrition experiments performed on First Nations children (see Mosby 2013). As mentioned earlier, the question in how far trauma can be represented also refers to the extent to which children should be exposed to trauma. Leaving gaps in illustrations and storylines could therefore also be seen as a means of omitting certain details from a child's eyes and ears.

Notwithstanding the cruel context of both books, the narrations balance the atrocity of the residential school system and enjoyable and aesthetic storytelling for children. Through references to cultural and collective identity, colourful illustrations and episodic indications of gaps in memory and representation, these picturebooks develop specific stylistic devices for depicting trauma for children. Thus, they show that traumatic experiences are, despite the difficulties that surround the articulation of trauma, only unspeakable to a certain extent and that trauma fiction can indeed function as a support in working through (see French, in Watson 2000). Just as Shin-chi becomes an agent at residential school by stealing food and escaping to the river, also the author becomes an agent in unveiling and publishing of her ancestors' past and thus enabling healing for herself and the community.

Intertextuality as a Form of Cultural Connections and Survival

Beyond the visual intertextual reference, also the text as such can be considered. In her extended work on *Trauma Fiction* (2004), Anne Whitehead includes a chapter analysing the interplay of trauma narratives and intertextuality. For her, this device has different functions, such as a resurfacing of past traumata, determination of a character in the present, or also enabling forgotten and silenced voices to tell their own story (see Whitehead 2004: 85-86). In the picturebooks at hand intertextuality is used to remind of past injustices while at the same time providing hope and continuity of cultures and traditions. Yet, as extended reading experiences and cultural knowledge are necessary for identifying such references, this should be reserved for advanced learners or university students. According to Hallet (2010) intertextual references allow to identify characteristics of other cultures and support their understanding which makes it part of ICC as well.

"[U]ntil the roses bloom in the spring and the salmon have returned to our river" (Campbell 2005: n.p.) is reminiscent of phrases that were repeatedly used in treaties between the British colonies in North America and the Haudenosaunee and other agreements with Native Americans and First Nations people. Regarding matters of trade, settlement and easing violent conflicts of the different parties involved, peace was said to last "as long as the sun shines upon the earth; as long as the waters flow; as long as the grass grows green".[14]

The relevance of such treaties for First Nations peoples becomes visible when also today First Nations refer to those treaties in fighting against the government's plan to build and extend hydro power plans, for example in British Columbia (BC Hydro dams, Hales 2014).[15] Although this promise was included in the treaties between the government and First Nations, there are countless cases in which they were not kept, hydro power plants were built and the tar sand industry ignored negotiated land rights. The inclusion of a similar phrase right at the beginning of *Shi-shi-etko* foreshadows the impact the residential school will have not only on the girl herself, but also her family and community. Although the mother sends "my girl" to residential school, it can be assumed that the girl may no longer be her girl because the education children received at residential school was an education according to British colonial standards and did not echo any of the traditions and knowledge important to First Nations people. In fact, after years at residential school some of the children returned home as strangers to their own land and community, because they had forgotten their language and cultural routines were foreign to them. This alienation is the topic of *Not my Girl* by Christy Jordan-Fenton and Margaret Pokiak-Fenton mentioned earlier, in which mother and daughter need to go through an intense process of getting to know each other again after the daughter spend years at residential school cut off from her family. Alice Masak French reflects comparable experiences (1977). At the same time, the initial quote is included in a double page which shows mother and daughter standing in the shallow water of the creek, greeting the sun in the early morning with open arms – an indication of a new beginning which raises hopes for a survival of cultural identity.

A similar hopeful undertone can be read into the father's "paddle song" he sings on the third last day before Shi-shi-etko has to leave for residential school. This can be understood as a direct reference to Tekahionwake's (1861-1913) long poem "The Song my Paddle Sings" first published in *The White Wampum* in 1895 which readers familiar with First Nations Literature might recall. While

[14] See *The Covenant Chain*, http://www.iroquoisdemocracy.pdx.edu/html/covenantchain.htm

[15] See http://www.theecoreport.com/green-blogs/lifestyle/minorities/firstnations/site-c-how-long-until-the-sun-stops-shinning-grass-does-not-grow-and-the-rivers-dry-up/

paddle songs are not uncommon in First Nations literature, this references reveals interesting parallels. Tekahionwake translated into English means "two-lives"[16] or "double wampum"[17] and indeed, the author, daughter of a Kahniakenhaka (Mohawk) chief of mixed ancestry and a white mother, combines "two literary traditions [...]: the oral legends of the Iroquois and English Romanticism" (New 2002: 555). "The Song My Paddle Sings" reflects the pride in her aboriginal heritage. When Shi-shi-etko repeats her father's paddle song, she not only shows that she has learnt and memorized it, but the intertextual reference to this poem also indicates that Shi-shi-etko herself may be able to combine both the education at residential school and the teachings of her family and community. Additionally, just as Tekahionwake's poems and legacy have remained vivid within First Nations traditions and memory so will Shi-shi-etko and her cultural identity after she returns from residential school.

In *Shi-shi-etko* the mother wants her daughter to remember "the ways of our people", but many children returned to their families and had forgotten about traditions, routines and also the language. Yet, the "elders carried forward, carried on with parts, survived, this is what people should contemplate, even though they were children this doesn't change their strength" (CBC interview with Campbell 2014). And further

> as children they remembered so much of our culture, going back to the communities, and able to carry through that strength, there was a period where people didn't practice cultural activities, but it came back ... now everybody is going strong again and bringing those things back ... our elders were children at that time and they are still able to remember and practice... be proud of the land, the territory you come from ... there are stories within stories of where our ancestors and our elders come from. (ibid.)

While the First Nations, Métis and Inuit have had to face multiple disruptions in their existence in Canada, those intertextual references to cultural products[18] reveal that their past struggles and achievements are not forgotten but remain visible in the present. Both books reveal that people have "retained their lan-

---

[16] http://www.manataka.org/page1998.html

[17] http://www.thecanadianencyclopedia.ca/en/article/pauline-johnson/

[18] A further example that could be mentioned is the parallel of Shi-shi-etko leaving the bag of memories filled with springs under a tree and a scene in Jeannette Armstrong's *Whispering in Shadows* (2000), in which Penny buries copper under a tree, both of which resembling offerings to nature. While *Shi-shi-etko's* offering should protect her family and community, one way of reading Penny's offering could indicate that she seeks healing for herself. "Penny" is also the term for the currency coin, which in the past was made of copper. In fact, references to the "Shining Woman of Copper" can be found multiple times in the novel (e.g. 98, 286).

guage and their culture and continue to work toward healing and reconciliation" (100 Years of Loss: n.p.).

5. Crossover to School and University Classrooms

In addition to the didactic aspects that were mentioned before, crossing over from trauma fiction to learning environments, different aspects need to be taken into consideration. First and foremost, this regards the audience and learner group for whom teaching environments are to be planned. I believe that second language learners of a similar age group as the intended audience will be overwhelmed, not necessarily by the language and style of the picturebooks, but rather by their content and context. As indicated in the reading of *Shi-shi-etko*, though, this book could be used to engage young learners in reflecting about saying goodbye to beloved people and thinking of experiences that are important to share before a farewell. Also the analysis of the colour code and the fragmentation that is used in both books can allow already young learners to engage with the analytical skills necessary for developing intercultural awareness. Content-wise, however, this topic may be rather demanding for primary school students so that their potential for intermediate and advanced learners as well as university students can be emphasized. Conceptually, I already mentioned that trauma fiction for children lends itself for engaging with multimodal narratives and inquiry-based learning. Yet, the larger frame in which such picturebooks are contextualized are scenarios of inter- and transcultural learning as well as interdisciplinary teaching.

As elaborated in an earlier section, the development of ICC has become the key aspect of foreign language education. Next to Byram's model of ICC, scholars such as Bredella and Christ (1993), Bredella (2002, 2010), Burwitz-Melzer (2003) and Surkamp and Nünning (2008) have repeatedly elaborated on literature's potential to develop ICC and understand otherness. They agree that through reading multicultural literature, learners can engage with the protagonists' experiences, can change perspectives and develop empathy and understanding of the other culture. Learning about other people's realities increases their awareness of otherness and challenges their egocentric perspectives. Yet, as I have elaborated in detail (see Alter 2015), it is essential to engage with a variety of texts and pay close attention to the representation of otherness in order to avoid a further establishment of stereotypes and prejudices. The consideration of postcolonial fiction in general, and trauma fiction for children more specifically, is an important extension to texts that are commonly read in ELT (see Alter 2015). Based on their serious historical background, they also entail a cognitive challenge that more experienced learners may enjoy compared to literary analyses that focus on stylistic device and their interpretation. Trauma fiction allows to cognitively engage with the circumstances a text is founded on and motivates to investigate such backgrounds. Grounded on a literary reading experience, more advanced students can explore non-fictional text and trace the creation of (trauma) fiction seeing history as a starting point.

A short novel about residential school that would be suitable for intermediate learners is *As Long as the Rivers Flow* by Larry Loyie (2005). The readers follow Lawrence's last summer before he enters residential school. Like in *Shi-shi-etko*, also the protagonist of this story spends a lot of time with his family and in nature. For him, this last summer is the time when he learns and enjoys other skills important in daily life, such as sewing and making moccasins, berry picking, hunting and story-telling. Similar to *Shi-shi-etko*, the focus is not on the school experience, but on the days the family spends together before their son has to leave. Apart from this context, it offers a credible representation of First Nations cultures and could therefore support students in challenging common stereotypes of First Nations peoples in this specific historic background, but also beyond.

Picturebooks can unfold additional potential with more advanced learners when they are read from a stronger analytical and meta-perspective compared to younger learners' reader-response approach that focusses on changing perspectives and relating the text to the self (Bredella / Burwitz-Melzer 2004). In particular, picturebooks about controversial issues (Koehnecke 2001) or trauma fiction lend themselves to be investigated in the advanced English classroom or at university. As experienced learners can cognitively perform on a higher level, it is beneficial to explore with them how an author processes traumatic experiences in the plot and how the illustrators manage to illustrate those. With university students one can expect that they have fundamental background knowledge of First Nations history, and that they, therefore, understand the historical background. Additionally, they could actually be familiar with a few texts the picturebooks refer to and therefore be able to unveil some of the intertextual references that are included in *Shi-shi-etko* and *Shin-chi's Canoe*. In the advanced ELT classroom, intertextual knowledge could be achieved through group work or learning at stations. When the application of picturebooks in advanced classes and at university speaks to students' cognitive and aesthetic development, those factors contribute to an increase of students' literary literacy, a concept that has gained significance in current TEFL discourses as well (see Burwitz-Melzer 2013: 55-70, Lütge 2012: 191-202).

Just as this essay traces some current criticism of trauma theory, even if only in highlights, university students could engage with this topic in a similar outline: they can read early academic texts on trauma theory and use postcolonial trauma texts to critically reflect upon those early accounts. Such an inductive approach could then lead to exploring Craps' and Gibbs' texts and compare their criticism to the students' own results. In the context of cultural studies, students could explore the incidents beyond the residential school system which continuously added to the trauma of First Nations, Métis and Inuit people. At the same time they could differentiate the colonizers' influence on the indigenous population while distinguishing the positive aspects of the relationships as well.[19] This would prepare future teachers to use texts such as *Shi-shi-etko* and *Shin-chi's Canoe* in their own classrooms, as it is essential that they not only develop the background knowledge but are also comfortable with this topic and make sure that a respective atmosphere is created.

Using various examples of history, university students could investigate how authors balance the demands of a child audience on the one hand and the reflection of the truth of the past's atrocity on the other. Cultural and literary studies classes could engage in in-depth reflections of trauma fiction for children and analyse those texts according to their content, context and representation of trauma. Example texts could be:

- Roberto Innocenti's *Rose Blanche* (1985), a picturebook about a little girl that watches the street from her window as it fills up with Nazi soldiers. Especially striking about the book are the detailed descriptions of the girl's sensual perception of her surrounding and her joyful and innocent voice which is dramatically disrupted as she follows one of the trucks to the forest and discovers a concentration camp.
- Toshi Maruki's *Hiroshima No Pika* (1982), an account of a little girl that witnesses the Hiroshima bombing.
- Maira Kalman's *Fireboat: The Heroic Adventures of the John J. Harvey* (2002), about the boat that was too old to still be used in New York, but regained an important task on 9/11 when all the help the city could get was needed after the attacks on the World Trade Center.
- Andrea Patel's *On that Day* (2002), which offers a very hopeful post-9/11 message to children.

Surely, these books as such are not free of controversy but rather invite students to critically reflect upon aspects such as ideology and propaganda that may subtly be transmitted. Additionally, those examples were published in different decades, so that students may also investigate a change of representation of

[19] As is for example mentioned in Michael Kusugak's afterword to Artic Stories (1998).

trauma, particularly when books from different time frames reflect on a similar trauma.

The picturebook examples discussed and introduced above cross over between trauma fiction and children's literature, social studies and history, cultural and literary studies and art, and thus allow university students to apply knowledge gained in different academic fields. Such learning and teaching is beneficial for an interdisciplinary reading of those texts which also contributes to students' development of a network of knowledge and competences.

6. Conclusion

This essay applied a critical reading of trauma theory to picturebooks for children that reflect upon the residential school experience in Canada. Between 1830s and 1996 approximately 150,000 children were removed from their families, dislocated from their land and brought to government- and Church-run schools that tried to civilize those children, a policy that is often referred to as "Kill the Indian to save the Child." Writing about her people's experiences, First Nations, Métis and Inuit authors such as Nicole Campbell or Margaret Pokiak-Fenton not only regain voice to make public and correct this devastating past, but also help against forgetting it as well as offering documents of their individual, but also collective processes of working-through. Especially the choice of picturebooks as a form of trauma fiction leaves an intense impact as "[o]f all contemporary genres of children's literature, the picture book offers the most dramatic and/or ironic testimony to trauma, precisely because the genre is usually presumed innocent" (Kidd 2005: 137). In both picturebooks *Shi-shi-etko* and *Shin-chi's Canoe* this innocence is not only reflected through the protagonists who long to be with their family, but also through the telling usage of colours and fragmentation in the illustrations.

Craps' and Gibbs' approaches to trauma theory have certainly added very important reconsiderations of a paradigm that so far fell short of a more holistic perception of trauma and a non-Western perspective. This is also reflected in my reading of the picturebooks as trauma is not necessarily presented in disrupted narrations characterized by nightmarish flashbacks or limited to individual experiences. Rather, as the analysis revealed, trauma can indeed be collective and caused by continuous oppression, as is the case in First Nation, Métis and Inuit history in North America.

What is additionally interesting about *Shi-shi-etko* and *Shin-chi's Canoe* is that the author has not experienced the residential school system herself, but heard of the stories from her family and community. Therefore, even when the younger generation was not directly affected by this policy, the intergenerational impact has such magnitude that also for them processes of healing are essential in order to cope with collective traumatization of the past. Only if storytelling continues can children be educated about the reasons of current living conditions and would it be possible that stories can "grown over the wound like a second skin" (Schwab 2006: 96).

Yet, despite the collective atrocity of residential school experiences, their individuality renders any generalization impossible. Therefore, more investigations and research is necessary in the research of trauma fiction and its role in (foreign language) education. From a cultural studies perspective, additional critical research needs to be conducted with regards to Native trauma and the bias entailed in any Eurocentric terminology.

Crossing over to ELT and university education, this essay emphasized the picturebooks potential to develop ICC, especially in view of the cognitive dimension and its influence on the affective level. Through engaging with trauma fiction for children, students can be prepared for an emphatic encounter with this bleak era of Canadian history. Through references to actual events, cultural reflection could gain a more thorough and meaningful level of communication.

In sum, I believe that writing, publishing, reading and especially teaching trauma fiction in different age groups as part of ICC in ELT, has become a necessity in order to learn about and from other cultures and be provided with a holistic image of a particular culture. Attempts of understanding otherness need to take the historic and social-cultural development of a culture into account. Picturebooks are one means of giving already younger learners insights into such developments.

Bibliography

100 Years of Loss. http://www.legacyofhope.ca/downloads/100-years-of-loss-booklet.pdf (24/10/14).

Alter, Grit (2011). Living between Two Worlds – Künstlerische Darstellungen zum Leben der Inuit analysieren und verstehen. *Englisch 5-10*, 16, 30-33.

Alter, Grit (2015). *Inter- and Transcultural Learning in the Context of Canadian Young Adult Fiction*. Münster: Lit-Verlag.

Armstrong, Jeannette (2000). *Whispering in Shadows*. Penticton: Theytus.

Armstrong, Jeannette (1985). *Slash*. Penticton: Theytus.

Armstrong, Jeannette (1983). *Neekna and Chemai*. Penticton: Theytus.

Armstrong, Jeannette (1982). *Enwhisteetkwa (or Walk in Water)*. Penticton: Okanagan Indian Curriculum Project/Okanagan Tribal Council.

Ashcroft, Bill / Griffiths, Gareth / Tiffin, Helen (1998). *Key Concepts in Post-Colonial Studies*. New York: Routledge.

Ashcroft, Bill / Griffiths, Gareth / Tiffin, Helen (1989). *The Empire Writes Back*. New York: Routledge.

Barker, Debra K.S. (1997). Kill the Indian, Save the Child: Cultural Genocide and the Boarding School. *American Indian Studies: An Interdisciplinary Approach to Contemporary Issues*. New York. Peter Lang, 47-68.

Bell, Thorsten / Urhahne, Detlef / Schanze, Sascha / Ploetzner, Rolf (2010). Collaborative Inquiry Learning: Models, Tools, and Challenges. *International Journal of Science Education* 3(1), 349-377.

Bland, Janice (2013). Introduction. In: Bland, Janice / Lütge, Christiane (Eds.). *Children's Literature in Second Language Education*. London: Bloomsbury, 1-12.

Bland, Janice / Lütge, Christiane (2013) (Eds.). *Children's Literature in Language Education*. London: Bloomsbury.

Bradford, Claire (2011). Multiculturalism and Post-colonialism. In: Grenby, M.O. / Reynolds, Kimberly (Eds.). *Children's Literature Studies – A Research Handbook*. New York: Palgrave Macmillan, 162-170.

Bradford, Claire (2007). *Unsettling Narratives. Postcolonial Readings of Children's Literature*. Waterloo: Wilfrid Laurier University Press.

Bredella, Lothar (2010). *Das Verstehen des Anderen. Kulturwissenschaftliche und Literaturdidaktische Studien*. Tübingen: Narr.

Bredella, Lothar / Burwitz-Melzer, Eva (2004). *Rezeptionsästhetische Literaturdidaktik: Mit Beispielen aus dem Fremdsprachenunterricht Englisch*. Tübingen: Narr.

Bredella, Lothar (2002). *Literarisches und interkulturelles Verstehen*. Tübingen: Narr.

Bredella, Lothar / Christ, Herbert (Eds.) (1993). *Zugänge zum Fremden*. Gießen: Verlag der Ferber'schen Universitätsbuchhandlung.

Bruchac, Joseph (2004). *The Winter People*. St. Louis: Turtleback Books.

Burwitz-Melzer, Eva (2013). Approaching Literary and Language Competence: Picturebooks and Graphic Novels in the EFL Classroom. In: Bland, Janice / Lütge, Christiane (Eds.). *Children's Literature in Language Education*. London: Bloomsbury, 55-70.

Burwitz-Melzer, Eva (2003). *Allmähliche Annäherungen: Fiktionale Texte im interkulturellen Fremdsprachenunterricht der Sekundarstufe I. Beiträge zur Gießener Fremdsprachendidaktik*. Tübingen: Narr.

Butzkamm, Wolfgang (2011). Why Make Them Crawl if They Can Walk. Teaching with Mother Tongue Support. *RELC Journal* 42(3), 379 - 391.

Butzkamm, Wolfgang (1973). *Aufgeklärte Einsprachigkeit: Zur Entdogmatisierung der Methode im Fremdsprachenunterricht*. Heidelberg: Quelle & Meyer.

Byram, Michael (1997). *Teaching and Assessing Intercultural Communicative Competence*. Clevedon: Multilingual Matters.

Campbell, Nicola (2008). *Shin-chi's Canoe*. Toronto: Groundwood Books.
Campbell, Nicola (2005). *Shi-shi-etko*. Toronto: Groundwood Books.
Campbell, Nicola. *Nicola I. Campbell, author of Shin-Chi's Canoe.* http://www.cbc.ca/books/bookclub/2009/11/nicola-i-campbell-author-of-shin-chis-canoe.html (24/10/14).
Campbell, Maria (1977). *Little Badger and the Fire Spirit*. Toronto: McClelland and Stewart.
Campbell, Maria (1973). *Halfbreed.* Lincoln: University of Nebraska Press.
Caruth, Cathy (1996). *Unclaimed Experience: Trauma, Narrative, and History*. Baltimore: Johns University Press.
Caruth, Cathy (1991). Unclaimed Experience: Trauma and the Possibility of History. *Yale French Studies* 79, 181-192.
Connolly, Paula T. (2008). Retelling 9/11: How Picture Books Re-Envision National Crises. *The Lion and the Unicorn* 32(3), 288-303.
Covenant Chain, The. http://www.iroquoisdemocracy.pdx .edu/html/covenant-chain.htm (24/10/14).
Craps, Stef (2013). *Postcolonial Witnessing: Trauma Out of Bounds*. New York: Palgrave Macmillan.
Craps, Stef / Buelens, Gert (2008). Introduction: Postcolonial Trauma Novels. *Studies in the Novel* 40(1/2), 1-12.
French, Alice Masak (1991). *The Restless Nomad*. Winnipeg: Pemmican Publishing.
French, Alice Masak (1977). *My Name Is Masak*. Winnipeg: Peguis Publishing.
Gibbs, Alan (2014). *Contemporary American Trauma Narratives*. Edinburgh: Edinburgh University Press.
Haig-Brown, Celia (1988). *Resistance and Renewal: Surviving the Indian Residential School.* Vancouver: Arsenal Pulp Press.
Hales, Roy (2014). BC: SITE C, "As Long as the Sun Shines, the Grass Grows & the Rovers Flow". http://www.theecoreport.com/green-blogs/lifestyle/minorities/firstnations/site-c-how-long-until-the-sun-stops-shinning-grass-does-not-grow-and-the-rivers-dry-up/ (24/10/14).
Hallet, Wolfgang (2010). Intertextualität und Intermedialität. In: Carola Surkamp (Ed.), *Metzler Lexikon Fremdsprachendidaktik.* Stuttgart: Metzler, 127-128.
Hallet, Wolfgang (2008). Visual Culture und Literatur: Die neuen multimodalen Romane und die Literaturdidaktik. In: Eva Burwitz-Melzer (Eds.), *Fremdsprachen Lehren und Lernen. Themenschwerpunkt: Lehren und Lernen mit literarischen Texten* 37, 141-153.
Innocenti, Roberto (1985). *Rose Blanche.* Mankato: Creative Editions.
Ipellie, Alootook (1993). *Artic Dreams and Nightmares*. Penticton: Theytus Books.
Johnston, Basil H. (1988). *Indian School Days*. Toronto: Key Porter Books.
Jordan-Fenton, Christy / Pokiak-Fenton, Margaret (2014). *Not my Girl.* Toronto: Annick Press.

Jordan-Fenton, Christy / Pokiak-Fenton, Margaret (2013). *When I Was Eight.* Toronto: Annick Press.

Jordan-Fenton, Christy / Pokiak-Fenton, Margaret (2011). *A Stranger at Home.* Toronto: Annick Press.

Jordan-Fenton, Christy / Pokiak-Fenton, Margaret (2010). *Fatty Legs*. Toronto: Annick Press.

Kalman, Maira (2002). *Fireboat: The Heroic Adventures of the John J. Harvey.* New York: Puffin.

Kennedy, Mark (2014). At Least 4,000 aboriginal children died in residential schools, commission finds. *National Post*, Jan 3, 2014. http://news.nationalpost.com/2014/01/03/at-least-4000-aboriginal-children-died-in-residential-schools-commission-finds/ (24/10/14).

Kertzer, Adrienne (2002). *My Mother's Voice: Children, Literature, and the Holocaust*. Peterborough: Broadview.

Kidd, Kenneth (2005). 'A' is for Auschwitz: Psychoanalysis, Trauma Theory, and the "Children's Literature of Atrocity. *Children's Literature* 33, 120-149.

Koehnecke, Dianne (2001). *Smokey Night* and *Crack*: Controversial Subjects in Current Children's Stories. *Children's Literature in Education* 32(1), 17-30.

Kusugak, Michael / Vladyana, Krykorka (1998). *Artic Stories*. Toronto: Annick Press.

LaCapra, Dominick (2001). *Writing History Writing Trauma*. Baltimore: John Hopkins University Press.

Lane, Dorothy F. (2006). The Language of Trauma. *CCL/LCJ Canadian Children's Literature/Littérature canadienne pour la jeunesse* 32(1), 170-179.

Legacy of Hope Foundation. http://www.legacyofhope.ca/home (24/10/14).

Leys, Ruth (2000). *Trauma: A Genealogy*. Chicago: University of Chicago Press.

Ligocka, Roma (2003). *The Girl in the Red Coat*. New York: Random House.

Ligocka, Roma (2000). *Das Mädchen im roten Mantel*. München: Droemer Knaur.

Lim, Huai-Yang (2008). Review Shin-chi's *Canoe*. *CM XV* (7). http://umanitoba.ca/cm/vol15/no7/shinchiscanoe.html (24/10/14).

Loyie, Larry (2005). *As Long as the Rivers Flow.* Toronto: Groundwood Books.

Lütge, Christiane (2012). Developing "Literary Literacy"? Towards a Progression of Literary Learning. In: Eisenmann, Maria / Summer, Theresa (Eds.). *Basic Issues in EFL Teaching and Learning*. Heidelberg: Winter, 191-202.

Lunn, Janet (1981). *The Root Cellar.* Lester and Orpen Dennys.

Lynch-Brown, Carol / Tomlinson, Carl M. / Short, Kathy G. (2011). *Essentials of Children's Literature*. Boston: Pearson.

Maruki, Toshi (1982). *Hiroshima No Pika*. New York: Lothrop, Lee & Shepard.

May, Jill (1995). *Children's Literature and Critical Theory: Reading and Writing for Understanding*. New York: Oxford University Press.

Mosby, Ian (2013). Administering Colonial Science: Nutrition Research and Human Biomedical Experimentation in Aboriginal Communities and Residential Schools, 1942–1952. *Histoire sociale/Social history* 46(91), 145-172.
Mosioner, Beatrice (Culleton) (1984). *April Raintree.* Winnipeg: Pemmican Publication.
Mosioner, Beatrice (Culleton) (1983). *In Search of April Raintree.* Winnipeg: Pemmican Publication.
Mourão, Sandie (2012). English Picturebook Illustrations and Language Development in Early Years Education. Unpublished PhD-Thesis. Aveiro: University of Aveiro, Portugal. http://ria.ua.pt/handle/10773/9180 (19/10/15).
New, William H. (Ed.) (2002). *Encyclopedia of Literature in Canada*. Toronto: University of Toronto Press.
Nilsen, Alleen P. / Donelson, Kenneth L. (2009). *Literature for Today's Young Adults*. Boston: Person.
Nodelman, Perry / Reimer, Mavis (2002). *The Pleasures of Children's Literature*. Boston: Allyn & Bacon.
Norton, Donna E. (2011). *Through the Eyes of a Child: An Introduction to Children's Literature.* Boston: Pearson.
O'Dell, Scott (1970). *Sing Down the Moon.* Boston: Houghton Mifflin.
Patel, Andrea (2002). *On that Day.* Berkeley: Tricycle Press.
Rahn, Suzanne (1991). An Evolving Past: The Story of Historical Fiction and Nonfiction for Children. *The Lion and the Unicorn* 15(1), 1-26.
Risager, Karen (2012). Introduction: Intercultural Learning: Raising Cultural Awareness. In: Eisenmann, Maria / Summer, Theresa (Eds.). *Basic Issues in EFL Teaching and Learning*. Heidelberg: Winter, 143-155.
Robinett, Jane (2007). The Narrative Shape of Traumatic Experience. *Literature and Medicine* 26(2), 290-311.
Said, Edward (1978). *Orientalism.* New York: Vintage Books.
Saunders, Rebecca / Aghaie, Kamran Scot (2005). Introduction: Memory and Mourning. *Comparative Studies of South Asia, Africa and the Middle East* 25(1), 16-29.
Schindler's List, director Steven Spielberg, with Liam Neeson, Ben Kingsley, Ralph Fiennes, Caroline Goodall, Jonathan Sagall, Embeth Davidtz, Universal Pictures, 1993.
Schwab, Gabriele (2006). Writing against Memory and Forgetting. *Literature and Medicine* 25(1), 95-121.
Statement by the National Meeting on Indian Residential Schools (1991). http://www.cccb.ca/site/images/stories/pdf/apology_saskatoon.pdf (24/10/14).
Styvendale, Nancy (2008). The Trans/Historicity of Trauma in Jeannette Armstrong's *Slash* and Sherman Alexie's *Indian Killer*. *Studies in the Novel* 40(1/2), 203-223.
Surkamp, Carola / Nünning, Ansgar (2008). *Englisch Literatur unterrichten 1: Grundlagen und Methoden.* Seelze: Klett/Kallmeyer.

Tekahionwake / Pauline E. Johnson. Manataka American Indian Council. http://www.manataka.org/page1998.html (24/10/14).

Tekahionwake / Pauline E. Johnson. Pauline Johnson. http://www.thecanadian-encyclopedia.ca/en/article/pauline-johnson/ (24/10/14).

Van der Kolk, Bessel / van der Hart, Onno (1995). The Intrusive Past: The Flexibility of Memory and the Engraving of Trauma. In: Caruth, Cathy (Ed.). *Trauma: Explorations in Memory*, Baltimore: Johns Hopkins University Press. 158-182.

Watson, Christine (2000). Autobiographical Writing as a Healing Process. Interview with Alice Masak French. *Canadian Literature* 167, 32-42.

Whitehead, Anne (2004). *Trauma Fiction*. Edinburgh: Edinburgh University Press.

Wilhelm, Jeffrey D. / Wilhelm, Peggy J. (2010). Inquiring Minds Learn to Read, Write, and Think: Reaching all Learners through Inquiry. *Middle School Journal* 41(5), 39-46.

Zarowny, Marie (2009). Statement on Behalf of Congregations of Women Religious Involved in the Indian Residential Schools of Canada. http://www.ssabc.ca/story/statement-behalf-congregations-women-religious-involved-indian-residential-schools-canada (24/10/14).

PETER FREESE

"What, then, is the American, this new man?" (Crèvecœur): National Identity in a Country of Immigrants[1]

Having explained some relevant terms, I provide verbal, visual and auditory material on the history of the U.S. national anthem and its recent Spanish version as suitable means for introducing the concepts of national identity and national language into the EFL-classroom. I then sketch the gradual development of an 'American' identity, define unconditional assimilation, Americanization, Anglo-Saxon racialism, cultural pluralism, and multiculturalism as the basic attitudes the 'ones' have shown to the 'others' in the course of U.S. history, and demonstrate how these positions can be successfully taught through selected cartoons. Arguing that contemporary problems can only be understood in relation to the past, I outline the history of the "melting pot" concept from Crèvecœur's famous "Third Letter" through Zangwill's play to the ceremonies in Henry Ford's English Classes, and sketch such (in)famous expressions of Anglo-Saxon racialism as Josiah Strong's Our Country, *Senator Beveridge's speeches about the annexation of the Philippines, and Madison Grant's* The Passing of the Great Race. *Finally, I deal with the controversial relationship between one's national identity and one's language and show how different historical and contemporary American approaches to making immigrants learn English have a high transfer value for German EFL-learners and can increase their intercultural competence.*

The notion of 'national identity' is comparatively young and developed only in the mid-eighteenth century in connection with the establishment of nation states. In our present-day globalized world with supranational institutions, transnational economies, and waves of migrants moving across the globe, this notion is increasingly contested and some even consider it obsolete. Since an abstract debate about what 'national identity' means is beyond the limits of the

[1] On April 17, 2012, I opened the lecture series "CROSSOVERS: Postcolonial Studies and Transcultural Learning" at the English Institute of Münster University with a talk on this topic. Since I could not include the many visual texts and audio files I used in my presentation in the printed version, I have rewritten the text and incorporated material from earlier essays on "American National Identity in a Globalized World as a Topic in the Advanced EFL-Classroom," in Freese 2008 and "From Melting Pot to Quilt: Ethnic Diversity vs. National Identity," in Freese 2005c and 2006.

EFL-classroom, any thematic sequence should start with a motivating opening. With regard to the concept of identity, it is sufficient to recall that 'identity' as an individual's or a group's sense of self over time can only be developed in relation to others, and that both individuals and groups have multiple economic, cultural, political, national and other identities that are of different importance in different situations and result from the interaction between the self or group and others. As far as 'nations' go, one usually distinguishes between 'good' societies which are based on a social contract, open to all who want to join, and patriotic, and 'bad' societies which are based on ethnic characteristics or ideological tenets, limited to those who share these traits or beliefs, and nationalistic.

*****

In September 1814, the American lawyer and amateur poet Francis Scott Key, held captive aboard a British man of war during the Battle of Baltimore, observed how in a rainy night the British fleet bombarded Fort McHenry. When the Stars and Stripes was still flying triumphantly above the battered fort the next morning, he was inspired by his countrymen's bravery and wrote a poem about the "Defence of Fort McHenry," which opens with these lines:

> Oh, say can you see by the dawn's early light
> What so proudly we hailed at the twilight's last gleaming,
> Whose broad stripes and bright stars through the perilous fight,
> O'er the ramparts we watched, were so gallantly streaming?

Later, Key's brother-in-law combined the poem with the popular melody of a song about the pleasures of wine and women composed in Britain by John Stafford Smith in the 1770s. Text and music were published under the new title "The Star-Spangled Banner," and the song gradually became more popular. More than a century later, it was adopted as the national anthem of the United States of America by a law signed on March 3, 1931 by President Herbert Hoover. On January 27, 1991, Whitney Houston sang "The Star-Spangled Banner" with jazz chords and gospel rhythms at the Tampa Super Bowl and when her rendition was released as a single, it quickly rose to number 20 on the *Billboard* Hot 100 chart and sold 750,000 copies in the first week.

When the complex history of "The Star-Spangled Banner" (its spontaneous genesis in an ongoing war; its coupling of a serious text with the melody of an anacreontic love song; the long time it took to become the national anthem; its unusual success in the pop song charts) and its function as a formal expression of 'national identity' has been worked out with the help of such useful teaching material as Edward Percy Moran's romantic painting of Key in the act of writing his poem,[2] a facsimile of the original manuscript,[3] or a video of Whitney Houston's famous rendition,[4] teachers might present a YouTube clip on "Nuestro Himno."[5] From this clip the students will learn that in April 2006 a Spanish version of the American anthem was released to over 500 Spanish language radio stations across the United States, and they can then listen to this variant: "Amanece: ¿lo véis a la luz de la aurora / Lo que tanto aclamamos la noche al caer? / Sus estrellas, sus franjas flotaban ayer, / En el fiero combate en señal de victoria." (The day is breaking, do you see it? In the light of the dawn? What we so acclaimed at nightfall? Its stars, its stripes, flew yesterday in the fierce battle as a sign of victory). The co-existence of an English- and a Spanish-language version will raise the crucial questions of whether a national anthem should only be sung in the 'national' language, and of whether there is something like a 'national' language? Predictably, "Nuestro Himno" triggered a heated nation-wide debate about these questions, and President Bush felt compelled to declare, according to the *Seattle Times* of April 29, 2006, that "people who want to be U.S. citizens should learn English and 'ought to learn to sing the national anthem in English.'"[6] In this context, it would not only be interesting to have a group of students report on the major arguments exchanged in this debate,[7] but also important to make them recognize that the debate about a 'national language' is by no means only an American problem and to make them transfer the topic to their own daily existence in Germany. For this purpose they should visit the homepage of Hans Christian Ströbele, a member of the *Bundestag*,[8] where they will find both an audio clip of the third stanza of the *Deutschlandlied* sung in Turkish and Ströbele's comment on the feasibility of this version.

After this introductory unit, it becomes necessary to work out some basic knowledge about the evolution of a 'national identity' in the U.S. Whereas Germans had a linguistic and cultural identity of long standing before they became citizens of a politically united nation state as late as 1871, in the U.S. things happened in reversed order, since the American Revolution created a new political entity with a need for a national consciousness, which could nei-

---

[2] See http://www.baltimoreorless.com/2012/09/francis-scott-key-composes-the-star-spangled-banner/.

[3] See http://en.wikipedia.org/wiki/The_Star-Spangled_Banner.

[4] See http://www.dailymotion.com/video/x28chl_national-anthem-usa-whitney-houston_music.

[5] See http://www.youtube.com/watch?v=f4gP_pSOCz4.

[6] *Seattle Times*, April 29, 2006, http://seattletimes.com/html/nationworld/2002960428_anthem29.html.

[7] Using <nuestro himno + Bush> as their searchword, they will find pertinent material and discover that as early as 1919 the U.S. Bureau of Education commissioned a Spanish version of Key's text. But at that time the song was not yet the official national anthem, but just one patriotic song among others.

[8] See http://www.stroebele-online.de/dokumente/129925.html.

ther be derived from the diverse languages, religions, and nationalities of the settlers in the thirteen colonies nor defined in contrast to the cultural ancestors in Britain who had become the political opponents. Thus, Philip Gleason could state that "the United States defined itself as a nation by commitment to the principles of liberty, equality, and government on the basis of *consent*, and the nationality of its people derived from their identification with those principles." (1980: 31) Since around 1790 eight out of ten white Americans were of British derivation, there was of course also a certain disposition towards defining the new nation in terms of *descent*, and that is shown by the fact that Blacks and Native Americans were excluded for reasons of race. But the essential condition for becoming an "American" was not an immigrant's national, ethnic, linguistic or religious background, but their commitment to the universal ideas of equality and republicanism, their willingness to accept the English tradition of liberty, and their orientation towards a new and better future. This commitment made G. K. Chesterton observe that "America is the only nation in the world that is founded on a creed,"[9] and in 1917 this creed became known as the 'American Creed,' formulated in William Tyler Page's winning entry to a patriotic contest as, in his own words, "the summary of the fundamental principles of the American political faith as set forth in its greatest documents, its worthiest traditions, and its greatest leaders."[10] This creed, which was adopted by Congress in the following year, reads as follows:

> I believe in the United States of America as a government of the people, by the people, for the people; whose just powers are derived from the consent of the governed, a democracy in a republic, a sovereign Nation of many sovereign States; a perfect union, one and inseparable; established upon those principles of freedom, equality, justice, and humanity for which American patriots sacrificed their lives and fortunes. I therefore believe it is my duty to my country to love it, to support its Constitution, to obey its laws, to respect its flag, and to defend it against all enemies.[11]

Such an ideologically motivated identity concept made naturalization easy, and this is why during the period of mass immigration from the first federal law of 1790 to the naturalization law of 1906, free white immigrants, no matter what their nationality or language, could become American citizens by simply swearing that they had lived in the U.S. for five years, would renounce all hereditary titles and political allegiance to any other state, and would support the U.S. constitution.

---

[9] Quoted in Church 2002; here taken from http://www.thenation.com/doc/20020916/church.

[10] Quoted in http://en.wikipedia.org/wiki/William_Tyler_Page.

[11] See http://www.ushistory.org/documents/creed.htm.

But in a country which defined itself as Protestant in stark opposition to Catholicism, this openness changed when, in the half-century before the Civil War, immigration led to a massive growth of the Catholic population. In 1790 there had been only 35,000 Catholics, but when by 1860, mostly due to the influx of Irish fleeing from the potato famine, their number had grown to 3.1 million, religion began to play a major role in the definition of national identity. Anti-Catholicism led to the short-lived Know-Nothingism and to bitter fights over educational policy. New public schools were set up as 'Americanizing' institutions meant to counter the detrimental effects of the parochial schools founded by the Irish immigrants. Consequently, national identity was no longer a primarily ideological notion, but also religion, education, and cultural customs and values became important ingredients. A cartoon about the unwelcome arrival of the Catholic "Propagation Society" intent upon converting Brother Jonathan, the fictional personification of the U.S., could be used to demonstrate the widespread anti-Catholic feelings,[12] and Thomas Nast's famous cartoon about "The American River Ganges: The Priests and the Children" from *Harper's Weekly*, September 30, 1871 would provide excellent teaching material.[13]

Ill. 1: Thomas Nast, The American River Ganges: The Priests and the Children, 1871

This scathing cartoon deals with the divisive issue of whether parochial schools should receive public support. It shows the U.S. Public School in ruins, with the

12 See http://lcweb2.loc.gov/service/pnp/cph/3a30000/3a31000/3a31300/3a31382r.jpg.

13 See http://www.yale.edu/glc/archive/1106.htm.

Stars and Stripes flying upside down as a distress signal and with Tammany Hall in the background displaying the Papal Tiara and the Irish Harp. Boss Tweed and his henchmen are leading teachers to the gallows and sacrificing the children to the crocodiles, and only a lonely teacher with a Bible is trying to interfere. Closer inspection reveals that the heads of the crocodiles are cunning Irish faces with bishops' miters. Here, then, Nast exposes what he considers the hostile attack of undemocratic Catholicism upon God's own Protestant country.[14]

In the last quarter of the nineteenth century, the proverbial 'melting pot' notion,[15] which dates as far back as to Crèvecœur and was popularized by Zangwill, became the leading concept, and although it presumed to be tolerant and cosmopolitan, its proponents took it for granted that the new immigrants would merge into the existing mould. There were exceptions on racial or, better, racist terms such as the Chinese Exclusion Act of 1882, which defined the Chinese as unassimilable and thus unfit for citizenship,[16] and with ever growing immigration waves scepticism about the working of the melting pot grew. Thus, by the beginning of the twentieth century the concept of 'Americanization' gained ground, and conformity to the cultural majority in language, religion, manners, and values was considered a prerequisite for becoming American. 'Americanization,' however, meant different things, and whereas, after the U.S.'s entry into World War I, the anti-German campaign against 'hyphenation' called for an abdication of the immigrants'

Ill. 2: The Mortar of Assimilation, 1889

[14] Further pertinent cartoons can be found in Freese 1999: 248-271 or reprinted in Freese 2002: 51–77 and in Freese 2010: 239-253.

[15] The cartoon on the next page, "The Mortar of Assimilation," *Puck Magazine,* 26 June 1889 (http://museum.msu.edu/museum/tes/immigration.htm) shows Miss America stirring the pot of American "Citizenship" with the big ladle of "Equal Rights," and everybody is willing to be 'melted,' with the exception of a rebellious Irishman.

[16] See the texts and pictures provided in Freese 2005a: 17-19.

home cultures,[17] less stringent 'Americanizers' concentrated on educating the newcomers in order to acquaint them with and integrate them into their host culture.

Proponents of 'Anglo-Saxon Racialism' such as Josiah Strong in his book *Our Country* (1886), Madison Grant in his vitriolic study *The Passing of the Great Race* (1916) and Lothrop Stoddard in *The Rising Tide of Color* (1920) were even more fanatic. They mixed theories of Anglo-Saxon superiority with Darwinian notions of evolution and romantic ideas of a *Volksgeist* in order to reject inferior races, and they played a crucial role in bringing about the restrictive immigration laws of the 1920s with their quota systems, their literacy test, and the Dillingham Commission's distinction between welcome 'old' and unwelcome 'new' immigrants.

But parallel to such exclusivist – and often decisively racist – attitudes, Horace Kallen's notion of "cultural pluralism" as proposed in his 1915 essay "Democracy versus the Melting Pot: A Study of American Nationality,"[18] gained ground. His supporters rejected Americanization and Anglo-Saxon Racialism as expressions of narrow ethnocentrism, turned the acronym WASP from a laudatory tag into an ethnic slur, and understood the U.S. no longer as a nation with a shared identity, but as a political unity consisting of diverse cultures. Therefore, "ethnicity assumed greater salience as an element in the national identity than it has had at any other time," and "during the first quarter of the twentieth century, the ethnic factors of 'race,' nationality, language, [...] were the issues that sprang immediately to mind when Americans asked themselves, 'What does it mean to be an American?'" (Gleason 1980: 46) Whereas thus, after the Irish influx, Catholics played a central role in the emergence of religion and later on Jews like Kallen were responsible for the emergence of ethnicity as salient ingredients of America's national identity, in the 1950s and '60s the status of Blacks moved to the front.

As a war against totalitarianism, World War II had strengthened the original ideological perception of America's national identity, but now such a perception became questionable. The Swedish social scientist Gunnar Myrdal famously defined the contradiction between the treatment of Blacks and the central tenets of the country's self-image as *An American Dilemma* (1944) and understood this dilemma, in a revealing phrase, as the decisive obstacle to "the gradual realization of the American Creed" (quoted in Church 2002). The discrepancy

---

[17] See the cartoon "Removing the Hyphen", http://www.butterflystorm.com/Work/GermanTexts/Removing%20the%20Hyphen.htm (27/03/2015).

[18] For this essay, which Kallen would later extend into his comprehensive study *Cultural Pluralism and the American Idea* (1956), see http://home.apu.edu/~rgeib/edu-526/melting-pot-v-salad-bowl/.

between lofty American ideals as pronounced in the Declaration of Independence and a faulty American reality as expressed in the treatment of Blacks led to the Civil Rights Movement and made Martin Luther King exclaim "I have a dream that one day this nation will rise up and live out the true meaning of its creed." (King 1963 quoted in Freese 2011: 23) Two laws passed in 1965, the Voting Rights Act, which ended the abridgement of the right to vote on the basis of race or colour, and the Immigration Act, which abolished the discriminatory national origin quotas, clearly show that race and ethnicity had become crucial criteria for defining the American identity. At the same time, the old ideological foundations were weakened by the crisis of national confidence triggered by the Vietnam War.

A surge of particularist group interests, in which the promotion of Black Power, Black Pride, and Black Studies was followed by the Brown Power of Chicanos and the Red Power of Native Americans, resulted in a wave of ethnic self-assertion. New research in European immigration challenged the notion that immigrants had been radically uprooted from their original cultures and found their ethnicity a more durable heritage than previously believed. Marcus Lee Hansen formulated the influential Hansen's Law: "What the son wants to forget the grandson wishes to remember." (1952: 492-500) And Oscar Handlin opened his study *The Uprooted* with a sentence that became proverbial: "Once I thought to write a history of the immigrants in America. Then I discovered that the immigrants *were* American history." (1953: 3) One manifesto of this reorientation was Michael Novak's *The Rise of the Unmeltable Ethnics* (1972), which rejects Americanization as a mere euphemism for "WASPification" and calls for a replacement of WASPs by PIGS, i.e., Poles, Italians, Greeks and Slavs.

In the turbulent sixties, the traditional definition of an American as a believer in the American creed was either replaced by new ethnic definitions, which drew their appeal from the damages done to the older concept, or the concept of national identity was rejected altogether. The insistence on internal ethnic differences and the denial of a shared creed became even stronger in the 'culture wars' of the 1980s and 1990s, when 'multiculturalism' became the war cry and *e pluribus plures* replaced *e pluribus unum*. (see Freese 1996: 155-170) The hallowed assumptions of American self-understanding were decried as patriarchal, racist, and hegemonic and exchanged for an insistence on the differences of gender, class, race, ethnicity, and sexual preference. The classic literary canon was rejected as the works of dead white Protestant males and replaced by a more 'hospitable' canon admitting hitherto excluded women, gays, lesbians,

African Americans, Native Americans, and Chicanos.[19] The 'grand narratives' of old were rejected as unduly privileged; and the bird's-eye view of the U.S. as a homogeneous whole was replaced by the cultural contestation of the bits and pieces of a 'multicultural' society in increasing fragmentation. Radical critics even maintained that the U.S. as a nation state was no longer an apt subject of research and teaching.[20]

What this simplified survey has shown is that

1) in the course of its history, America's national identity has always oscillated between the *unum* and the *plures*, the unifying power of a shared creed and the diversifying tendencies of many ethnicities, and that
2) the question as to which and how many immigrants are to be admitted to the U.S. and how they are to be assimilated has been and still is of decisive importance for America's national identity.

It is important to add, however, that this brief survey, which was simplified for teaching purposes, traces only what was long considered the 'mainstream' version of the evolution of America's national identity. For a comprehensive picture, it would have to be complemented by the history of the millions of Blacks who were brought to the New World against their will and whose contribution to the national identity of the U.S. was completely neglected for a long time.

*****

Since it does not seem advisable that teachers pass the preceding information to the students in a talk and chalk presentation, they might use selected cartoons in order to establish a provisional inventory of the basic attitudes which the 'ones' have shown towards the 'others' in the course of U.S. history.

The earliest position was that of *unconditional assimilation* inviting all immigrants, independent of their race, religion and language, with the exception of 'savage' Indians and 'primitive' Blacks, to take part in Jefferson's great experiment and to begin with God's blessing a better and fuller life in the 'New Canaan' of America. This position is most clearly expressed in the Austrian immigrant Joseph Keppler's cartoon "Welcome to All" (1880), which depicts the U.S. as an "Ark of Refuge" with Uncle Sam as a second Noah, and makes the queue of hopeful immigrants enter the ark in pairs as in the biblical precedent. America is portrayed as chosen by God to save humankind from the dark cloud of European wars, and a large poster lists the crucial differences between the Old and the New World: "no oppressive taxes / no expensive kings / no com-

---

[19] For a discussion of the often faddish application of 'multiculturalism' in EFL-teaching see Freese 2000 or reprinted in Freese 2002: 11-30.

[20] See Radway 1999.

pulsory military service / no knouts or dungeons." While these slogans tell the immigrants what they will be spared in America, a smaller poster tells them what they can expect, namely: free education, free land as provided by the *Homestead Act* of 1862, free speech as guaranteed by the *First Amendment*, free ballot, and – Keppler's tongue-in-cheek addition – free lunch, which of course does not exist.[21]

Ill. 4: Joseph Keppler, Welcome to All, 1880

This cartoon is an exact visual complement of the closing lines from Emma Lazarus' famous sonnet *The New Colossus*:

> Give me your tired, your poor,
> Your huddled masses yearning to breathe free,
> The wretched refuse of your teeming shore.
> Send these, the homeless, tempest-tost to me.
> I lift my lamp beside the golden door. (Freese 2005a: 8)

By 1893 the situation had changed, for too many were coming; and now the inhabitants of what Thomas Paine had called "the asylum for the persecuted lovers of civil and religious liberty from *every part* of Europe" (Paine 1925: 127), began to fear that America might become what they decried as the 'dumping ground' for European refuse. Consequently, the new position of *Americani-*

[21] The American adage "There's no such thing as a free lunch" means that one gets nothing for free. For its origins and its use in economic theory see http://www.phrases.org.uk/meanings/tanstaafl.html.

zation came into being, meaning that only those would be admitted who were willing to adopt the values and customs of the ones already there. Keppler depicted this change by confronting a hopeful newcomer with five well-fed and elegantly dressed 'Americans,' who prevent him from entering the country. But their shadows betray that once they, too, were poor immigrants and reveal what they looked like when they arrived. With the iconographic shorthand of his times, Keppler identifies them, from left to right, as an Englishman with a stable-boy's brush, a Jew with a peddler's tray, an Irish field hand, a German

Ill. 5: Joseph Keppler, Looking Backward, 1893

Michel with his *Zipfelmütze*, and a Scandinavian with a hunter's fur cap and backpack. His cartoon parallels Thomas Bailey Aldrich's poem *Unguarded Gates*, which changes Lazarus' "Mother of Exiles" into a "white Goddess" and skeptically asks:

> O Liberty, white Goddess! Is it well
> To leave the gates unguarded? On thy breast
> Fold Sorrow's children, soothe the hurts of fate,
> Lift the down-trodden, but with hand of steel
> Stay those who to thy sacred portals come
> To waste the gifts of freedom. (Aldrich 1907: vol. 2, 71f)

Here Keppler shows that apart from the Native Americans, who were exterminated or crowded into reservations, all Americans are immigrants and that this makes the self-righteous rejection of new immigrants by old ones unacceptable.

The next, and still more xenophobic, position is that of *Anglo-Saxon racialism*, as expounded by Madison Grant and his rabid pseudo-science of Anglo-Saxon superiority in *The Passing of the Great Race*. Grant's position is cleverly anticipated in an 1882 cartoon about the feared genetic decline resulting from uncurbed immigration. It deals with "Unrestricted Immigration and Its Results – A Possible Curiosity of the Twentieth Century: The Last Yankee," and shows the last specimen of the endangered species of the tall and slim Yankee surrounded by representatives of diverse immigrant groups, whose stunted figures and demented faces testify to their inferior racial heritage. In the background, a German *Michel* with his *Zipfelmütze* looks out of a window above "Boomelheimer's Delicatessen," and a French *Marianne* observes the spectacle from a window above "Jean Boucois' Americaine Bakery." A shop-sign that advertises "Yan-kee – Amelican Laundry" conjures up a third ethnic stereotype, namely that of the Chinese laundryman who cannot pronounce an 'r' and thus tries in vain to assume 'Yankee' status.

Ill. 6: Unrestricted Immigration and Its Results, 1882

These positions did not follow one another but existed side by side, and at the very time at which Grant deplored the decline of the Anglo-Saxon master race, Horace Kallen introduced his concept of *cultural pluralism*. Finding the melting pot notion not only impossible but also undesirable, he pleaded for tolerant ethnic coexistence and visualized the U.S. society as an orchestra in which each ethnic group plays its own instrument but all sounds merge into a grand American symphony. A dramatic historical change was necessary before this hopeful image could become at least temporary reality. When in April 1917 the United States entered the war against Germany, the common enemy made Americans forget their internal strife. This is illustrated by a government poster for the first Liberty Loan program. The wicked enemy makes the hostile ethnic groups come together, and the slogan which creates an unknown kind of cohesion reads "Americans All!" Thus, the 'honour roll' now includes all ethnic groups from Pappandrikopolous, the Greek, to Gonzales, the Spaniard, and from Knutson, the Swede, to Kowalski, the Pole.[22]

Ill. 7: Americans All, 1917

After World War II the position of cultural pluralism was strengthened by a growing interest in the cultural achievements of non-mainstream groups and the insights of immigration research, and this development took place against the background of what U.S. soldiers had learned overseas. The new concept of America as a political unity with cultural diversity was labelled *multi-ethnicity*, and now non-WASP Americans proudly professed their ethnic heritage, which is most clearly shown in a 1977 Pan Am advertisement announcing that "All of us come from someplace else." It shows a small Italian village street and suggests that "just once, you should walk down the same street your great-grandfather walked." The accompanying text reads:

Ill. 8: All of us come from someplace else, 1977

Picture this if you will. A man who's spent all his life in the United States gets on a plane, crosses a great ocean, lands. He walks the same streets his family walked centuries ago. He sees his name, which is rare in America, filling three pages in a phone book. He speaks haltingly the language he wishes he had learned better as a child. As America's airline to the world, Pan Am does a lot of things. [...] But nothing we do seems to have as much meaning as when we help somebody discover the second heritage that every American has.

[22] The two Keppler cartoons in color and the two poems by Lazarus and Aldrich are arranged as a mini-sequence in Freese 2005a: 8f.; the "Last Yankee" cartoon and the Liberty Loan Poster in color can be found in ibid.: 27 and 21.

These five visual texts form an informative mini-sequence for the EFL-classroom. They introduce the positions of Unconditional Assimilation, Americanization, Anglo-Saxon Racialism, Cultural Pluralism and Multi-Ethnicity and their analysis results in a useful referential grid. In a highly simplified but nevertheless legitimate version, these positions can even be reduced to plausible formulas.

1. With *unconditional assimilation* the members of different ethnicities are 'melted' into a new and better species, Zangwill's "coming superman": $A + B + C > D$.
2. With *Americanization* those who come later are expected to adopt the values and manners of those who are already there: $A + B + C > A$.
3. With *Anglo-Saxon racialism* only those are welcome who belong to the 'master' race: $A = A$.
4. With *cultural pluralism, multi-ethnicity* (historical variations of what today we call *multiculturalism*) all groups have the right to preserve their particular values and manners: $A + B + C > A + B + C$.

These formulas, which encompass the most common attitudes the ones have held toward the others in the course of American history, are not only helpful for all further work, but also have great transfer value for German students who are confronted with similar attitudes ranging from the xenophobic *Stammtisch* slogan 'The boat is full' to the Green Party's hopeful vision of a 'multicultural bazaar.'

In the contemporary U.S. both the revival of ethnicity and the widespread doubts as to the salience of the creed have led to what some diagnose as a crisis of nationality, and it was in a climate defined by the 'culture wars' of the eighties and nineties, the lasting shock of 9/11, and the wars in Iraq and Afghanistan that Samuel P. Huntington published his answer to the question of what it means to be an American in his bestseller *Who Are We? America's Great Debate* (2004). For him "the distinct Anglo-Protestant culture of the founding settlers" provided the unifying element for all later immigrant groups, namely, "the English language; Christianity; religious commitment; English concepts of the rule of law, the responsibility of rulers, and the rights of individuals; and dissenting Protestant values of individualism, the work ethic, and the belief that humans have the ability and the duty to try to create a heaven on earth, a 'city on a hill.'" He states that this heritage has been lost, and the traditional American identity is threatened by a growing number of disruptive forces in reaction to which it might develop in four directions:

> 1. a creedal America, lacking its historic cultural core, and united only by a common commitment to the principles of the American Creed [similar to Habermas' *Verfassungspatriotismus* in Germany];
> 2. a bifurcated America, with two languages, Spanish and English, and two cultures, Anglo-Protestant and Hispanic;
> 3. an exclusivist America, once again defined by race and ethnicity and that excludes and/or subordinates those who are not white and European;
> 4. a revitalized America reaffirming its historic Anglo-Protestant culture, religious commitments, and values and bolstered by confrontations with an unfriendly world;
> 5. some combination of these and other possibilities. (Huntington 2004: xvii)

It would be interesting to speculate which of these identities will result from the combination of a growing stream of Hispanic and Asian immigrants, the impact of cosmopolitan intellectuals who reject the concept of 'nation' as obsolete, the leaders of global corporations who want to profit from the dismantling of national borders, and militant multiculturalists who reject the idea that an immigrant society should try to achieve cultural unity. And it would be fascinating to join in on the debate on whether Huntington is right when he argues that these developments jeopardize the coherence of the U.S. and its future as a liberal democracy and that only a revival of a civic patriotism on a religious basis can stop the ongoing disintegration.[23]

*****

Speculations about ongoing developments might be interesting, but from an educational perspective it is more important to make the students recognize that contemporary problems can only be understood if their historical roots are taken into consideration. In order to heed James Baldwin's crucial insight that "the past is all that makes the present coherent," (1969: 4) some seminal historical texts must be studied.

An indispensable text is the famous "Third Letter" in Michel-Guillaume Jean de Crèvecœur's *Letters from an American Farmer* (1782), which is not only one of the most often quoted American texts, but also the earliest attempt at addressing the issue of American identity. Crèvecœur asked "What, then, is the American, this new man?" and he answered:

> He is neither an European, nor the descendant of an European, hence that strange mixture of blood, which you will find in no other country. [...] *He* is an American, who, leaving behind him all his ancient prejudices and manners, receives new ones from the new mode of life he has embraced, the new government he obeys, and the new rank he holds. He becomes an American by being received in the

[23] See, e.g. Jim Sleeper's review (http://hnn.us/articles/4987.html) or Francis Fukuyama's comments (http://www.slate.com/id/2101756).

> broad lap of our great Alma Mater. Here individuals of all nations are melted into a new race of men, whose labours and posterity will one day cause great changes in the world. (quoted in Freese 2005a: 13f)

With this observation, which stresses the newness and the promise of the 'American' identity as evolving through a process of assimilation, he founded an influential national myth. A century later it was taken up by the British Jew Israel Zangwill, who had David Quixano, the hero of his influential play *The Melting Pot*, rhapsodize:

> America is God's Crucible, the great Melting-Pot where all the races of Europe are melting and reforming! – the real American has not yet arrived. He is only in the Crucible, I tell you – he will be the fusion of all races, perhaps the coming superman. (quoted in Freese 2006: 29)

Ill. 9: The 'Melting Pot' Exercises in Ford's English Classes, 1916

The consequential change of Crèvecœur's theoretical notion of 'melting' into Zangwill's concrete metaphor of the 'melting pot' was most directly translated into reality by Henry Ford, who was very keen on 'Americanizing' his immigrant workers and whose Sociological Department checked whether they adopted the desired American habits such as washing regularly and brushing their teeth and thus deserved to receive the five-dollar daily wage which Ford offered in 1914. All his immigrant workers had to attend compulsory English classes, at the end of which they went through a graduation ceremony that illustrated their transformation in the mythic American 'melting pot.' The *Ford Times* of 1916 published a photograph of the ceremony together with the following comment:

> The "Melting Pot" exercises were dramatic in the extreme: A deckhand came down the gang plank of the ocean liner, represented in canvas facsimile. "What cargo?" was the hail he received. "About 230 hunkies," he called back. "Send'em along and we'll see what the melting pot will do for them," said the other and from the ship came a line of immigrants, in the poor garments of their native lands. Into the gaping pot they went. Then six instructors of the Ford school, with long ladles, started stirring. "Stir! Stir!" urged the superintendent of the school. The six bent to greater efforts. From the pot fluttered a flag, held high, then the first of the finished product of the pot appeared, waving his hat. The crowd cheered as he mounted the edge and came down the steps on the side. Many others followed him, gathering in two groups on each side of the cauldron. In contrast to the shabby rags they wore when they were unloaded from the ship, all wore neat suits. They were American in looks. And ask anyone of them what nationality he is, and the reply will come quickly, "American!" "Polish-American?" you might ask. "No, American," would be the answer. For they are taught in the Ford school that the hyphen is a minus sign.[24]

This combination of a visual and a verbal text provides suitable teaching material for the 'melting pot' concept, and concerning the feasibility of this concept, teachers might refer to two texts that demonstrate the profound changes in its evaluation. In 1959, the historian Arthur M. Schlesinger Sr. counted the idea of the melting pot among America's ten greatest contributions to civilization (see 1959: 67), but only four years later Nathan Glazer and Daniel Patrick Moynihan laconically observed in their study of the ethnic makeup of New York City that "the point about the melting pot [...] is that it did not happen." (Glazer / Moynihan 1963: v)

The position of Anglo-Saxon Racialism and the degree to which the notion of 'race' dominated the national identity discourse at a particular time, can be taught by means of representative excerpts from Josiah Strong's *Our Country* (1885), Senator Beveridge's speeches on the annexation of the Philippines (1900), and Madison Grant's *The Passing of the Great Race* (1916). Strong predicted the eventual victory of the supreme Anglo-Saxon race in the American West:

> The Anglo-Saxon is the representative of two great ideas, which are closely related. One of them is that of civil liberty, [...] The other [...] is that of a pure *spiritual* Christianity [...] these are the forces which, in the past, have contributed most to the elevation of the human race, and they must continue to be, in the future, the most efficient ministers to its progress. It follows, then, that the Anglo-Saxon [...] sustains peculiar relations to the world's future, is divinely commissioned to be, in a peculiar sense, his brother's keeper. [...] Does it not look as if

---

[24] The photograph and the text are available in Freese 2005b: 88. The text might be profitably compared with a description of the Ford ceremony in Jeffrey Eugenides' Pulitzer Prize-winning novel *Middlesex* (2002) which is reprinted in ibid.: 89.

> God were not only preparing in our Anglo-Saxon civilization the die with which to stamp the peoples of the earth, but as if he were also massing behind that die the mighty power with which to press it? [In the near future the world] will enter upon a new stage of its history – *the final competition of races, for which the Anglo-Saxon is being schooled* [...]. (reprinted in Freese 2011: 37)

Senator Beveridge elevated America as God's chosen country ordained to bring democracy to the rest of the world:

> God has not been preparing the English-speaking and Teutonic peoples for a thousand years for nothing but vain and idle self-contemplation and self-admiration. No! He has made us the master organizers of the world to establish system where chaos reigns. He has given us the spirit of progress to overwhelm the forces of reaction throughout the earth. He has made us adepts in government that we may administer government among savage and senile peoples. [...] And of all our race he has marked the American people as His chosen Nation finally to lead in the regeneration of the world. This is the divine mission of America, and it holds for us all profit, glory, happiness possible to man. We are trustees of the world's progress, guardians of its righteous peace. (reprinted in Freese 2011: 40)

And Madison Grant deplored the admission of immigrants of inferior racial stock and predicted America's ethnic suicide:

> [...] the new immigration [...] contained a large and increasing number of the weak, the broken and the mentally crippled of all races from the lowest stratum of the Mediterranean basin and the Balkans, together with hordes of the wretched, submerged populations of the Polish ghettos. Our jails, insane asylums and almshouses are filled with this human flotsam and the whole tone of American life, social, moral and political has been lowered and vulgarized by them. These immigrants adopt the language of the native American, they wear his clothes, they steal his name and they are beginning to take his women, but they seldom adopt his religion or understand his ideals and while he is being elbowed out of his own home the American looks calmly abroad and urges on others the suicidal ethics which are exterminating his own race. (reprinted in Freese 2005a or b: 26f)

These passages provide the necessary background for any debate about contemporary problems such as the need for new immigration legislation.

*****

The introductory unit on the English and Spanish versions of the American national anthem has shown that one's national identity is intricately related to one's language. For a long time it was taken for granted that German citizens speak German, French citizens speak French, and so on, and this is why the fathers of the German *Grundgesetz* did not deem it necessary to declare that the official language of the *Bundesrepublik* was to be German, and why the Founding Fathers did not state in the Constitution that English should be the official language of the United States.[25] According to the *Harvard Encyclopedia of American Ethnic Groups*, more than 130 ethnic groups make the U.S. one of the most heterogeneous countries in the world, but linguistically is has always been surprisingly homogeneous, since most of the newcomers strove to learn English as fast as possible, a fact that is frequently illustrated by the night-school scene as a standard ingredient of immigration literature. Admittedly, there were always non-participatory groups such as the Old Order Amish, the Pennsylvania Dutch or the Lubavitcher Jews that clung to their mother tongues and spoke both a private and a public language. But on the whole, the linguistic integration of immigrants was no problem, and President Theodore Roosevelt's laconic observation that every immigrant should be given a chance to learn English, but "if, after say five years, he has not learned English, he should be sent back to the land from whence he came," (quoted in Worsnop 1993: 705) exemplifies the traditional position.

In the EFL-classroom, an awareness of the language problem created by the English and Spanish versions of the national anthem can be created with a short text by Sandra Cisneros. Her excellent novel *The House on Mango Street* (1991) contains a little vignette which is titled "No Speak English" and offers a moving comment on the immigrant's linguistic dislocation. It tells about a Mexican who, after years of toil, has finally earned enough money to bring his wife and their little baby to Chicago, where she stays in her room because she speaks no English. The text ends like this:

> *¡Ay! Mamacita*, who does not belong every once in a while lets out a cry, hysterical, high, as if he had torn the only skinny thread that kept her alive, the only road out to that country. And then to break her heart forever, the baby boy who has begun to talk, starts to sing the Pepsi commercial he heard on T.V. No speak English, she says to the child who is singing in the language that sounds like tin. No speak English, no speak English, and bubbles into tears. No, no, no, as if she can't believe her ears.[26]

Another suitable EFL-text is Nicolasa Mohr's short story "The English Lesson" (1977) about two Puerto Ricans attending classes in "Basic English, Tuesday

[25] The widespread myth that German had almost become the official language of the U.S. is not true. Arndt 1976 shows that this myth goes back to two events. Seven years after the passing of the Constitution, German-American citizens from Virginia petitioned the Third Congress that all federal laws should be printed in 3,000 copies in German and English, but the House of Representatives rejected this request with a small majority. There are vague reports that in the legislative assembly of Pennsylvania a petition for making German the official language narrowly failed.

[26] Cisneros' vignette can be found in Freese 2005a: 52. An audio version of the text as read by Cisneros' herself is available on the CDs accompanying Freese 2007.

evenings from 6.30 to 8.00, at a local public school" in New York.[27] And the funniest treatment is Leo Rosten's *The Education of H*Y*M*A*N K*A*P*L*A*N* (1937), a series of stories about a Yiddish-speaking immigrant who goes to "the American Night Preparatory School for Adults" (9) to learn English and makes such hilarious mistakes as conjugating 'to die' as "die, dead, funeral" (109) and 'to fail' as "fail, failed, bankrupt" (15), and declaring that his wife has "high blood pleasure" (115).[28]

Officially, any immigrant who applies for citizenship in the U.S. must prove that he or she has a sufficient command of English and a basic knowledge of civics. This is explained in detail in what would be a very useful teaching tool in EFL-courses, namely, the booklet *Welcome to the United States: A Guide for New Immigrants*, and the basic historical facts can be taught with an even better tool, namely, a helpful set of *Civics Flash Cards*[29]. But reality is much more complicated. The 1968 *Bilingual Education Act* was the first federal law that recognized the needs of so-called LESA (= Limited English-Speaking Ability) children and provided money for special programs (see Thernstorm 1980: 619-629), in 1974 the Supreme Court ruled in *Lau v Nichols* that the San Francisco School District had to provide assistance to non-English-speaking Chinese students,[30] and an increasing number of Spanish-speaking immigrants insisted on bilingual schools that began to flourish in the multicultural climate of the eighties and nineties. How crucial the issue of bilingual education has become is shown by some relevant Census figures of 2000. In that year, 42.8% of all school children between five and seventeen in California, 26.7% in New York, and 15.7% in the country at large were children of immigrant mothers. If one adds the numbers of children between one and four, the figures rise to 43.7% for California, 28.8% for New York and 17.9% for the total country. This means that in California almost one half, in New York more than a quarter, and in the whole country about a sixth of all school children were children of 'foreigners' who needed special linguistic and cultural tuition to be integrated, and it can be safely assumed that meanwhile these figures have grown. For this task there are four competing strategies, namely

---

[27] An annotated edition of Mohr's story is available in Freese 2012: 103-122.

[28] Leo Rosten (1908-1997) emigrated from Poland into the U.S. in 1911. During the Great Depression he taught English to recent immigrants in night-school. His enormously successful books *The Education of H*Y*M*A*N K*A*P*L*A*N* (1937), the sequel, *The Return of H*Y*M*A*N K*A*P*L*A*N* (1959), and the completely rewritten combination of both, *O K*A*P*L*A*N! My K*A*P*L*A*N!* (1976) result from this experience.

[29] Both are published by the U.S. Citizenship and Immigration Services in Washington.

[30] For details see http://www.nabe.org/Resources/Documents/Advocacy%20page/LauvNichols.pdf.

1. maintained bilingual education with native-language instruction continued alongside English,
2. transitional bilingual education with native-language instruction being gradually phased out,
3. English-only education, sometimes with 'structured immersion' programs in which the level of English is geared to the students' comprehension (US-English[31]), and
4. bilingual education instructing English-speaking and non-English-speaking children in both languages (English Plus[32]).

The influential 'U.S. English' organization demands that official government business must be conducted solely in English at all levels, with the exception of the fields of public health, safety services, and tourism. On the federal level, this demand has not yet been implemented. In 1996, the House of Representatives passed the "Bill Emerson English Language Empowerment Act," but the Senate has not yet considered it. In May 2006, however, the Senate passed S2611, a "Comprehensive Immigration Reform Act," as an alternative to H.R.4437, the much more radical "Border Protection, Antiterrorism, and Illegal Immigration Control Act of 2005" passed by the House of Representatives.[33] S2611 contains an unspecified clause about English as the national language, but in view of the fact that the two bills triggered the biggest demonstrations in memory all over the country[34] and that illegal immigration is widely considered a crucial problem[35] it is surprising that so far Congress has all but neglected the linguistic implications of mass immigration.

On the state level, the situation is different. By now, 31 states have passed "Official English" laws and have created a complicated situation.[36] In California, for example, the influential "Save Our State" lobby fights against what they

---

[31] See http://www.us-english.org/.

[32] See http://ourworld.compuserve.com/homepages/JWCrawford/engplus.htm.

[33] The complete texts of the two laws are available under http://www.cbo.gov/ftpdocs/72xx/doc7208/s2611.pdf and under http://www.govtrack.us/congress/bill.xpd?bill=h109-4437. A helpful comment on the present state of the debate on how to deal with undocumented Americans is Grunwald 2013.

[34] Material about the demonstrations on May 1, 2006, known as the Great American Boycott or the Day Without Immigrants, can be found under http://en.wikipedia.org/wiki/Great_American_Boycott.

[35] See; e.g., Tumulty, Karen (2006), "Who Gets to Be an American?", and the polls in *Time*, 10 April 2006.

[36] The map is taken from the U.S.English homepage, http://www.us-english.org/view/13. See also the homepage of ProEnglish: English Language Advocates, http://www.proenglish.org/official-english/state-profiles.

deem a threatening 'invasion' by foreigners, and extremely xenophobic documents like this decidedly racist driving license[37] are being circulated in the internet.

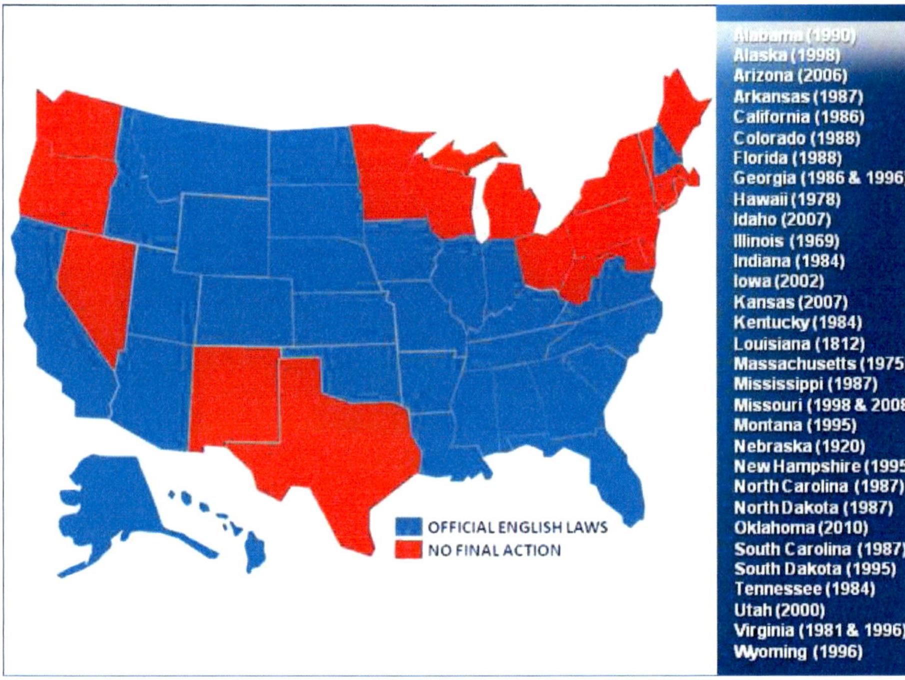

Ill. 10: States with (blue) and without (red) Official English Laws, 2012

Generally speaking, doubts about the usefulness of bilingual education seem to grow and there is an increasing concern about establishing English as the national language. In 2000, for example, John Micklethwait pointed to the Californian *Proposition 227*, which

> replaced bilingual education, which around half the students with poor English were receiving, with crash courses in English. Bilingual education, originally invented as a way to steer funds to poor people in the southwest, has always produced disappointing results. It is now merely a sop to the teachers' unions. Since bilingual education was banned in California about a year ago, test scores have risen. Even more tellingly, the students who were put on the English crash course or into mainstream classes are well ahead of those still stuck in bilingual ones. ("A Raw Deal": 13)

Thereby he took up what Arthur M. Schlesinger Jr. had observed as early as 1992 as what was then still a minority position:

[37] See http://lighthousepatriotjournal.wordpress.com/2006/06/27/california-responds-to-forest- fires.

> [...] bilingualism has not worked out as planned; rather the contrary. Testimony is mixed, but indications are that bilingual education retards rather than expedites the movement of Hispanic children into the English-speaking world and that it promotes segregation more than it does integration. It nourishes self-ghettoization, and ghettoization nourishes racial antagonism. [...] Using some language other than English dooms people to second-class citizenship in American society. [...] The bilingual campaign has created both an educational establishment with a vested interest in extending the bilingual empire and a political lobby with a vested interest in retaining a Hispanic constituency. [...] bilingualism is an elitist, not a popular, movement [...] institutional bilingualism remains another source of the fragmentation of America, another threat to the dream of "one people." (1992: 108ff.)

Ill. 11: A "Mexifornia" Driver Licence

The material on this controversial issue is almost endless; and a detailed analysis would have to relate it to the gradual abolition of affirmative action, a hotly debated issue.[38] As far as German EFL-teaching is concerned, a suitable expository text would be Charles Krauthammer's 2006 essay "In Plain English: Let's Make It Official," and among the books that deal with what is the largest bilingualism issue, namely the English-Spanish conflict, there are at least two that offer promising material for the students. In 1998, the successful Latino entrepreneur Lionel Sosa published his bestseller *The Americano Dream: How Latinos Can Achieve Success in Business and in Life*, in which he defined the mastery of English as the necessary requirement for economic success:

> [...] it is essential for Latinos dealing with Anglo businesses to speak the same language. By this I don't mean just being fluent in the language of business – English. I mean understanding those subtleties that are part of any communication, things that are implied or left unsaid, a kind of code that can be learned only by acute observation and practice. (1999: 105)

---

[38] See, e.g., *Proposition 209*, which voters passed in California in 1996, which stipulates that "the state shall not discriminate against, or grant preferential treatment to, any individual or group on the basis of race, sex, color, ethnicity, or national origin in the operation of public employment, public education, or public contracting," and which caused great changes in hiring practices and university admissions. The complete text is available under http://Vote96.ss.ca.gov/Vote96/html/BP/209text.htm.

More than a decade earlier, the Chicano intellectual Richard Rodriguez had already delivered a brilliant plea for learning English as a prerequisite for cultural integration in his moving autobiographical book *Hunger of Memory* (1982).

*****

Some basic knowledge about the United States as an immigrant society is an indispensable prerequisite for an understanding of 'America,' and the crucial role which a shared language plays with regard to the formation of a national identity is also of direct importance for German learners, in whose courses there is a growing number of fellow students who, or whose parents, speak a first language other than German. Consequently, an examination of the answers given to Crèvecœur's question "What then, is the American, this new man?" in the course of U.S. history is important both with regard to the United States as a topic to be taught in the EFL classroom and German students as the learners to be educated and provided with the ability of transcultural understanding.

Bibliography

"A raw deal." *Economist* [London, England] 11 Mar. 2000: 12+. *The Economist Historical Archive, 1843-2011.*

Aldrich, Thomas Bailey (1907). *The Writings of Thomas Bailey Aldrich.* Boston and New York: Houghton Mifflin.

Arndt, Karl J. R. (1976). German as the Official Language of the United States of America. *Monatshefte für deutschen Unterricht, deutsche Sprache und Literatur* 68 (2), 129-150.

Baldwin, James (1969). *Notes of a Native Son.* London: Corgi Books.

Beveridge, Albert J. (1908). *The Meaning of the Times and Other Speeches.* Indianapolis: Bobbs-Merrill.

Church, Forrest (2002). The American Creed. *The Nation.* http://www.thenation.com/doc/20020916/church.

Cisneros, Sandra (1991). *The House on Mango Street.* New York: Random House.

Crèvecœur, J. Hector St. John (1981). *Letters from an American Farmer and Sketches of 18th-Century America*, ed. by Albert E. Stone. New York: Penguin American Library.

Eugenides, Jeffrey (2002). *Middlesex.* New York: Farrar, Straus and Giroux.

Freese, Peter (1996). Universality vs. Ethnocentricity, or; the Literary Canon in a Multicultural Society. *Zeitschrift für Anglistik und Amerikanistik* 44 (2), 155–170.

Freese, Peter (1999). Between Assimilation and Nativism: Popular Expressions of the Changing Concepts of American Identity. In: Hagenbüchle, Roland / Raab, Josef (Eds.). *Negotiations of America's National Identity* (Vol. II). Tübingen: Stauffenburg, 248-271.

Freese, Peter (2000). The Chances and Limits of 'Intercultural Understanding' in the Advanced EFL-Classroom. *Literatur in Wissenschaft und Unterricht* 33 (3), 247–263.

Freese, Peter (Ed.) (2002). *Teaching 'America': Selected Essays.* München: Langenscheidt-Longman.

Freese, Peter (Ed.) (2005a). *From Melting Pot to Multiculturalism: E pluribus unum?* (8th enl. ed.). München: Langenscheidt.

Freese, Peter (2005b). *From Melting Pot to Multiculturalism – Resource Book.* (6th rev. ed.). München: Langenscheidt.

Freese, Peter (2005c and 2006). From Melting Pot to Quilt: Ethnic Diversity vs. National Identity. *Mitteilungsblatt des FMF Niedersachsen* 20 (2), 18-39 and *Mitteilungsblatt des FMF Westfalen-Lippe* 24 (1), 8-21.

Freese, Peter (Ed.) (2006). *Israel Zangwill, "The Melting Pot"* (2nd ed.). München: Langenscheidt.

Freese, Peter (2008). American National Identity in a Globalized World as a Topic in the Advanced EFL-Classroom. In: Freese, Peter (Ed.), *Ethnic Visions of the United States of America* (*American Studies Journal*, No. 51 [Spring 2008], http://asjournal.zusas.uni-halle.de).

Freese, Peter (2010). Die amerikanische Einwanderungsgeschichte im fortgeschrittenen EU anhand von politischen Karikaturen und Werbeanzeigen. In: Hecke, Carola / Surkamp, Carola (Eds.). *Bilder im Fremdsprachenunterricht: Neue Ansätze, Kompetenzen und Methoden.* Tübingen: Narr, 239-253.

Freese, Peter (Ed.) (2011). *The American Dream: Humankind's Second Chance?* (14th enl. ed.). München: Langenscheidt.

Freese, Peter (Ed.) (2012). *New York Stories* (8th ed.). München: Langenscheidt.

Glazer, Nathan / Moynihan, Daniel Patrick (1963). *Beyond the Melting Pot: The Negroes, Puerto Ricans, Jews, Italians, and Irish of New York.* Cambridge, MA: MIT Press.

Gleason, Philip (1980). American Identity and Americanization. In: Thernstrom, Stephan (Ed.) *Harvard Encyclopedia of American Ethnic Groups.* Cambridge, MA., and London: The Belknap P of Harvard University Press, 31-58.

Grant, Madison (1918). *The Passing of the Great Race or the Racial Basis of European History* (rev. ed.). New York: Scribner's Sons.

Grunwald, Michael (2013). Immigrant Son. *Time* (International Edition) 181(6), 24-30.

Handlin, Oscar (1953). *The Uprooted: From the Old World to the New*. London: Watts and Co.

Hansen, Marcus Lee (1952). The Third Generation in America. *Commentary* 14, 492-500.

Huntington, Samuel P. (2004). *Who Are We? America's Great Debate*. New York: Simon and Schuster.

King, Martin Luther (2011). I Have a Dream. In: Freese, Peter (Ed.). *The American Dream: Humankind's Second Chance?* (new, enl. ed.). München: Langenscheidt, 22-24.

Krauthammer, Charles (2006). In Plain English: Let's Make It Official. *Time* 167(24), 112.

Novak, Michael (1972). *The Rise of the Unmeltable Ethnics; Politics and Culture in the Seventies*. New York: Macmillan.

Paine, Thomas (1925). Common Sense. In: Van der Weyde (Ed.). *The Life and Works of Thomas Paine* (Vol. II). New Rochelle, NY: Thomas Paine National Historical Association, 93-182.

Radway, Janice (1999). What's in a Name? Presidential Address to the American Studies Association, 20 November, 1998. *American Quarterly* 51 (1), 1-32.

Rodriguez, Richard (1983). *Hunger of Memory: The Education of Richard Rodriguez*. New York: Bantam Books.

Rosten, Leo (1970). *The Education of H*Y*M*A*N K*A*P*L*A*N*. Harmondsworth: Penguin Books.

Schlesinger, Arthur Jr. (1992). *The Disuniting of America: Reflections on a Multicultural Society*. New York: W.W. Norton and Co.

Schlesinger, Arthur M. Sr. (1959). America's Influence: Our Ten Contributions to Civilization. *Atlantic Monthly* 203, 65-69.

Sosa, Lionel (1999). *The Americano Dream: How Latinos Can Achieve Success in Business and in Life*. New York: Plume Books.

Strong, Josiah (1963). *Our Country: Its Possible Future and Its Present Crisis*. Ed. by Jürgen Herbst. Cambridge, MA: The Belknap P of Harvard University Press.

Thernstrom, Abigail M. (1980). Language: Issues and Legislation. In: Thernstrom, Stephan (Ed.). *Harvard Encyclopedia of American Ethnic Groups*. Cambridge, MA and London: The Belknap P of Harvard University Press, 619-629.

Tumulty, Karen (2006). Who Gets to Be an American? *Time* (10 April 2006), 30-40.

Worsnop, Richard L. (1993). Bilingual Education. *CQ Researcher* 3(30), 697-720.

Internet Sources[39]

http://en.wikipedia.org/wiki/Great_American_Boycott
http://en.wikipedia.org/wiki/The_Star-Spangled_Banner
http://en.wikipedia.org/wiki/William_Tyler_Page
http://hnn.us/articles/4987.html
http://home.apu.edu/~rgeib/edu-526/melting-pot-v-salad-bowl
http://lcweb2.loc.gov/service/pnp/cph/3a30000/3a31000/3a31300/3a31382r.jpg
http://lighthousepatriotjournal.wordpress.com/2006/06/27/california-responds-to-forest-fires
http://museum.msu.edu/museum/tes/immigration.htm
http://ourworld.compuserve.com/homepages/JWCrawford/engplus.htm
http://seattletimes.com/html/nationworld/2002960428_anthem29.html
http://Vote96.ss.ca.gov/Vote96/html/BP/209text.htm
http://www.baltimoreorless.com/2012/09/francis-scott-key-composes-the-star-spangled-banner/
http://www.butterflystorm.com/Work/GermanTexts/Removing%20the%20Hyphen.htm
http://www.cbo.gov/ftpdocs/72xx/doc7208/s2611.pdf
http://www.dailymotion.com/video/x28chl_national-anthem-usa-whitney-houston_music
http://www.govtrack.us/congress/bill.xpd?bill=h109-4437
http://www.nabe.org/Resources/Documents/Advocacy%20page/LauvNichols.pdf
http://www.phrases.org.uk/meanings/tanstaafl.html
http://www.proenglish.org/official-english/state-profiles
http://www.slate.com/id/2101756
http://www.stroebele-online.de/dokumente/129925.html
http://www.us-english.org/
http://www.us-english.org/view/13
http://www.ushistory.org/documents/creed.htm
http://www.yale.edu/glc/archive/1106.htm
http://www.youtube.com/watch?v=f4gP_pSOCz4

Audio Material

Freese, Peter (Ed.) (2007). *Viewfinder Special*. München: Langenscheidt ELT, CD2, No. 34.

[39] All internet sources were last accessed 4/10/2012.

WERNER DELANOY

The Case of Gloria Anzaldúa: Translating a Postcolonial Perspective into (English) Language Education

The following article aims to interconnect (English) language education with postcolonial issues and translation practices through the prism of a particular case study. In more concrete terms, attention is drawn to the Mexican-American scholar and writer Gloria Anzaldúa and her two books for children, and to how these books were discussed in a concrete translation project carried out with English language students. In the first part of the article, Gloria Anzaldúa's work will be related to postcolonial debates, the focus being on her trans-modern perspective and on her understanding of cultural hybridity. In the second part, a case is made for a power-critical approach to culture-learning in ELT contexts. Moreover, translation is presented as a pedagogical tool which can encourage careful and (self-)reflective forms of text reception and text creation. Finally, Gloria Anzaldúa's books for children come in two languages – English and Spanish. Therefore, they can also open up space for connecting English language education to a plurilingual agenda.

1. Introduction

Gloria Anzaldúa (1942-2004) is a Mexican-American scholar and writer whose work defies easy labels. Therefore, placing it under a postcolonial banner does not do full justice to her writings. Yet there is a postcolonial dimension to her work. Also the multi-dimensionality of her thinking is typical of current post-colonial theory-building where postcolonial concerns interconnect with other power-critical positions. Finally, the focus on postcoloniality poses a challenge to German ELT teaching, which, so far, has only paid insufficient attention to such a perspective. Thus, in this article postcoloniality is also emphasized in order to widen the scope of English language education.

Translation is a key term in Postcolonial Studies where it is used as a metaphor for what happens when people, texts, ideas or institutions move and are moved from one cultural context to another. Indeed, the term encourages sustained and detailed reflection upon how such moves affect source and recipient domains. Thus, a focus on translation gives particular attention to how

Anzaldúa's work is presented in an ELT context, and how ELT practices in turn may undergo change in the light of such contact. However, translation will not only be used as a metaphor for cultural transfer. In addition, a case will be made for reactivating translation as a textual practice to invite careful and (self)critical readings.

In the first section of this article attention is drawn to how Anzaldúa's writings relate to some major postcolonial concerns, the focus being on her notion of cultural hybridity and on the trans-modernity of her approach. Moreover, her two books for children will be introduced to further discuss her concept of (postcolonial) empowerment. In the second part, some general reflections on translation, postcoloniality and English language education will be followed by a concrete translation project. In this project Anzaldúa's children's books crossed manifold linguistic and cultural borders. Although the project was carried out in an ELT context, it also includes a plurilingual dimension.

2. Gloria Anzaldúa: A Postcolonial Thinker and Writer

Postcolonialism is a problematic term since the prefix *post* may suggest that colonialism has come to an end (see Wildburger 2006: 131). Yet, despite its limitations the term is still used to discuss what Enrique Dussel (2013: 15) calls "the unfinished and incomplete project of decolonisation". What are the aims of such a project? From its very beginning postcolonialism has aimed for independence from foreign control. While first, political independence was sought, the programme – with national sovereignty achieved – then turned to decolonizing the mind (see Loomba 1998: 12, 185). As for mental independence, postcolonial thinkers and writers have shown particular interest in developing *trans-modern* perspectives which reach beyond western and Eurocentric concepts of modernity (see Young 2003: 113; Dussel 2013: 167). Moreover, while in early postcolonial texts the binarism between coloniser and colonised played a central role, current approaches emphasize that the two perspectives have become implicated in each other (see Loomba 1998: 182). Thus, syncretic concepts of culture have replaced models suggesting cultural homogeneity and easy cultural separability. Finally, while postcolonialism has always engaged with colonial and neo-colonial oppression, more recent approaches have also turned to the power inequalities inside postcolonial societies, thus linking a postcolonial agenda to other power-critical programmes (e.g. feminism).

How does Gloria Anzaldúa's work relate to these postcolonial concerns? First, her approach is trans-modern in orientation, since Anzaldúa grounded her approach in indigenous religion, mythology and folklore. Secondly, she is strictly opposed to a monolithic conception of culture, stressing cultural hybridity and interconnectedness in her concept of the *New Mestiza*. Finally, in her work postcolonial concerns intersect with a feminist agenda. In the following reflections, her understanding of trans-modernity and her concept of the New Mestiza will be further discussed with reference to Anzaldúa's theoretical texts and her books for children.

Gloria Anzaldúa's Trans-modern Perspective

People in the west often claim to have a monopoly on modernity and enlightened thinking. From a postcolonial perspective, this claim is part of a hegemonic programme justifying the west's right to intellectual and economic domination and exploitation. Dussel (see 2013: 14), for example, argues that this myth of superiority makes Western modernity appear in a highly favourable light, while simultaneously masking its will to dominate, exploit and silence others. Postcolonial thinkers like Dipesh Chakraparty (see 2008: 44), Dussel (see 2013: 14f.) or Mohamed Turki (see 2010: 116f.), thus, have questioned western and Eurocentric narratives of progress by emphasizing their complicity in (post)colonial suppression and exploitation. Simultaneously, they have shifted attention to 'native' concepts to delink the notion of modernity from western role models.

With this aim in mind, Dussel (2013: 167) makes a case for a "trans-modern" agenda to show that postcolonial cultures have their own rich histories and are capable of independent concept-formation. What he means by *trans-modern* is a move beyond western and Eurocentric models by uncovering forgotten histories, silenced voices and marginalized perspectives which are relevant to the present. For Dussel (see ibid.: 167), a trans-modern approach does not reject western critical thinking out of hand. Moreover, he (see ibid.: 166) argues against uncritical approval or glorification of native models which themselves are neither frozen in time nor innocent of power inequalities. To his mind (see ibid.: 181), the transition to transmodernity is an arduous, (self)critical, unstable and lengthy process of resistance and self-determination. Because of its instability and the cultural power of western concepts, he argues against western participation in this undertaking, fearing that otherwise the project may be hijacked by outside forces. Dussel (ibid.: 168, 178) or Marwan Kraidy (2005: 155), therefore, attribute particular importance to a "south-to-south" or "east-to-east" dialogue to help transmodernity take root in postcolonial societies.

How does Anzaldúa's concept compare to this notion of transmodernity? On the one hand, she does not share Dussel's protectionist attitude. For Anzaldúa, everybody in favour of power-critical concerns can become involved in her programme. As for her concept of the *New Mestiza*, she states that "progressive whites who have friends from different worlds and who study different cultures become intellectual mestizas" (Anzaldúa 2009: 210). She adds that "they may not be emotional [...] and biological mestizas", yet their empathy, sensitivity and political awareness connect them to like-minded people. Also, for Anzaldúa (2007: 239) or Ania Loomba (1998: 182) a clear separation between western and non-western perspectives is impossible, since after a shared history spanning more than 500 years these perspectives have become implicated in each other. This does not mean that a (temporary) retreat cannot advance intellectual independence, but in line with Robert Young's (2003: 3) play on words, such independence will also remain "in dependence" of perhaps unsolicited influence. Finally, from a cultural learning perspective, where the addressees live in a European country, Anzaldúa's approach invites a cross-cultural dialogue to forge new power-critical alliances. This is one of the reasons why her approach was chosen for this article.

On the other hand, in line with Dussel, Anzaldúa's approach includes a transmodern dimension. She reclaims an indigenous past dating back to the ancient Tolmecs and to the early Aztecs. In her concept, she refers to Toltec religion and mythology which in her view radically fuses opposites. A good example is the earth-goddess Coatlicue who combines good and bad, life and death, beauty and horror and stasis and movement (see Anzaldúa 2007: 68). To her mind, Coatlicue provides a foundation for a holistic understanding of life including a spiritual dimension. She uses this foundation to criticize dualistic concepts, which, according to her, can be found both in later Aztec and in western positions. In this respect, she is critical of both indigenous and western perspectives. For Anzaldúa, however, a Toltec perspective is an ideal which she does not question. Here - in my view - she falls short of Dussel's understanding of transmodernity which rules out any uncritical acceptance or glorification of a native past.

Anzaldúa's transmodernity not only links back to Toltec religion and mythology. She also looks for voices silenced during colonial times. For example, she reintroduces and re-evaluates the character of Malinali (Cortez' translator and lover) and the legend of *la Llorona*. As for the latter, she rewrites the story as a book for children. The title of the book is *Prietita and the ghost woman/ Prietita y la Lorona* (1995a), the story coming in two languages (English and Spanish) with both versions written by Anzaldúa. The illustrations are provided by the Mexican-American artist Christina Gonzalez.

In this story, Prietita, a young Mexican-American girl living in the borderlands between the U.S. and Mexico, serves her apprenticeship with the village healer, a woman called *la curandera*. One day, Prietita's mother falls ill, and *la curandera* sends the girl on a quest for the healing plant to cure the mother's disease. The plant, however, can only be found in the carefully guarded and dangerous *King Ranch*. Prietita gains unauthorized access to this territory, and what follows is a journey through the night, where, feeling lost, she meets a series of helpers. The most powerful is *la Llorona* who directs her to the healing plant and who guides her back to safety. Back home she reports her experience to people from her village. In this story a common legend is rewritten. In the legend, *la Llorona*, which in Spanish means 'weeping woman', kills her children and is then turned into a hostile water spirit, who is condemned to look for lost children who she captures and abducts. In Anzaldúa's text, however, *la Llorona* is turned into a guardian angel helping lost children accomplish their mission.

This rewriting is in line with a trans-modern agenda. According to Edith Vásquez (2005: 66), the legend has undergone significant transformation over the centuries. While the figure of *la Llorona* first warned indigenous people of the brutality of the Spanish conquerors, she became the monster who captured and killed children during colonial times. For Anzaldúa (2007: 52), this figure is no longer an ogre. Instead, like Malinali, she becomes one of the mothers of "la gente Chicana" who protects and guides her children. Anzaldúa rewrites the story by making *la Llorona* a spiritual medium for postcolonial and female empowerment. On the one hand, Anzaldúa recaptures the positive image of the early colonial *Llorona*. On the other hand, she rewrites the story with a postcolonial agenda in mind, where *la Llorona's* function is no longer that of the lone warner of Spanish imperialism. Instead, the setting is now the present with its still existing social divisions, and *la Llorona* becomes the helper of the young who take initiative and risks for the well-being of the poor and underprivileged. In the story the risk-taker is a young girl, her teacher is a wise woman, and the spiritual helper is female, too. In other words, socio-cultural transformation is made possible by women with the young leading the way and the old acting as powerful helpers.

Let me just add that in the story the older women - *la Llorona* and *la curandera* - are both trans-modern helpers. *La Llorona* connects back to a positive pre-colonial past and through her new transformation she becomes a powerful support for a modern agenda. Prietita's teacher – *la curandera* – is not a doctor or healer in a conventional European and western sense. Her approach is more holistic including herbal and spiritual healing, and it is in line with a social and humanitarian agenda

The New Mestiza

One of the major changes in culture studies in the past 40 years is the shift from a monolithic understanding of culture to viewing cultures as hybrid and heterogeneous entities. Following Kraidy (2005: 59), a good example for this shift in approach is Edward Said's work. In *Orientalism*, Said (1978) still discusses the west as a monolith in its hegemonic treatment of oriental cultures, this treatment leading to an unbridgeable gap between the two. This position, however, is revised in *Culture and Imperialism*, where he states that "all cultures are involved in one another, none is single and pure, all are hybrid, heterogeneous, extraordinarily differentiated, and unmonolithic" (Said 1994: xxv). Meanwhile, cultural hybridity has become a *conditio sine qua* non in culture studies. Moreover, cultural hybridisation has been discussed under the banner of transculturality, and the latter has been opposed to the concepts of inter- and multiculturality. This is not the place, however, to further engage in this debate (for a detailed discussion, see: Delanoy 2012a). Suffice it to say, that cultural interconnectedness is a highly important characteristic of culture formation in a global modernity. Yet, any one-sided valorization of the concept should be avoided. As postcolonial studies have shown, cultural hybridisation is a complex and varied phenomenon which must be situated in specific contexts and subjected to power-critical analysis (see Kraidy 2005: vi, 3; Loomba 1998: 178-181).

Gloria Anzaldúa is a proponent of a hybrid concept of culture. Indeed, her main book – *Borderlands / La Frontera: The New Mestiza* (2007, first published in 1987) – is a manifesto for cultural hybridity both in terms of form and content matter. On formal levels, the book mixes autobiography, history, culture theory, philosophical speculation and poetry, and brings together different languages (e.g. English, Spanish, TexMex, Nahuatl). Content-wise, Anzaldúa makes a case for divergent and power-critical thinking, where tolerance for ambiguity and frustration is developed, where unpleasant truths are addressed, and where "severed and separated pieces" are integrated in new formations, which are more inclusive plus in line with an egalitarian and democratic society (Anzaldúa 2007: 101). For Anzaldúa (see ibid.: 102), such a new mestiza life approach is pain- and stressful, thus placing considerable demands on its proponents. Yet, it is also a creative and satisfying process with high energy levels, which – to be successful – needs the support of others.

Therefore, similar to the Marxist credo of "workers of all nations unite" she calls for a coalition of the oppressed and like-minded, where –as already mentioned – everybody can join the new mestiza movement. Despite the leading role of women, the concept is not against men as such, but against oppressive power structures. The way I read Anzaldúa, women are given this role because they are subject to both (neo)colonial and patriarchal oppression, the latter also being a characteristic of postcolonial societies. Thus, women are the victims of multiple forms of oppression. On the one hand, this heightens their sensitivity to such oppression. On the other hand, liberation has to start with them to make sure that a postcolonial programme is wide enough in scope to address external and internal discrimination.

Of course, Anzaldúa gives her trans-modern approach a female face. In more concrete terms, she reclaims a Toltec goddess and reinterprets the roles of female historical and legendary characters to create a new foundation for social liberation. Also, she creates characters like Prietita to show how her programme can be translated into concrete action. However, Coatlicue - in her fusion of opposites - not only serves a feminist agenda but can also reconnect men and women. Moreover, in her other book for children, Anzaldúa shows that her notion of liberation also benefits men, who when oppressed need to be helped, and when clinging to "macho" beliefs need to be brought to reason (see Anzaldúa's [2007: 105] comments on *macho* culture).

So far, I have only referred to one of Anzaldúa's books for children, namely to her rewriting of the legend of *la Llorona*. In the other book – *Friends from the other side / Amigos del otro lado* (1995b) – Anzaldúa together with the illustrator Consuelo Méndez draw attention to the humanitarian implications of the new mestiza concept. In this story, which predates *Prietita y la Llorona/ Prietita and the ghost woman*, Prietita meets the slightly younger Joaquin, an illegal Mexican immigrant who has settled in Prietita's village. In the course of the story, she protects him from a gang of boys living in the same village. Moreover, she introduces Joaquin to *la curandera* to cure his rash, plus she hides the boy and his mother from *la migra* (the border police) in *la curandera's* house, when they search the village for illegal immigrants. Finally, Prietita contacts some of the neighbour women to find job possibilities for Joaquin and his mother. At the end of the story, *la curandera* is so impressed with Prietita's courage and humanity that she offers to take her under her wings.

Prietita is presented as a role model for the new mestiza concept. She is a cultural hybrid (Mexican American) and lives in the borderlands, where multiple divisions need to be overcome. Indeed, the village boys see Joaquin as an unwanted foreigner and intruder despite their common language and similar appearance. Thanks to Prietita's intervention, Joaquin and his mother can be better integrated into the social world of the village. Prietita acts in the interest of a more humane society where the weakest are cared for and protected from oppression. She is even prepared to break the law when her civil disobedience serves a higher form of justice. Finally, she can draw on a network of helpers who again are mainly women. The men in the story need to be helped as is the case with Joaquin. In addition, their physical and verbal aggression needs curbing. Indeed, Prietita confronts the boys attacking Joaquin by calling their misguided male identity into question.[1] Also, the two policemen are given wrong information to prevent them from executing discriminatory laws. In other words, the men portrayed – because of their problematic identities and their implication in social systems of injustice – cannot act as an avant-garde for advancing the new *mestiza* concept.

3. Translating Gloria Anzaldúa's Books for Children into English Language Education

In this section an approach will be suggested which – metaphorically speaking – views engagement with postcoloniality as cultural translation, that is to say as a careful, ongoing, self-reflexive and open-ended re-contextualisation process. The recipient context is German EFL education, and the focus is on how meaning is made of postcolonial texts and perspectives in this learning context. As for concrete texts, the focus is on Anzaldúa's books for children. Finally, a project will be introduced where these texts – in a literal sense – are translated into different languages and cultural contexts.

Translation, Postcoloniality and English Language Education

As mentioned before, *translation* serves as a key metaphor in postcolonial studies. Hence, any movement across cultures can be studied as a translation process, where source and recipient domains enter into specific relationships. Moreover, postcolonial critics view translation as a political act (see Spivak 1993: 179 f.; Young 2003: 141), where the question of „who controls the means of translation" is of crucial importance (see Kraidy 2005: 152). Also, a case is made for a particular type of translation. According to Michael Cronin (2003: 142) a distinction must be made between "translation as assimilation" and "translation as diversification". While the former assimilates the alterity of other perspectives to one's own position, the latter aims for making differences visible. Thus, proponents of translation as diversification have expressed particular interest in the „remainders", i.e. the elements that resist and defy assimilation attempts (Cronin 2003: 159; also see: Chakrabarty 2008: xiii-xiv). To make such translation possible a high dose of (self)critical meta-reflection is required (see Cronin 2003: 141). Indeed, critical meta-reflection is paramount for all translation, since translators always select and prioritize certain elements of source texts, thus privileging particular aspects and creating only partial re-

[1] The words used by Prietita are: „What's the matter with you guys? How brave you are, a bunch of *machos* against one small boy. You should be ashamed of yourselves!" (Anzaldúa 1995b: n.p.).

presentations (see Tymoczko 1999: 55). Finally, a postcolonial perspective as suggested by Anzaldúa implies a close relationship with the text to be translated. *Close* here also means that the translator shares an intellectual and emotional interest in helping the oppressed. This position overlaps with Dussel's or Young's postcolonial perspectives, where sympathy for the pain and the suffering of the poor and oppressed is of central importance (see Dussel 2013: 104; Young 2003: 111f.).

There are manifold parallels between this notion of translation and a concept of dialogue as suggested by a power-critical hermeneutics after Gadamer (see Kögler 1992) which has served the present author as a basis for a particular cultural-learning approach (see Delanoy 2007: 50-52, Delanoy 2012a: 161-162). Such a hermeneutics views all understanding as partial, selective and open to re-definition which is in line with Tymoczko's notion of translation as selective re-presentation. Moreover, understanding is seen as people bound, contextually situated and as subject to power claims and inequalities, the latter making these hermeneutics compatible with power-critical schools of thought such as postcolonial studies. Such a hermeneutics also argues against assimilating or uncritically giving oneself to other viewpoints. Indeed, the power of dialogue rests in the possibility to (self)critically learn from others, which implies a high dose of meta-reflection. Furthermore, understanding is viewed as a lived experience where respect, sympathy and care for other people play a crucial role. Finally, dialogue ideally is shaped by equal partners sharing a concern for a democratic world.

Yet, there are also differences between this concept of dialogue and a postcolonial position as advocated by Anzaldúa. Anzaldúa's trans-modern approach includes a spiritual dimension, which is clearly absent in a post-Gadamerian hermeneutics.[2] Indeed Chakrabarty (see 2008: 10-16) views such a dimension as a common element in postcolonial concepts, although other postcolonial thinkers, for example Said (see 2004: 11), have emphasized the secularity of their programme.

Another moot point is the question of who is in control of translations. In this article, Anzaldúa's position is filtered through my western and otherwise limited understanding of postcoloniality. This raises the questions of whether I

[2] However, in this respect there is some affinity between Gadamer's hermeneutics and Anzaldúa. For Gadamer (1990: 75-76), the work of art permits irrational flashes of fundamental insight into the whole of existence, which gives aesthetic experience a quasi-religious dimension. Similarly, Anzaldúa (2007: 60) speaks of *la facultad*, i.e. an "instant sensing … without conscious reasoning", where again far-reaching and holistic experience (including spiritual insight) becomes possible.

have a right to act as a mediator, and of how reliable my translation is. As for the right to mediate, the openness of the concept of the new mestiza invites such initiative on my part, provided that I (self)critically engage with Anzaldúa's position. Reliability is a different issue. According to Spivak (see 1995: 24f.), the postcolonial critic and writer is faced with the dilemma of wishing to speak on behalf of the "subaltern" (oppressed) and not being able to do so because of his/her detachment from their life worlds. Following Spivak, this raises doubt not only about my but even about Anzaldúa's position. Anzaldúa's life history, however, shows that she suffered multiple forms of oppression, which makes her a reliable source even by Spivak's standards. As for my own reliability, I follow a post-Gadamerian hermeneutics which is less sceptical than Spivak's position. While this hermeneutics emphasizes the partiality of all understanding and concomitantly a continuous need for (self)critical reflection, it also believes in the possibility to partly understand and help others despite cultural and experiential differences.[3]

As a textual practice translation has a long tradition in the philologies. As such it played a central role in foreign language learning before communicative language learning became the dominant paradigm. With the communicative turn, however, it no longer proved compatible with the experiential and utilitarian learning programmes of the day. In the light of recent socio-cultural developments, i.e. in the context of a globalised and *liquid* modernity, the educational significance of translation, however, is being rediscovered. A "liquid modernity", i.e. an age where "nothing can [...] keep its shape for long" (Bauman 2000: 4), can be highly averse to focussed, careful, (self)critical and ongoing reflection (see Delanoy 2012a: 163f.). However, such reflection is indispensable in such a social context. A liquid modernity implies that people live in unstable worlds where the responsibilities for success or failure increasingly lie with the single person. Indeed, the single person is constantly faced with making important decisions, which because of global interconnections may have repercussions going far beyond the personal and local. Hence, an education is needed where deep reflection coupled with wide-reaching cultural awareness can be learned and practised. In my view, translation can contribute to such education provided that it can be integrated into experiential learning programmes.

As indicated in the introduction, a focus on postcoloniality and translation also shifts attention to how the recipient domain – English language education - is

[3] In my view, a more optimistic perspective is also confirmed by successful cross-cultural political and economic initiatives. A good example is SEWA (Self-Employed Women's Association), where aid workers (non-Indian and Indian) have worked with poor Gujarati women to improve their life conditions (see Nussbaum 2000: 15f.).

affected by this topic and approach. Indeed, its impact can already be seen in my choice of terminology. In other words, I do not speak of *language learning* but of *language education* to emphasize that engagement with postcolonial perspectives connects language learning with educational issues. Moreover, postcolonialism implies the inclusion of power-critical dimensions, which according to Laurenz Volkmann (2012: 171) - by and large - have been absent from German ELT practices and the theories concerned with it. Thus, German ELT approaches are faced with a new challenge on both practical and theoretical levels. Postcolonial perspectives often require students to move "outside the[ir] comfort zone[s]" (Johnston / Mangat 2012: 35f.), since their recipients may be confronted with unpleasant and conflict-ridden realities. Thus, to put it simply, language education enriched by postcolonial perspectives is not a feel-good programme, where multicultural diversity and transcultural mixing can be celebrated in general terms and on superficial levels. Following Said (2003: 55), such a programme requires the shift from a "smug" humanism to a perspective, where education is "an unsettling adventure in difference" serving the discovery of new perspectives in the interest of a more democratic world. Indeed, translation is deliberately chosen as an approach for such learning, since it requires patient attention to detail and ongoing meta-reflection. Such an approach can help prevent superficial understanding and the normalization of difference. However, it also places considerable demands on the learners both as a learning approach and in terms of content matter.

Finally, the subject English itself is affected. On the one hand, postcoloniality has widened the scope of English Studies considerably, and it has helped to de-centre British and U.S.-American perspectives. On the other hand, there is a danger that in English Studies postcoloniality is only treated as an Anglophone problematic. Indeed, Anzaldúa's work was also chosen because her approach – culturally and linguistically – comprises Hispanic, Anglophone and indigenous perspectives. Furthermore, as a textual practice translation can also help decentre English as the dominant linguistic medium by creating space for other languages.

Translating Gloria Anzaldúa's Books for Children

Gloria Anzaldúa's children's books have been chosen for translation projects for different reasons. First, content-wise they can irritate readers because of the civil disobedience portrayed, the preference given to female characters, the support offered to illegal immigrants, or the rewriting of existing legends. Indeed, despite its intended addressees (young children) these topics make the books a challenge for older readers, too. Moreover, the comfort zone is not transgressed too far, since in both books the protagonist succeeds in her mission, being aided by highly positive helpers. Thus, postcoloniality can be experienced as a perspective with potentially positive outcomes, which makes the texts a good starting point for introducing postcolonial issues. Also, the language used is simple, and therefore it does not get in the way of translation. In other words, the learners are not side-tracked by unknown words or complicated syntactic structures, and, thus, can focus their attention on the linguistic and cultural *remainders* to be dealt with in the translation process. Finally, German or Austrian classrooms have become multicultural and multilingual, and translating the texts into languages other than German can give English language education a plurilingual dimension.

So far, translation projects have been carried out with university students of English at the universities of Vienna and Klagenfurt in Austria. In all instances, the text to be translated was *Friends from the other side/ Amigos del otro lado*. As for the task-as-workplan, the students were invited to either produce a literal or a cultural translation into a language of their own choice. While the aim of a literal translation is to stay as faithful as possible to the source text, a cultural translation requires the transfer of the source text into a new setting (see Eco 2006: 18). To keep the task within manageable limits only between three and five pages had to be translated, which the students could choose themselves. Because of the presence of monolingual speakers of English and bilingual speakers of English and Spanish, some alternative tasks needed to be added to the original workplan. In concrete terms, cultural translations could also be written in English, thus making it possible for monolingual English speakers to stay within their language. As for bilingual speakers of English and Spanish, they were offered the possibility to write a cultural translation in one of the two languages. Moreover, they were invited to take a close look at the differences between Anzaldúa's English and her Spanish text. Finally, all students were instructed to look at both the written text and the illustrations, and - in the case of cultural translations - to reflect upon image-related differences.

The translation projects have been discussed in another article where the main focus is on plurilinguality and English language education (see Delanoy 2012b). As for the main findings, translating the text did encourage motivating, engaged, highly reflective and repeated readings, permitting manifold insight into linguistic and cultural differences. The two translation approaches – literal and cultural translation – offered specific possibilities, yet also posed particular limitations (see ibid.: 435f). The literal translations fostered close attention to detail, in some cases however they also inhibited engagement with the text on more general meaning levels. On the other hand, the cultural translations encouraged a more general approach. At the same time, important detail was ignored, which, in some instances, led to a normalization of Anzaldúa's perspective. Indeed, the strengths and limitations of the two approaches became palpable and discussible when the different approaches were compared and contrasted in classroom discussions.

In the discussion process, one of the roles of the teacher (the present author) was to focus attention on the *remainders*, i.e. the bits defying one-to-one correspondences. On the level of detail, a case in point is the item *la curandera*, which implies a combination of medicinal, spiritual and social healing. None of the translations offered could equal the polysemy of the term, and reflection upon the gaps in meaning permitted insight into Anzaldúa's trans-modern programme. Another detail concerned the mesquite tree, which is repeatedly referred to in the written text and in the illustrations. The mesquite tree (the German translation is *Süßhülsenbaum*) is the tree on which Prietita sits. It has strong roots and can survive in difficult terrain, which in symbolic terms may signal the robustness and rootedness of the new mestiza. In some of the cultural translations, the problem of finding an equivalent (for example in a Viennese setting) was discussed, and again the remainders led to further engagement with Anzaldúa's programme. Finally, let me just add that English, being the only language shared by all students, was used as the lingua franca to discuss the various translations, which included texts in Italian, Bosnian, Slovak, Russian and Turkish.

So far, no similar project has been conducted with reference to *Prietita and the Ghost Woman/ Prietita y la Llorona*. On the one hand, this is due to the book currently being out of print. On the other hand, the project I have in mind goes beyond my own seminar rooms, requiring cooperation with some of the local Klagenfurt schools.[4] In concrete terms, I am aiming for a cultural translation of the book into a Carinthian setting. Indeed, wailing women and other female water sprites play an important role in Klagenfurt legends. According to Dieter Jandl (see 2000: 8-10), the name *Klagenfurt* is derived from the old German word for wailing woman (*chlaga*). Moreover, in Old Slovene the name for wailing woman is *cvilja*, and the name of the place where such a woman lives is *cviljovec*, which comes close to the Slovene name for Klagenfurt (*Celovec*). Let me just add that German and Slovene-speaking Carinthians have shared a troubled history since the late 19th century. Hence, students from Klagenfurt high schools will be invited to write German and Slovene versions of the *la Lorona* text to create a bilingual book for children, which presents a posi-

---

[4] The schools to be chosen for the project should include one of the two bilingual Klagenfurt high schools with Slovene and German as the main languages of instruction. Moreover, contributions from another high school with a special arts focus are particularly welcome, since the translations will also extend to the illustrations.

tive new founding myth for a Carinthia where the two communities can meet as equals. Simultaneously, the various linguistic and cultural problems will be addressed which arise when the *la Llorona* text is translated into this setting.

Furthermore, the text(s) to be produced in this project will include written text and pictures. Thus, a multimodal approach is required which is compatible with the principles discussed. Such an approach is suggested by proponents of the *New London Group*, whose perspective on multiliteracies includes power-critical and emancipatory dimensions (see Cope / Kalantzis 2000: 3 f.). However, a multimodal approach also further complicates the project design. Indeed, such a project requires a transdisciplinary approach where arts classes need to be included. Finally, it must be noted that the project is still in its infancy, and whether it will ever see the light of day is still an open question. Yet in potential the project includes what I see as the central objectives when translating Anzaldúa's postcolonial perspective into a new context. First, some of the thrust of Anzaldúa's concept is carried over into a new context, since – in line with her emancipatory position – two antagonistic (Carinthian) perspectives will be connected as equals. Secondly, the creativity which comes with postcolonial renewal can spill over into both language and arts classes. Finally, the focus on translation requires careful and continuous reflection upon the differences between Anzaldúa's text and its translations.

4. Conclusion

By way of conclusion, let me sum up what I see as the main cornerstones when introducing postcolonial perspectives into ELT contexts:

First, the inclusion of power-critical perspectives is indispensable. However, the power-critical perspectives to be dealt with go beyond western and eurocentric models, thus requiring particular attention to their trans-modern specificity and difference. Because of the potentially highly challenging content-matter such learning is no plain sailing. However, in a globally interconnected world struggling with colonial legacies and gross social inequalities, such learning can help address practices of oppression in the interest of a more equitable and democratic world. Moreover, the creativity required to develop new perspectives gives teachers and learners a special role. In other words, they are invited to join a new alliance of change agents.

Secondly, engagement with postcolonial perspectives requires what Said (2003: 61) calls a "philological" approach, i.e. "... a detailed, patient scrutiny of and a lifelong attentiveness to the words and rhetorics by which language is used by human beings who exist in history". Translation is such an approach, and as a careful and ongoing textual practice it can draw attention to differences which may go unnoticed otherwise. In the light of the demands placed on the learners, however, a pedagogy is needed which makes translation motivating and manageable for particular learner groups. In the projects discussed in the previous section, a highly optimistic postcolonial perspective was chosen to help learners gain access to postcolonial worlds. Also, a text was selected which in terms of linguistic difficulty would not overstretch the students' abilities. Finally, adjustments were made to the workplan to give all students a chance to participate in the project.

Thirdly, postcolonial studies help de-centre dominant and entrenched viewpoints. In an ELT context, therefore, special attention should be given to perspectives situated in cultural and linguistic borderlands. On the one hand, such a context encourages moves beyond an Anglo-centrism where either the UK or the USA remains a continuous point of reference. On the other hand, such a borderlands approach permits the inclusion of other languages, thus connecting English language education to plurilingual learning. Because of their multiculturality and multilinguality Gloria Anzaldúa's writings are a good example for such de-centring.

Finally, the approach suggested in this article is of course partial, limited and open to re-definition. From my hermeneutic perspective, such limitations can be partly overcome through a dialogue with people thinking differently. The article, therefore, is an invitation to colleagues to challenge the views presented and to join a new alliance of English language educators wishing to incorporate postcolonial perspectives into ELT classrooms.

Bibliography

Anzaldúa, Gloria (2009). The New Mestiza Nation. In: Keating, AnaLouise (Ed..). *The Gloria Anzaldúa Reader*. London and Durham: Duke University Press, 203-216.

Anzaldúa, Gloria (2007). *Borderlands. La Frontera. The New Mestiza. Third Edition*. San Francisco: Aunt Lute Books.

Anzaldúa, Gloria / Gonzalez, Maya Christina (1995a). *Prietita and the Ghost Woman. Prietita y la Llorona*. San Francisco: Children's Book Press.

Anzaldúa, Gloria / Méndez, Consuelo (1995b). *Friends from the Other Side. Amigos del Otro Lado*. San Francisco: Children's Book Press.

Bauman, Zygmunt (2000). *Liquid Modernity*. Cambridge: Polity.

Chakrabarty, Dipesh (2008). *Provincializing Europe. Postcolonial Thought and Historical Difference. With a New Preface by the Author*. Princeton and Oxford: Princeton University Press.

Cope, Bill / Kalantzis, Mary (2000). Introduction. Multiliteracies. The Beginnings of an Idea. In: Cope, Bill/ Kalantzis, Mary (Eds.). *Multiliteracies and the Design of Social Futures*. New York: Routledge, 3-8.

Cronin, Michael (2003). *Translation and Globalization*. London and New York: Routledge.

Delanoy, Werner (2007). Dialogue as a Perspective for English Language Learning. In: Kindermann, Wolf (Ed.). *Transcending Boundaries. Essays in Honor of Gisela Hermann-Brennecke*. Berlin: LIT, 49-69.

Delanoy, Werner (2012a). From 'Inter' to 'Trans'? Or: Quo Vadis Cultural Learning? In: Eisenmann, Maria / Summer, Theresa (Eds.). *Basic Issues in EFL Teaching and Learning*. Heidelberg: Winter, 157-167.

Delanoy, Werner (2012b). Mehrsprachigkeit als Perspektive: Gloria Anzaldúas *Friends from the Other Side/ Amigos del Otro Lado*. In: Hammer, Julia/ Eisenmann, Maria/ Ahrens, Rüdiger (Eds.). *Anglophone Literaturdidaktik. Zukunftsperspektiven für den Englischunterricht*. Heidelberg: Winter, 425-439.

Dussel, Enrique (2013). *Der Gegendiskurs der Moderne. Kölner Vorlesungen*. Wien and Berlin: Turia + Kant.

Eco, Umberto (2006). *Quasi dasselbe mit anderen Worten*. München: Hanser.

Gadamer, Hans Georg (1990). *Wahrheit und Methode. Grundzüge einer philosophischen Hermeneutik.* (6th ed.). Tübingen: J.C.B. Mohr.

Jandl, Dieter (2000). *A Brief History of Klagenfurt*. Klagenfurt: Heyn.

Johnston, Ingrid / Mangat, Jyoti (2012). *Reading Practices, Postcolonial Literature, and Cultural Mediation in the Classroom*. Rotterdam: Sense Publishers.

Kögler, Hans-Herbert (1992). *Die Macht des Dialogs. Kritische Hermeneutik nach Gadamer, Foucault und Rorty*. Stuttgart: J.B. Metzler.

Kraidy, Marwan M. (2005). *Hybridity or the Cultural Logic of Globalization*. Philadelphia: Temple University Press.

Loomba, Ania (1998). *Colonialism / Postcolonialism*. London and New York: Routledge.

Nussbaum, Martha C. (2000). *Women and Human development. The Capabilities Approach*. Cambridge: Cambridge University Press.

Said, Edward (1978). *Orientalism*. London and Henley: Routledge & Kegan Paul.

Said, Eward (1994). *Culture and Imperialism*. London: Vintage.

Said, Edward (2004). *Humanism and Democratic Criticism*. Basingstoke: Palgrave.

Spivak, Gayatri Chakravorty (1993). *Outside the Teaching Machine*. New York and London: Routledge.

Spivak, Gayatri Chakravorty (1995). Can the Subaltern Speak? In: Ashcroft, Bill / Griffiths, Gareth / Tiffin, Helen (Eds.). *The Postcolonial Studies Reader*. London and New York: Routledge, 24-28.

Turki, Mohamed (2010). *Humanismus und Interkulturalität. Ansätze zu einer Neubetrachtung des Menschen im Zeitalter der Globalisierung*. Leipzig: Edition Hamouda.

Tymoczko, Maria (1999). *Translation in a Postcolonial Context*. Manchester: St. Jerome.

Vásquez, Edith M. (2005). La Gloriosa Travesura de la Musa Que Cruza / The Misbehaving Glory(a) of the Border-Crossing Muse: Transgression in Anzaldúa's Children's Stories. In: Keating, AnaLouise (Ed.). *Entre Mundos / Among Worlds. New Perspectives on Gloria Anzaldúa*. New York: Palgrave Macmillan, 63-75.

Volkmann, Laurenz (2012). Intercultural Learning and Postcolonial Studies. In: Eisenmann, Maria / Summer, Theresa (Eds.). *Basic Issues in EFL-Teaching*. Heidelberg: Winter, 169-180.

Wildburger, Eleonore (2006). The Postcolonial Mind: Reading Indigenous Australian Texts in the Foreign Language Classroom. In: Delanoy, Werner / Volkmann, Laurenz (Eds.). *Cultural Studies in the EFL-Classroom*. Heidelberg: Winter, 131-141.

Young, Robert J.C. (2003). *Postcolonialism. A Very Short Introduction*. Oxford: Oxford University Press.

MARK STEIN

Mobile Writers, Porous Texts: Teju Cole's and Mohsin Hamid's Textual Translocations

This essay engages the idea of crossovers by focussing on modes of translocal representation and the circulation of narratives of porosity. Despite its brevity, the chapter roams widely, connecting 'twitter litter' to novels by Teju Cole and Mohsin Hamid, and Judith Butler's concept of 'grievable lives' to textual translocations. The concept of porosity is deployed here in order to account for spatial and textual connections which these 'cultural products' fashion, exploit and transform at the same time. Porosity has the potential to render borders – despite their evident and frequently harmful function of division and separation – as connectors, as membranes, which foster and modulate traffic, connection and cross-fertilisation.

> Precisely because a living being may die, it is necessary to care for that being so that it may live. Only under conditions in which the loss would matter does the value of the life appear. Thus, grievability is a presupposition for the life that matters. (Butler 2009: 14)

> [D]iasporas always leave a trail of collective memory about another place and time and create new maps of desire and of attachment [... collective memories] whose archaeology is fractured.
> (Appadurai / Breckridge 1986: i)

1. Obama's Daughters, Jonas Brothers, Predator Drones

When President Obama held his annual White House Correspondent's Dinner on May 1st, 2010, the Jonas Brothers, a boy band that was quite successful at the time, was on the guest list. These dinners are held in order to build relationships with journalists and traditionally this is achieved by the President's address containing lots of jokes and banter. Obama's speechwriters and he himself showed a remarkable lack of judgement when it came to the following joke:

> The Jonas Brothers are here. They're out there somewhere. Sasha and Malia are huge fans, but boys, don't get any ideas. Two words for you: predator drones. You will never see it coming. ("Obama Jokes" 00:00:01-00:00:20)

The frequent (and frequently illegal) use of predator drones by the US outside their national territory, in the Middle East and elsewhere, is one of the less than proud legacies of the Obama Presidency. Unmanned aerial vehicles are used not only to invade foreign territory for reconnaissance, but also in combat when equipped with warheads. This has led to an estimated number of 3.500 to 4.700 deaths in fifteen years (see Matthews 2013). Obama has achieved reducing the proportion of civilian deaths amongst predator drone casualties since taking over from the Bush administration. At this point, we can only speculate how Donald Trump's Presidency will affect this number. Aided by the UK, the US remain the only nation using drones extraterritorially and Obama faced questions from a range of American and international pressure groups who doubted the lawfulness of their use and critiqued especially American and non-American civilian drone victims. The persistent use of remote killing machines since 9/11 is one poignant reminder that national borders have increasingly become subject to trespassing. But they are not only a reminder of the porosity of state borders which have, with a wide range of technological advances, become a lot harder to police. Obama's fantasy of protecting his daughters from members of the boy band is more than a slip-up; the flippant threat of deploying predator drones not only draws on the heteronormative tenet that girls require protection from boys whilst at the same time presupposing that the Jonas Brothers might find Obama's daughters attractive. The private and the public are traversed with ease, showing a personal facet of Obama, his role as father, all with the aim of making him more amiable to the Fourth Estate. The incredible insouciance with which the President – after all the recipient of the 2009 Nobel Peace Prize, right at the start of his first term of office – rhetorically deploys lethal weapons in order to keep his loved ones safe is a measure of the power this office wields. By extension, of course, Obama wishes to be seen not only as keeping safe his daughters, but the American people at large. The fact that the 'joke' was successful — which is suggested by the transcript recording laughter — also points to the *topicality* of the subject of predator drones, a question to be addressed in the context of some short stories by Teju Cole (below).

2. Premise and Objectives

This short essay is premised on the notion that the presumed border between the texts we read, the cultures we breathe, and the effects we wield, the difference we seek to make in the world – politically, socially, interpersonally, ecologically, historically, – is marked by *porosity*: By leakage, seepage, organic, vital exchange, breathing pores, connection, intersection, transference, and transgression. When suggesting that "[d]espite all our desperate, eternal attempts to separate, contain and mend, categories always leak", Trinh Minh-ha (1989: 94) speaks to the requirement and the need of academics to establish and to work within categories; to question them; to reform them; and to move beyond them. As meaning-making animals, we cannot but categorize, compartmentalize, create boxes – even whilst we remain aware that they are, of necessity, provisional at best. Trinh Minh-ha calls these efforts not only eternal but, significantly, desperate too; we do rely upon categorisation, discrimination, on distinguishing one from the other. As we discriminate between different texts and authors, different genres and formats, different literary periods, etc., we actively insert separations, introduce rifts and create spaces of containment. And yet, she reminds us, categories always leak. We may wish to mend them, but there's leakage; little holes; big holes. According to Minh-ha, categories are then always already 'imperfect' with respect to their function of separating. Rather than separation, their function might, in the end, be a modulation and a tempering of flows, of connections, of exchange. It is this question of the border as a connector that I'm beginning to explore here.

My interest lies furthermore with narrative, diaspora, the global in its many shapes and forms, contemporary notions of the postcolonial, and how they intersect with and impact upon each other. How, then, has postcolonial studies been shaped under the signs of the global and the diasporic? Conversely, how has the unforeseen and unparalleled expansion of postcolonial paradigms across copious academic disciplines, to universities around the globe, into popular culture, and into grassroots movements, how has the dare I say *colonial* expansion of the postcolonial had its own specific impact on how we conceptualize what Gilroy and Spivak call the planetary?

How has narrative form responded to spatial boundaries becoming increasingly permeable, a reality for many but by no means all of us on this planet? Certainly, increasingly permeable spatial boundaries also pertain to and indeed affect communications, mediatisation, trade and commerce, ecological degradation, etc. How have those processes turning space into place themselves been altered by transnationalism, by time-space-compression, and by some of the most pressing global issues? – Among them increased migration (and increasingly perilous migrations) inside zones of crisis and beyond them, within the Middle East and Africa, and into Europe, North America, and elsewhere; mandate-free international warfare relying upon new remote-controlled armaments; proliferating nuclear threat; not to mention the sustained and profound instability at the heart of core financial, administrative, and political systems.

Today, numerous disciplines take an interest in social, cultural, political and economic connections between individuals, social formations, locations and institutions that cut across the nation state and span the globe. Steven Vertovec has noted that "globalization has entailed the increasing extent, intensity, velocity, and impact of global interconnectedness across a broad range of human domains" (2009: 2). One such human domain is constructed by the texts and the cultures that we study, tokens of human expression, and building blocks of the disciplines that we mould and inhabit.

3. Twitter-length Short Stories

I've already indicated my interest in the porosity of textuality and of literary texts. Texts that do not just re-inscribe pre-texts, as intertextuality would have it, but which prick and puncture other texts and penetrate and perforate distinct locations. There is seepage, then, to be observed in this kind of textuality. Let's turn to a short story that is in fact so short that we can easily reproduce it here in full:

> Mrs Dalloway said she would buy the flowers herself.
> Pity. A signature strike leveled the florist's.
> (@tejucole, 14 Jan 2013, 6:04 PM)

End of quote. End of story. Here's another one:

> Okonkwo was well known throughout the nine villages and even beyond. His torso was found, not his head.
> (@tejucole, 14 Jan 2013, 6:15 PM)

And one final example:

> Call me Ishmael. I was a young man of military age. I was immolated at my wedding. My parents are inconsolable.
> (@tejucole, 14 Jan 2013, 6:06 PM)

The pattern at work in these three very short pieces is easily recognizable; we are familiar with part of the storyline from the news we consume, and another part from the classics we've read. In the first example of porous textuality, a three-sentence story relates Virginia Woolf's 1925 novel *Mrs. Dalloway* to the contemporary 'War on Terror' which the US mostly leads outside its own territory, but within its self-declared global sphere of interest – frequently with the help of unmanned drones. Cole published this story on Twitter in 2013, and has Mrs Dalloway killed in a London flower shop by way of a "signature strike". The second example of twitterature takes liberties with Chinua Achebe's *Things Fall Apart* (1959), again using the novel's opening sentence and, again, cutting the story *very* short by eradicating the protagonist at the outset. Tragic hero and famous wrestler Okonkwo is dismembered so that only his torso remains. In example three, Herman Melville's *Moby-Dick* (1851) is killed off within a few lines, with narrator Ishmael being immolated before he can draw you and me into his story of Captain Ahab and the whale, leaving behind his grieving widow and parents.

There are seven porous short stories like that by Cole which translocate canonical literary texts into the War on Terror by lifting their well-known opening lines and amalgamating them with by now formulaic news items on the dirty work of predator drones. In effect, heroes and heroines of world literature are snuffed out – apparently for the greater good. Or at least for the USA's greater good, as in the so-called war on terror. Mrs Dalloway, Ishmael, Joyce's Buck Mulligan, Ralph Ellison's invisible man, Kafka's Josef K., Achebe's Okonkwo, and Camus' *l'étranger*: they all suffer a similar fate. Remote killing machines, euphemistically called drones, rewrite and thereby undo literary history – in Cole's literary imagination. On one level, the stories reproach us as students of literature in the following way. They imply – scandalously – that as readers of these canonical texts we might care more about the loss of life when it affects our named literary heroines and heroes, from Dalloway to Okonkwo. When it comes to the frequently nameless victims who actually do get killed on "our" behalf, much in the way that Cole describes, we find it harder to engage with real deaths than with fictionalized ones. Judith Butler has developed the concept of 'grievability' in several essays since the late 1990s, developing it further and connecting it to her notion of 'precariousness' in her 2009 study *Frames of War: When Is Life Grievable?* Whilst the above literary heroines and heroes are 'grievable', the frequently nameless victims of the war on terror that populate our news stories are mostly not. Cole's stories precisely pinpoint this outrage.

On the other hand, we observe that Cole certainly entertains the un-writing of these well-known novels which he effectively eliminates when cutting them so very short. By way of synecdoche, these literary eradications stand in for all those real life-stories that can no longer unfold due to collateral damage, as the chilling euphemism goes:

> Unintentional or incidental injury or damage to persons or objects that would not be lawful military targets [...] Such damage is not unlawful so long as it is not excessive in light of the overall military advantage anticipated from the attack. ("Collateral damage", Dept. of Defense 2001: 76)

Sufficient military advantage to one side would seem to condone civilian casualties on the other, according to this source. Porous borders around nation states can, apparently, be crossed with legitimacy as long as these breaches ensure sufficient militarily advantage to the West. This rationale is reliant upon a clear distinction between two military opponents and the spaces they defend and attack. However, this clear division is not only questioned but also in fact eradicated by these short stories. Cole's brief stories are an objection against an unscrupulous and self-serving justification, a strident protest against this rationale; they question its validity and point to the implication of a wider public. Cole's texts are not only provocative, designed to engage with modern predator drone warfare, a topic we were only beginning to understand in 2003, when Cole published his stories on Twitter. They do not just connect two different story-lines, one canonical, the other ephemeral. Significantly, his short stories actively correlate distinct geographical spaces. In fact, London and the Middle East are not just linked in the first example; they are irrevocably conjoined and effectively treated as one seamless space: a translocation. Cole's twitter stories are literary translocations that draw on a conception of space that suspends our knowledge of geography and makes porosity visible (see Döring / Stein 2012; Munkelt / Schmitz / Stroh / Stein 2013). A porosity that belies if not eradicates a clear distinction between two military opponents and the national spaces they defend and attack, thereby undermining the rationale that underpins the logic of collateral damage. A seamless porosity which is achieved through technology, modern warfare, questions of responsibility, but, importantly, also through translocal representation and the circulation of narratives of porosity.

The *jouissance* which Cole's short short stories embody at the formal level (but not the content level), his joy of tampering with the classics, may account for the fact that these stories have been profusely re-twittered and become popular. His twitter work can be considered a type of e-activism that has ensured that there is now more of an awareness of predator drones and their lethal consequence borne out in the Middle East. With 264,000 followers on Twitter, Cole is well-placed for this kind of cultural work. Significantly, by insisting on spatial seamlessness, on porosity, Cole positions his readers ('followers') in the very spaces affected by signature strikes. His literary tweets create translocations that speak to those who allegedly benefit from the American war on terror whilst at the same time (metaphorically) placing his addressees in the very areas under attack.

4. Open Cities

Teju Cole's bio is infused with porosity and translocation; it is marked by crossovers and intersections. He was born in the United States in 1975 and raised in Nigeria. When he came back to the US in 1992, aged 17, he was both, a migrant (with an American passport), and a returning expat (who had spent almost no time in the US) – thereby inhabiting two mutually exclusive, porous categories. A writer, art historian and photographer, Cole studied African art history, medicine and holds a PhD in art history. Apart from short stories and 'twitter litter' (above), he is known for his photography, which has been exhibited in India and the United States. He has received wide acclaim for his novels *Every Day Is for the Thief* (2007, republ. 2014) and especially *Open City* (2012); his eclectic essays have now been collected as *Known and Strange Things* (2016).

Open City is a fascinating novel – although nothing much happens in it! Julius, the thirty-year old half-Nigerian, half-German narrator, takes extended walks across multiracial New York. He meets a broad range of people, including Saidu, a Liberian man held in a detention centre in Queens for two years, a facility he visits to please his then girl-friend; a shoe-shiner from Haiti; Moroccan migrant-intellectual Farouq and his friend Khalil in Brussels; he keeps his distance from an African American postal worker, from an African cab driver. We learn about his library that includes Peter Altenberg's *Telegrams of the Soul*, Barthes's *Camera Lucida*, Tahar Ben Jelloun's *The Last Friend,* and Appiah's *Cosmopolitanism* amongst other titles. The narrator has pertinent and incisive comments to make – on music, art, art theory. Julius holds a fellowship in psychiatry at Columbia Presbyterian hospital. In the first chapters, wandering through Manhattan in the dreariness of November, his dark thoughts suggest that he himself is enduring a suicidal mood. On the banks of the Hudson, he muses: "How easy it would be, I thought, to slip gently into the water here, and go down to the depths." (Cole 2011: 56) The text can be read as a *psychogramme*, a record of Julius' fluctuating mental states, which are in turn intimately linked to the different parts of the metropolis he traverses:

> Each neighborhood of the city appeared to be made of a different substance, each seemed to have a different air pressure, a different psychic weight: the bright lights and shuttered shops, the housing projects and luxury hotels, the fire escapes and city parks. (Cole 2011: 6f)

Julius appears morbid, desperate and vulnerable – and yet confident assessments such as the above also point to an empowered and self-assured subject, used to a certain amount of (arguably male) privilege.

Julius prolonged engagement with the metropolis he navigates seems to allow him to disengage from himself. He is always keenly aware of elsewhere – spatially, historically. When at home he listens to his internet radio in order to have access to stations from Europe and elsewhere, rather than local ones. In different ways, he constantly makes connections to different locations as well as to different historical periods. He thus points to New York's 'blind spots' such as when he evokes a palimpsest history of the site we now know as Ground Zero:

> But atrocity is nothing new, not to humans, not to animals. […] This was not the first erasure on the site. Before the towers had gone up, there had been a bustling network of little streets traversing this part of town. […] all of them had been obliterated in the 1960s to make way for the World Trade Center buildings, and all were forgotten now. Gone, too, was the old Washington Market, the active piers, the fishwives, the Christian Syrian enclave that was established her in the late 1800s. The Syrians, the Lebanese, and other people from the Levant had been pushed across the river to Brooklyn […] And before that? […] The site was a palimpsest, as was all the city, written, erased, rewritten. There had been communities here before Columbus ever set sail, before Verrazano anchored his ships in the narrows, or the black Portuguese slave trader Esteban Gómez sailed up the Hudson; human beings had lived here, built homes, and quarreled with their neighbors long before the Dutch ever saw a business opportunity in the rich furs and timber of the island and its calm bay. Generations rushed through […] and I, one of the still legible crowd […] wanted to find the line that connected me to my own part in these stories." (Cole 2011: 58f)

The narrator of *Open City* considers himself a part of the "still legible" – not coherent but rather disorganised – "crowd". Significantly, members of this "crowd" relate differently to Ground Zero, given not only the complex history of this space, but given, too, the complex matrix of connections that informs each and every individual. Belonging, then, *is* constructed, not given, according to Julius, but the reconstruction of such belonging – the "find[ing of] the line that connected [him] to [his] own part in these stories" – endows him and by extension others with agency. Julius is not enslaved by his past, or by his family background, but rather *selectively inscribes* himself into the stories he uncovers and passes on.

Julius's description of Ground Zero renders it a specific type of location; he describes it as a *paradigmatic* translocation. It is not just the former grounds of the twin towers that went up in smoke at 9/11; in Julius's reading, the site remains connected to its earlier incarnations and uses. The crowd that is "still legible" survives in inscriptions, archives, memorials and cenotaphs; it is made up of named individuals who lead or have lead grievable, valuable lives. The victims of 9/11 have been mourned, their names are preserved for posterity, remembered, memorialized. However, as Judith Butler cautions, public grieving is not equally afforded all victims:

> After the attacks of 9/11, we encountered in the media graphic pictures of those who died, along with their names, their stories […] [T]here was considerably less public grieving for non-US nationals, and none at all for illegal workers. (Butler 2009: 38)

Cole points to a different but related absence; the individuals and populations formerly associated with the same site, the traders and customers of Washington Market, the earlier Levantine residents, the victims of the slave trade, Dutch settlers and colonists, native Americans who preceded them all: their names have – bar a few exceptions – been forgotten and their individual lives are not grievable.

Cole's reading of the palimpsest history of Ground Zero and the city beyond not only brings to the fore but also raises objections against such a selective memory which remembers the recent but disremembers earlier victims. The palimpsest history questions what differentiates remembered from forgotten lives and warns against immoderate mourning which has the potential to blot out earlier suffering and loss. If the price paid for (selectively) mourning the victims of the 9/11 events amounts to disregarding colonial violence, slavery, and exploitation, then responsible mourning involves a translocal practice which reaches out to different communities, engages diverse cultures, and discrete historical periods. This nexus emerges more clearly when, not far from Ground Zero, Julius discovers a plaque commemorating New York's African burial ground, a covert (because overgrown) reminder of slavery in the city. Frustratingly, there is no access to this significant cemetery holding 15.000 to 20.000 blacks, "most of them slaves", whose lives are now not mourned: The "land had been built over and the people of the city had forgotten that it was a burial ground" (Cole 2011: 220). We are merely given a fairly inexact estimate – and no names. It seems, the 'weight' of these deaths, their value, lies in the large number, not in their individual lives. The unnamed individuals interred there cannot be mourned; their substantial number allows merely for collective recognition – at best.

In this way, *Open City* directs our attention to a society which is not only divided in its present moment but which has historically been riven – despite its immigrant foundations. Not only the exploitative, disenfranchising, expropriative, and genocidal relations with native Americans are frequently elided, both in history books and official commemoration as well as at a more local level. The foundational discrimination between distinct, heterogeneous, and overlapping immigrant groups along the lines of culture and faith (Christians, Jews, Muslims), ethnicity (Anglo, Western European, Irish, Eastern European, South Asian, East Asian, North African, sub-Saharan African), and legal status (free, chattel; citizen, resident, 'illegal') suggests that the 'land of the free', as the 'Star-Spangled Banner' has it, does not mete out freedom in equal measure. Whilst Butler, in the context of international war, also observes the translocal "division of the globe into grievable and ungrievable lives" (2011: 38), Cole's focus is firmly on divisions within the space of the heterogeneous nation-state; on the outrage of discrepant public grieving for different social groups, past and present.

Metaphorically, New York is the novel's open city, inasmuch as Julius assesses its openness, its ability and disposition to embrace and absorb settlers, migrants, refugees, foreigners, visitors, slaves; not only today but also in history. However, the title also recalls a strategy of self-preservation codified in international law. When a city is about to be captured in the course of war, declaring it an 'open city' seeks to minimise deaths and the city's destruction by halting military defence and giving up fortifications. Brussels, the city Julius visits, was declared an open city during World War II. It might seem a counter-intuitive strategy to defend and save city and population by *not* defending them; preventing the enemy force from inflicting destruction by not engaging the enemy. Nevertheless, from Athens to Manila, from Krakow to Paris, from Rome to Hamburg, several cities were declared open during World War II.

However, we can also recognize Julius's own strategy of not quite engaging through the lens of this technical term. Whilst his knowledge is wide-ranging, if not encyclopaedic; whilst his walks and his confidence allow him to traverse the metropolis; whilst his travels and ancestry connect him to several countries and continents, Julius typically does *not* engage personally, but rather in an abstract, impersonal way. He passes on information and also judgements – which are, significantly, not necessarily specific to him. His own position remains in the dark and can hardly be ascertained by the reader. Julius does not defend himself against stimuli from the outside; he absorbs them and transmits them onwards. He acts like a conductor, conveying a charge. He is, in a word, porous.

We do not learn a great deal about Julius because he is reticent when it comes to information about himself. It takes the reader thirty pages or so to find out that he is from Africa, which is revealed unhurriedly through oblique hints such as: "I turned around to see his black cowl melt into an unlit doorway. In the Harlem night, there were no whites" (Cole 2011: 18). Not only does he engage with Yoruba cosmology, he also relates, "I knew Idi Amin well, so to speak, because he'd been an indelible part of my childhood mythology" in the context of discussing the film *The Last King of Scotland.* Precisely because these clues are inconclusive, this way of conveying his background might make the reader question how important it is to know whether or not Julius is in fact of African descent. However, Julius's Nigerian labour migrant background *does* have a bearing on the novel in several ways. While studying medicine in Madison, Wisconsin, Julius had an unpleasant experience at a dinner party where the host, an Indian doctor, who was affected by the expulsion from Uganda of tens of thousands of Indians by Idi Amin in 1972, announces that "when I think about Africans I want to spit" (Cole 2011: 30): "The bitterness was startling. It was an anger that, I couldn't help feeling, was partly directed at me, the only other African in the room. The detail of my background, that I was Nigerian, made no difference, for Dr. Gupta had spoken of Africans" (Cole 2011: 31).

When Julius encounters Moji in Manhattan, he does not recognize her, while she is able to call out his name. The elder sister of a childhood friend, Moji charges him with sexual assault at a teenage party back in Nigeria. Whilst the narrator does make space in his narrative for Moji's side of the story, he neither confirms nor denies her charges. Hence, Julius takes no responsibility as a (potential) offender. The narrator also evades his responsibility of sanctioning or contesting the account. He passes on Moji's story about their encounter without engaging with it, which is provocative in itself, given the serious nature of her allegations. Moji only remains legible in his account because she inserts her name into his story; without her intervention, she would have been left out from Julius's story and become ungrievable.

In the course of the novel, it becomes clear that his connection to the continent is significant in various ways. Nevertheless, time and again, Julius is wary of being claimed both by Africans and African Americans, be it on account of his phenotype, be it on account of a presumed shared ancestry, history, culture, or experience of discrimination: His often abrupt behaviour makes plain that he is "in no mood for people who tried to lay claims on me" (Cole 2011: 40). However, when it seems worthwhile to him, Julius himself advances the very claims he so detests. He greets Farouq by asking: "How are you doing, my brother?" (Cole 2011: 101) when he hardly knows him. He first terms this his "aggressive familiarity" but then decides that, because he is planning to use Farouq's internet café regularly, "it was best to make friends" (Cole 2011: 102). *Open City* shows Julius's engagement with the classifications African and African American; in the process Julius demonstrates that these categories leak, are marked by porosity. He does not dismiss the categories but finds basing claims on them difficult and emphasizes their heterogeneity and fuzzy borders. More generally, Julius roams the city and uncovers forgotten stories of migration, of suffering, of coercion. Yet he remains sceptical of social collectivities with firm borders. Despite his focus on historiography in multiracial New York, he emphasizes the porosity of social collectivities.

Both, literature and location, as well as the ways in which they continue to impact on each other, are complex phenomena. Whilst the earliest of English novels – Aphra Behn's *Oroonoko* (1688) and Daniel Defoe's *Robinson Crusoe* (1719) – are concerned with population transfer, with migration, with a globalized economy, and in some ways with translocation, this feature is in evidence more clearly and more self-consciously displayed in recent publications. In fact, many contemporary texts are marked by porosity and translocation, texts which themselves are examples of translocation. Mohsin Hamid's novel *The Reluctant Fundamentalist* (below) comes to mind, Kwame Kwei-Armah's 2003 play *Elmina's Kitchen*, some of Derek Walcott's poetry (think of his critique of tourism in *White Egrets*, think of *Omeros*), much of Caryl Phillips' work, Joseph O'Neill's *Netherland* (2008) – another 9/11 New York novel on translocation and diaspora which would fit into an expanded version of the present chapter. Translocation informs the thematics of Cole's *Open City* and in some ways has enabled the very production of this text; it certainly affected the *shape and form the book has*; and it has affected its *reception* too.

5. Reluctant Porosity: Mohsin Hamid's Take on 9/11

Mohsin Hamid's second novel *The Reluctant Fundamentalist* (2007) engages with the effects of 9/11 in a different way, a text marked by various translocal aspects. Pakistan-born Changez stands at the centre of Hamid's novel, a Princeton graduate who has just been hired by a New York firm specialising in ruthless evaluations of failing companies targeted for takeover. He undergoes a process of inward transformation following 9/11, which entails him ending his high-flying career, giving up the pursuit of his beautiful 'princess' Erica, and returning to Lahore. This is where he meets his American interlocutor: in a restaurant in the Old Anarkali district, Changez treats the nameless American (and us, the readers) to his life story. Told as a monologue, this understated, skilfully constructed development from fixation to disillusionment with America and with Erica, hovers the intersections of East and West. The novel is attentive to mutual misunderstanding, prejudice and distortion. Changez is uniquely placed between these cultural assemblages; he is, at different stages of his life, part of East *and* West. He identifies with the US, as well as with its enemies. He gives up the American dream when he finds it compromised, but his attachment to Erica is never entirely revoked. In that sense, the protagonist treads the porous line between Pakistan and the US, and finds himself unable to ever unequivocally subscribe to, and belong to, one or the other of theses regimes. He finds himself lost in translocation, never fully independent of one space whilst inhabiting the other.

With characteristic introspection, Changez describes his own response to the Twin Towers collapsing, as the US is brought to her knees:

> I smiled. Yes, despicable as it may sound, my initial reaction was to be remarkably pleased. [...] So when I tell you I was pleased at the slaughter of thousands of innocents, I do so with a profound sense of perplexity [...] I was the product of an American university; I was earning a lucrative American salary; I was infatuated with an American woman. So why did part of me desire to see America harmed? (Hamid 2007: 72f)

What interests me here, is how the transformation that Changez undergoes is actually *a stitching together* of distinct perspectives – perspectives pertaining to opposing life-worlds, cultures, and histories, perspectives that would appear to be anathema to amalgamation. Although the disillusioned protagonist does return to Pakistan, he does not return to an earlier self. Neither does he stay who he had become in the US. He has changed, as his name ('*changez*') suggests, and he keeps changing. When Changez watches the Twin Towers fall, he notes that "part of [him] desire[d] to see America harmed". Having appreciated the damage his firm inflicts on struggling companies around the world has made him self-critical; sceptical of his employers; and wary of the American Dream. He no longer fully subscribes to the ambitions of his American life but neither is he entirely free from them. It is from an in-between position that he raises the questions and expresses perplexity, as cited above.

It is telling that Changez was able to function quite ruthlessly, in sync with his employers' ideology, until he begins to put names and faces to those who are going to suffer from the evaluations he undertakes. When posted to Chile to evaluate a publishing house for a client of his employers, Changez meets the aging manager Juan-Bautista and is reminded of his maternal grandfather. He begins to question whether the financial value of the publishing house can properly account for the value which books themselves have in his eyes. For the first time he thoroughly grasps the consequences of his activities at Underwood Samson. Whilst their client would benefit from a lucrative investment opportunity, careers and livelihoods are destroyed and non-commercial values are at risk. When Changez allows himself to engage with the man and his life-world instead of only engaging with his accounts, Juan-Bautista's life becomes grievable.

The protagonist comes to view himself as a janissary once Juan-Bautista has strategically introduced him to the term, ultimately provoking Changez to abort his stint in Chile and quit his job. During the Ottoman Empire, for four hundred years, the janissaries had been the Sultan's exceedingly loyal household troops and bodyguards forged from captured Christian boys:

> There really could be no doubt: I was a modern-day janissary, a servant of the American empire at a time when it was invading a country with a kinship to mine [...] (Hamid 2007: 152)

The recognition of this analogy and of his own involvement if not even complicity with US imperial interests (empire, as Changez calls it) both further his transformation process and prompt him to give up his career. Historically, the janissaries, too, were social intermediaries placed between cultural assemblages, whose Christian heritage and professional loyalties clashed with each other. It is with these collaborators that Changez comes to identify at a moment of crisis – only to then radically change his affiliation and turn against the US as the novel progresses.

Changez response to 9/11 is not only related to his experiences at work. Before this date, he had been more able to dress in any way he chooses and explicitly relished this freedom:

> I was the only non-American in our group, but I suspected my Pakistaniness was invisible, cloaked by my suit, by my expense account, and—most of all—by my companions. (Hamid 2007: 71)

In a post-9/11 world, his freedoms are curtailed; leaving his smart suit in the closet and allowing him to be read as Muslim or Pakistani has become a risk. In the streets, Changez is stopped by police; at immigration, he is separated from his white American travel companions. For Changez and many Muslim Americans, the porous borders of his pre-9/11 existence are now much more heavily policed. But when it comes to the narrative perspective, porosity prevails.

The text engages with cultural difference by continuously comparing and contrasting (his) life in Pakistan with that in the US and in the process, it both commingles *and* differentiates the two. The porous, translocal quality in evidence in this text resides in this constant, effortless and demonstrative narrative movement across cultural divides. The US is repeatedly compared to the Mughal Empire, in an attempt to relativize American supremacy. The US's and Pakistan's shared history of British colonialism is also underscored. There is the linguistic crisscrossing as Changez reports on his interactions with different people. The enormous geographical scope of the text, its diegesis straddling almost the entire globe, from Chile to the Philippines, seems to grate with its narration from the very confines of Lahore's Anarkali market. This narrative situation echoes Jean-Baptiste Clamence's monologue narrated from an Amsterdam bar called Mexico City in Albert Camus's novel *The Fall* (1957). In more ways than one, *The Reluctant Fundamentalist* is modelled on *La Chute*, a text that was itself a comparatively early response to the fallout from colonialism.

The novel develops the thematics of translocation on several levels. Today's university system is one that resembles a global production line that needs raw materials from the global South for the benefit of the North, as the text critically notes:

> We international students were sourced from around the globe, sifted [...] until the best and the brightest of us had been identified. [...] In return, we were expected to contribute our talents to your society. (Hamid 2007: 4)

The global South here suffers so-called brain drain; the verb "sourced" suggests an analogy to forms of colonial economy in which raw materials were traded from the periphery to the colonial centre for refinement. The text also registers the revenue stream that especially US and UK universities receive from so-called 'third world' elites. Although this may resemble a problematic binary construction, *The Reluctant Fundamentalist* is actually deeply aware of complex global economic and cultural entanglements – and their long history. We can in fact observe in Changez's own family a pattern of studying abroad that points to a colonial legacy; Changez's father and his grandfather had studied in Britain, a reminder that Changez's own experiences are not entirely new.

The novel is marked by a strong tension, a sense of foreboding, a barely concealed threat of violence; this hinges on the question, who is the reluctant fundamentalist of the title, and what is, after all, a reluctant fundamentalist. This tension is palpable throughout the book, from the opening passage onwards:

> EXCUSE ME, SIR, but may I be of assistance? Ah, I see I have alarmed you. Do not be frightened by my beard: I am a lover of America. I noticed that you were looking for something; more than looking, in fact you seemed to be on a *mission*, and since I am both a native of this city and a speaker of your language, I thought I might offer you my services. (Hamid 2007: 1)

This intriguing lead-in is striking in several respects, one of them being the formality of its language; the English is somewhat quaint, slightly too polite and not quite what we expect from a contemporary US college graduate. But its 'courtliness' – the caricature of an upper-class English accent – still holds water in the context of Pakistani higher education. Arguably, this is owed to the colonial legacy of English in the Pakistani context; of course, English was bequeathed to India/Pakistan by its erstwhile colonizers and today, still, English is the language of tertiary education. There remain, too, boarding schools for the country's elite which are modelled on a type of English education now rare in the UK, more Victorian than contemporary, often conducted in a language that is slightly too rigid, too formal for comfort. This linguistic and historical crossover not only registers the long-standing interaction between East and West and the negotiation of power via linguistic register; the novel's beginning also raises the question of who is being addressed in this particular way. As a monologue, the text constructs its interlocutor and sensitizes its reader to the linguistic diversity that comes with the territory of cultural admixture. What Changez says and how he puts it also underscores the seriousness of his interrogation. Lastly, he also manages to insert a menacing hint of a threat to the novel's opening, pulling us in, producing a certain uneasiness.

The style of English employed here is also owed to Changez's *strategic* use of different registers and different accents in the course of his narrative. More importantly for my argument, his language is informed by a range of contexts, locations and historical moments: We are confronted with a *translocal* form of English that draws on distinct spaces rather than constructing an ostensibly authentic language deriving from a singular, specific location.

Changez's civility, so evident in this first paragraph, might be dubbed "sly civility" if we wanted to echo an argument Homi K. Bhabha put forward in the *Location of Culture* (1994: 93f). The novel opens by situating its narrator as a mimic man offering his services. His education enables him to act as *mediator*, being conversant with Urdu and English, knowing Pakistan and the US. He startles the unnamed and silent American; scares him, in fact. Whether it is his rhetoric or, as Changez himself assumes, his beard that is perceived as scary by his muted interlocutor, we do not know. However, at the beginning of the book he declares his love for America – a declaration that will be qualified as the story unfolds, as we have seen. His alertness, the incessant noticing, looking, reading all are characteristic of Changez's behaviour throughout the novel.

Changez points the finger at his American interlocutor, alleging that he is on a mission; but the exact nature of this mission is not revealed. Partial revelation of information through the narrator is how suspense and drama are built up here. The entire text consists of Changez's monologue; we only 'hear' from the American through him, indirectly, when Changez's responds to him, echoes him, or speculates on his feelings, as in the above passage. Whilst Changez gives us his life story, the sun sets, the skies darken, the bats come out and the tension between the two men (and the worlds they represent) tightens significantly.

As in English colonial writing, such as *Heart of Darkness* or *A Passage to India*, the other is not afforded a voice; instead, the other is ventriloquized. However, in this reversal of a colonial narrative style, Changez goes out of his way to understand the American's perspective and speculates about this feelings, motivations and aims. This monologue – which is actually and significantly an *implied dialogue* – also reaches out to its readership. The confessional mode, with its nod to Camus, implicates the readership because of the text's affective potential. We are required to keep our own prejudices in check – and not to fall into the traps laid out by the text. It is like an aside to the reader when we are cautioned:

> It seems an obvious thing to say, but you should not imagine that we Pakistanis are all potential terrorists, just as we should not imagine that you Americans are all undercover assassins. (Hamid 2007: 183)

The monologue, perhaps surprisingly, opens up space for its readers. The form does not only remind us of the artificiality of the literary construction. It also leaves blank spaces for the reader who is effectively required to fill in the other voices that make up the story. The acknowledged but largely absent other half of the narrative needs to be conjured up by the reader. This also accords with the different ways in which the text can be read, among them romance, thriller and political novel. The ambiguous ending fits into this analysis too:

> But why are you reaching into your jacket, sir? I detect a glint of metal. Given that you and I are now bound by a certain shared intimacy, I trust it is from the holder of your business cards. (Hamid 2007: 184)

One further effect of the monologue form of *The Reluctant Fundamentalist* is that the reader, in providing the missing half, becomes aware of her/his biases. Do you identify with the bearded Changez or with the clean-shaven American? Do you take Changez to be a fundamentalist, perhaps even a terrorist? Has he moved from focusing on 'the fundamentals' at Underwood Samson to indeed harming the US, as he insinuated? Alternatively, do you consider the American an agent of the state, an assassin, a hitman coming to get Changez because of his agitation against the US? With either choice, who is likely to win out? We have a cliffhanger before us, because on the closing page we cannot be sure whether the glint of metal is emitted by a gun or a cardholder, whether the danger is real or imaginary. These questions remain unanswered within the narrative.

Changez and his interlocutor enter each other's life worlds, with Changez apparently knowing the US much better than his opposite number does. At the level of narrative perspective, as I have stressed, the text effortlessly fluctuates between different life worlds and blends different locations, chronologies and perspectives. Porosity is intact at this level. However, when it comes to the protagonists, between them there is an enduring undertone of conflict, if not open verbal and physical aggression and indeed warfare. The protagonists get too close to each other for comfort; porosity seems to endanger them, allowing their respective antagonist to breathe down the other's neck. The narrative illustrates the tension between porosity residing at two different levels, that of narration and that of the diegesis.

6. Openings and Closings

Both, contemporary and historical texts require reading across disparate geographic and temporal space. In the context of globalisation and neo-imperialisms, not only unequal development and political instability but also violence and gender inequality continue to shape complex realities. While nation and narration, place and displacement, location and migration remain major paradigms of postcolonial critique, the postcolonial lexicon clearly indicates our concern with placement, movement and interconnection. Our understanding of what constitutes a specific location has dramatically changed in recent decades; this demands reading practices that reflect the communicative, political and aesthetic concerns of translocal representation. I have suggested above, that Cole's stories posted on twitter treat as *one space* the locations that direct drones and those that are targeted by them, placing his readers in both, thereby undercutting the binary logic used to legitimize the extraterritorial deployment of predator drones. The growing body of porous texts that – formally, linguistically and thematically – draw on and combine distinct and diverse cultural repertoires is an indication of the increasing relevance of postcolonial translocations today.

Reading diasporic novels such as *Open City* and *The Reluctant Fundamentalist*, – texts representing protagonists in diaspora, text written by diasporic authors, – requires an engagement with narrative gestures across time and space. Deploying the concept of porosity, this essay has engaged spatial and textual connections that the works by Cole and Hamid draw on, express and transform. Their porous short stories and novels treat borders (linguistic, cultural, national) not just as regimes of division but also as membranes through which connections are fostered and modulated.

Cole's and Hamid's novels offer a postcolonial perspective on 9/11 inasmuch as they critique forms of what can be termed US imperialism. Cole focuses on the uneven distribution of recognition, memory and grief when it comes to the history of ground zero. Mourning victims of the 9/11 events selectively, depending on their ethnicity, nationality and legal status, and paying no attention to the site's preceding connections with colonial violence, slavery, and exploitation, is assessed critically in *Open City*. Our attention is directed to a society that is socially and culturally divided – not only in the present moment but also from its historical inception. In the face of this, the text demands *responsible* mourning as a translocal practice that reaches out to different communities, engages diverse cultures and discrete historical periods; a practice that has the potential to render lives grievable. Hence, Cole focuses on divisions within the space of the heterogeneous nation-state; on the disunions within formations referenced as African American and African; on the disgrace of discrepant public grieving for distinct social groups, past and present.

Hamid represents New York as shutting down on his protagonist Changez once 9/11 has come to pass; whilst he enjoyed a wide range of freedoms before the attacks, in their aftermath these freedoms are increasingly curtailed. Placed between cultural assemblages, between Pakistan and the US, Changez is, at different stages of his life, part of East *and* West. He identifies with the US and he identifies with its enemies. The protagonist treads the porous line between Pakistan and the US, and finds himself unable to ever unequivocally subscribe to, and belong to, one or the other of theses regimes. Lost in translocation, Changez is never fully independent of one space whilst inhabiting the other. This is also reflected linguistically; Changez's language draws on a range of contexts, locations, historical moments and their lexicons. His is a *translocal* form of English that openly and self-consciously indexes a range of distinct times and spaces – instead of constructing an ostensibly authentic language, tied to a specific, singular location. Unlike in English colonial writing, where the other is not afforded a voice, Hamid's novel ventriloquizes Changez's silent American antagonist. In this reversal of a colonial narrative style, Changez seeks to understand the American's perspective and speculates about his feelings, motivations and aims. Given the text's affective potential, the implied dialogue reaches out to its readers who are required to keep their own prejudices in check, avoiding the traps laid out by the text.

The Reluctant Fundamentalist negotiates the legacy of colonialism in a postcolonial world and dramatizes the subtle impasses that can characterize exchange across permeable spatial, cultural, social and religious divides. Read through the concept of porosity, this novel allows us to see how textuality becomes an arena in which literary translocations are played out in order to constitute a postcolonial critique of US imperialism. Both, *Open City* and *The Reluctant Fundamentalist*, are good examples of cultural products representing and emerging from ever shifting grounds. In consequence, translocation is becoming increasingly significant. Texts are written with a view to their marketing in several languages and markets; authors move from one country to another; global audiences consume cultural products in different locales, creating demands in several marketplaces; national borders are fought over and redrawn, materially as well as textually, further undermining any sense of discrete and stable locations. Because the concept translocation can leave open points of departure and destination, translocation is distinct from 'dislocation' (which often implies a privileging of 'origins' over 'new' locations); translocation also denotes more than a simple 'change of location'. It is then not only a process (the transfer of people, cultural products and borders), but also signifies a new kind of location, a *trans*-location consisting of fractured and multiply connected spaces.

Bibliography

Appadurai, Arjun / Breckridge, Carol (1986). On Moving Targets. *Public Culture* 2, i-iv.

Camus, Albert (1957). *The Fall*. Transl. by Justin O'Brien. London: Hamish Hamilton.

Bhabha, Homi K. (1994). Sly Civility. In: Bhabha, Homi K. (Ed.). *The Location of Culture*. London: Routledge, 93-101.

Butler, Judith (2009). *Frames of War: When is Life Grievable?* London: Verso.

Cole, Teju (2016). *Known and Strange Things*. New York: Random House.

Cole, Teju (tejucole). "1. Mrs Dalloway said she would buy the flowers herself. Pity. A signature strike leveled the florist's." 14 January 2013, 06:04 PM.

Cole, Teju (tejucole). "2. Call me Ishmael. I was a young man of military age. I was immolated at my wedding. My parents are inconsolable." 14 January 2013, 06:06 PM.

Cole, Teju (tejucole). "6. Okonkwo was well known throughout the nine villages and even beyond. His torso was found, not his head." 14 January 2013, 06:15 PM.

Cole, Teju (2011). *Open City*. New York: Random House.

Cole, Teju (2007, repub. 2014). *Every Day Is for the Thief.* New York: Random House.

"collateral damage." US Dept. of Defense Dictionary of Military and Associated Terms JP 1-02. (12 April 2001, amended through 23 January 2002). http://www.bits.de/NRANEU/others/jp-doctrine/jp1_02(02).pdf.

Döring, Tobias / Stein, Mark (2012). Introduction. In: Döring, Tobias / Stein, Mark (Eds.). *Edward Said's Translocations. Essays in Secular Criticism.* New York: Routledge, 1-21.

Hamid, Mohsin (2007). *The Reluctant Fundamentalist*. London: Hamish.

Matthews, Dylan. (2013) Everything You Need to Know about the Drone Debate, in One FAQ. *Washington Post* March 8, 2013. https://www.washingtonpost.com/news/wonk/wp/2013/03/08/everything-you-need-to-know-about-the-drone-debate-in-one-faq/ (09/01/2017).

Munkelt, Marga / Schmitz, Markus / Stroh, Silke / Stein, Mark (2013). Introduction: Directions of Translocation – Towards a Critical Spatial Thinking in Postcolonial Studies. In: Munkelt, Marga / Schmitz, Markus / Stein, Mark / Stroh, Silke (Eds). *Postcolonial Translocations. Cultural Representation and Critical Spatial Thinking.* (Cross/Cultures 156 / ASNEL Papers 17). Amsterdam/New York: Rodopi, xiii-lxxviii.

Minh-ha, Trinh T. (1989). *Woman, Native, Other: Writing Postcoloniality and Feminism.* Bloomington: Indiana UP.

"Obama Jokes About Killing Jonas Brothers with Predator Drones." https://www.youtube.com/watch?v=WWKG6ZmgAX4 (18/01/2017).

Vermeulen, Pieter (2013). Flights of Memory: Teju Cole's Open City and the Limits of Aesthetic Cosmopolitanism. *Journal of Modern Literature* 37.1: 40-57.

Vertovec, Steven (2009). *Transnationalism.* Abingdon, UK: Routledge.

CHRISTIANE LÜTGE

Postcolonial Literature and Transcultural Learning in the EFL Classroom: Crossovers, Trodden Paths or Winding Roads?

Postcolonial literature and transcultural learning seem to share a natural connection. The ELT discourse on teaching cultural topics is increasingly concerned with texts by postcolonial authors. In fact, the experience of 'otherness' in literary texts is often regarded as the starting-point for processes of cultural learning and sometimes conceived of as a kind of 'magic formula' that may trigger a change of perspectives and foster mutual understanding. However, the critical implications of an alleged automaticity of the connections between postcolonial literature and transcultural learning should not be underestimated. If postcolonial literature is to play an adequate role in the EFL classroom, we need to go beyond superficial notions of functionalizing literary texts for didactic purposes. Likewise, some trodden paths and pitfalls lurking on the road towards transcultural learning should be taken care of.

1. Points of Departure

The teaching of literature in German EFL classrooms has undergone a considerable number of changes during the last twenty years. Complaints about a tendency towards fossilisation of the literary canon at schools were prominent in past decades and have led to a gradual opening for contemporary authors. This has significantly contributed to a profound interest in the so-called 'New English literatures', e.g. by postcolonial writers. The 'opening up' of cultural and literary perspectives with its beginnings in the 1970s and 1980s was rooted in a growing uneasiness about traditional concepts of *area studies*, the equivalent of the German concept of *Landeskunde* (see Eisenmann / Grimm / Volkmann 2010: vii). Teaching goals focusing on catalogues of general knowledge about so-called target cultures ranging from the notorious 'life and institutions' to topics such as 'fine arts' or 'political and governmental systems' were often geographically limited to Great Britain and the United States. The limitations in thematic scope and geography were criticised for projecting conventional concepts of culture and marginalizing regional, ethnic and other minorities (see Delanoy / Volkmann 2006).

Another major development that has influenced the teaching of literature in the EFL classroom is connected to the role it has been ascribed in the context of inter- and transcultural learning. Since the early 1990s the potential of literature for cultural learning has been emphasised. The teaching of foreign literature in its representation of linguistic and cultural otherness is seen as an ideal starting-point for reflections on the perspectivity of individual viewpoints. In comparing and contrasting their own values and world views to those of literary texts, learners can change and coordinate perspectives, a prerequisite for developing intercultural competence:

> Of special significance for intercultural understanding are post-colonial and minority texts, because they often dramatise intercultural conflicts and reveal causes for misunderstanding and misrecognition of others [...] (Bredella 2002: 14)

These allegedly 'natural' links between Postcolonial Studies and EFL teaching – namely with a view to literature didactics – have come under immense scrutiny over the past years following Bredella's famous statement from 2002. Since then, various publications have referred to the connections between postcolonial texts and inter- and transcultural learning:

- Antor (2006): on multiculturalism, interculturality and transculturality,
- Delanoy / Volkmann (2006): on new perspectives in Cultural Studies in ELT with a strong focus on inter- and transcultural learning,
- Delanoy (2013): on the shift from "inter to trans" and the general direction of cultural learning,
- Eisenmann / Grimm / Volkmann (2010): on teaching the New English Cultures and Literatures,
- Freitag-Hild (2010): on fictions of migration in the context of inter- and transcultural learning,
- Raddatz (2010): on the synergy effects of Postcolonial Studies and ELT,
- Doff / Schulze-Engler (2011): on transcultural perspectives on teaching the New Literatures in English,
- Volkmann (2012): on questions of connecting intercultural learning and postcolonial literature,
- Blell / Doff (2014): on binary oppositions in teaching about culture,
- Lütge (2015): on global aspects of cultural education,
- and Eisenmann (2015): on connections between postcolonial literature and transcultural learning.

On this road towards interdisciplinary contact, the concept of a mutual partnership between the fields of Postcolonial Studies and different forms of cultural learning has predominantly been established from the perspective of didactics and particularly in the context of teaching literature. In the following, I intend to look in more detail at the connections between these thematic fields and follow some of the theoretical trajectories shaping the discourse of crossovers and connections between them. The implicit assumption of their incommensurability as foregrounded in Volkmann's variation of Kipling's sceptical "and never the twain shall meet" will partly be taken up in some of the questions that I have found to be prevalent in this context: Are we in fact concerned with disciplinary crossovers or rather with following trodden paths – and possibly even truisms in the discourse of transcultural learning? What may be the hidden pitfalls or detours on this journey? Or are we following winding roads touching on different disciplinary fields with possibly fruitful but not always straight directions?

2. Connections

In recent years, transculturality has emerged as a new approach to culture particularly suited to exploring the hybridity of individual and collective identities and the cultural connections between people, texts and narratives in an increasingly globalized world. Transcultural approaches challenging the notion of national cultures as separate entities have become important in sociology (Beck 2008), philosophy (Welsch 1999), in literary and cultural studies (Antor 2006 Schulze-Engler / Helff 2009), in the fields of ELT pedagogy and in many interdisciplinary approaches focusing on questions of (teaching) contemporary – often postcolonial – literature (see Eisenmann et al. 2010, Delanoy 2013, Volkmann 2015).

Postcolonial Studies have developed an increasing prominence since the 1970s have been shaped by various influences and sources, among them the seminal works by Edward Said (1978), Gayatri Chakravorty Spivak (1990), Bill Ashcroft (2011), Bill Ashcroft, Gareth Griffiths and Helen Tiffin (2003), Homi K. Bhabha (1994) or Julie Mullaney (2010). Their critiques became instrumental not only in terms of detecting awkward cultural oppression or searching for an identity. They were also fundamentally influential for postcolonial theory itself with their demasking of dichotomies (us/them, West/East, white/black), most powerfully questioned by Said's critique of "Orientalism as a Western style of dominating, restructuring, and having authority over the Orient" (Said 1978: 3). The concept of 'hybridity' refers both to individual and collective identities and draws attention to the so-called 'third space' (see Bhabha 1984), cultural overlapping or generally 'in-betweenness' in contexts of cultural interaction. For Bhabha, hybridity is not to be seen in a negative sense of placelessness, but rather as a contact zone, a positive alternative for overcoming dichotomous concepts with a view to cultural and social identities in an increasingly globalized world (see Eisenmann 2015: 219). Cultural hybridity, a sense of 'in-betweenness', the diversity of identity markers beyond ethnicity and the gradual dissolution of fixed cultural boundaries have become important topoi in post-colonial literature(s), e.g. in Zadie Smith's *White Teeth*, Hanif Kureishi's *Buddha of Suburbia* or Qaisra Sharaz' "A Pair of Jeans". These and other texts from the postcolonial canon have entered the foreign language classroom, even if sometimes only in excerpts or as part of anthologies like *Many Voices – Many Cultures*, edited by Barbara Korte and Claudia Sternberg (1997).

The aforementioned concept of 'in-betweenness' is also important for EFL contexts and has partly been mirrored by concepts such as the 'third space' (Kramsch 1996), pointing to the fact that cross-cultural encounters are often established in what we might like to call pedagogic contact zones where mutual understanding may take place – at least partially. The potential of postcolonial texts for inter- and transcultural learning and the possibilities of connections between these newer postcolonial texts and transcultural learning have been received as fruitful.

Following a paradigm of Intercultural Communicative Competence Bredella's statement about the value of postcolonial and minority texts has reverberated in EFL literature. Postcolonial Literature in a broad sense has proved to be a highly productive paradigm with sub-topics featuring 'Black British Fiction' or 'Fictions of Migration'. The latter has been researched by Sommer (2001) and Freitag-Hild (2010) and is thematically not only a very current topic, but has already been mirrored in several anthologies put forward for the EFL classroom (see Korte / Sternberg 1997). Moreover, intermedial approaches and film analyses that have become increasingly important (see Lütge 2013) play a major role here. This includes films such as the almost notorious *Bend it like Beckham*, but also more recent film productions like Ayub Khan Dinh's *East is East*, Meera Syal's *Anita and Me,* turned into a film by Metin Hüseyin in 2002, or Mohsin Hamid's *The Reluctant Fundamentalist* and its 2012 film version. The latter was obligatory reading for the A-levels in North Rhine-Westphalia (Zentralabitur) in 2016, as part of the topic postcolonialism and migration – ethnic communities in 21st century Britain. Benjamin Zephaniah's poetry collection *We are Britain* and his novel *Refugee Boy* as well as Roddy Doyle's short story *New Boy* from 2005 and the film version from 2009 are other examples of connections between postcolonial texts and the EFL classroom.

Postcolonial theory has been challenged by hybridity as a concept. In fact, rather than two dichotomies of 'us' and 'them' fighting each other, diversity has come to the fore in a much broader sense. This is also true for developments in intercultural learning taking up postcolonial discourses and developing them into an understanding of transcultural learning. The shift of the prefixes 'from inter- to trans', a question posed by Werner Delanoy in his essay from 2013, illustrates the changing focus between different concepts of teaching cultural topics and indicates an ongoing discussion about the question of whether intercultural learning suggests a dichotomous view including essentialist notions of 'otherness', while transcultural learning may include more than that. At the same time, 'transcultural' as an umbrella term may also be thwarted for trying to comprise too much. The discussion about the adequate label for cultural learning in EFL and the underlying critique in this field has led to an increased awareness of the intricacies of teaching about culture. The question what the 'inter' actually stands for in intercultural learning and whether or not its extension into 'trans' clarifies or complicates the issue has not satisfactorily been answered yet. However, the two concepts interculturality and transculturality are not at all contradictory and belong together as part of an inseparable whole, which is why they must be interlinked in the interests of language and culture learning programmes (Eisenmann 2015: 222). The evolution of the prefixes, which does not exclude their individual importance, has been pointed out by Delanoy who suggests that "the time is ripe to make a transition from 'inter' to 'trans' to catch up with a changing world" (2013: 160). In this context, references to Wolfgang Welsch are numerous, as according to him

> transculturality is, in the first place, a consequence of the inner differentiation and complexity of modern cultures encompassing a number of ways of life and cultures, which may interpenetrate or emerge from each other (Welsch 1999: 194).

Welsch's concept of culture reflects processes of globalization and also includes references and links to concepts such as hybridity and 'third space', which describe postcolonial cultural developments from a cultural studies perspective. Internationally, one of the most influential scholars who worked on conceptualizations of cultures in a global age still is, however, Homi K. Bhabha, who in his seminal text *The Location of Culture* draws on ideas of Said to describe cultures within processes of hybridization (see Alter 2015). In the preface he links this hybridization to "global cosmopolitanism [...] that configures the planet as a concentric world of national societies extending to global villages" (Bhabha 1994: xiv). While the discussion about the right prefix, 'inter' or 'trans', and their potential development into yet another category, namely the 'global' dimension, is still ongoing in EFL contexts, it might be helpful to observe parallel discourses in postcolonial theory.

In fact, discussions about the adequacy of the terminology can also be witnessed in postcolonial studies. The label 'postcolonial' itself has been criticized for "embracing a vast diversity of cultural productions from very many different places and different histories under a single concept" (Döring 2007: 12). The obvious question here addresses the prefix again, the question what the 'post' in postcolonial stands for. While at first sight it may seem to imply an end to occupation or oppression, thus suggesting a chronological dimension, at closer inspection it rather stresses continuities and ongoing interactions between the colonizer and the colonized, as Mullaney suggests:

> It refers to what continues in the wake of colonization as what conditions pertain from first contact, to those conditions that are continually transformed and revivified by its powers in the aftermath rather than clearly demarcating the absence or withdrawal of colonial power as such. (Mullaney 2010: 3)

Additionally, the alternative label of the 'New Literatures' or the 'New English Cultures and Literatures' has been applied – again also alluding to the time dimension, but obviously deleting the 'colonial' part of the term. According to Schulze-Engler and Helff (see 2009: x), today the field of the 'New Literatures' has come to be seen as a world-wide network of Anglophone literatures and cultures with increasingly fuzzy edges. In fact, Indian authors not only write from India, but also from the Caribbean, from South Africa or elsewhere. Anglophone African literature extends to a variety of new diasporic locations in Europe and North America that have come into existence in the wake of migration, flight, and exile. Globally interlinked networks of ideas, texts and images are gaining importance. The idea of 'locating' culture and literature exclusively in the context of ethnicities or nations is rapidly losing plausibility throughout an "English-speaking world" (Schulze-Engler / Helff 2009: x) that has long since been multi-rather than monolingual.

On a different level, cultural difference can also be seen as a "moving target" in the context of "traveling cultures" (Clifford 1992) and "liquid modernity" (Bauman 2000). In fact, otherness may take place on different levels, in terms of ethnicity, gender, class or creed. An important aim, therefore, lies in the destabilization of the conventional binary model of 'self' and 'other', which has developed into one of the major aims in inter- and transcultural learning in an attempt to overcome stereotypes and long-established categories of cultural worldviews.

In the course of this development, the concept of 'writing back' (based on a famous quote by Salman Rushdie in a 1982 article in *The Times*) became widely known through the seminal study *The Empire Writes Back: Theory and Practice in Post-Colonial Literatures* by Ashcroft, Griffiths and Tiffin in 1989. 'Writing back' as a concept suggested a creative dialogue between cultures and led to reinterpretations of works from diverse backgrounds. While criticism of the earlier hegemonic colonial powers was exerted here, at the same time this was also about an establishment of identity which might belong to more than one cultural context. For EFL contexts postcolonial rewrites of original – traditional – texts were welcomed to the (inter-)cultural canon of literature in the classroom.

3. From Postcolonial Literature to Transcultural Learning – Shortcuts or Trodden Paths?

What Ngũgĩ wa Thiong'o (1986) called the need for "decolonising the mind" has been one of the driving forces of inter- and transcultural learning, in fact, it is an eminently important didactic task, not only considering the minds of people from former colonies but in developing an agenda for changing mind sets in EFL education. When extending our scope, we are faced with some of the key issues of language and culture teaching. Vital and controversial issues arise, leading to questions such as: "Which variety of English do we teach? What do we teach English for [...]? What do German school curricula prescribe, and where do they stand in need of further additions and adaptations?" (Eisenmann / Grimm / Volkmann 2010: ix)

It was in the 1990s that intercultural approaches to literary text became prominent. They reached a remarkable degree of recognition following the works of Lothar Bredella (Bredella 2002 and Bredella 2010abc), who was concerned with 'understanding otherness' and discourses surrounding the notion of the foreign language classroom as a hybrid 'third space' where learners must negotiate between the first culture and the foreign, the 'other' culture.

Bredella's notion of otherness is based on Gadamer's idea of a fusion of horizons, a merging of different concepts and implies the hybridization of viewpoints. It is opposed to concepts of the other's absolute otherness (Derrida 1982) or of concepts of otherness within the self (Kristeva 1991). Since the 1990s, the potential of postcolonial literature for intercultural learning – and recently with the addition of transcultural learning – has been transferred into the EFL classroom. As Bredella has pointed out,

> in the process of relating their own values and world views to the text, learners might change and co-ordinate perspectives and thus begin to understand the other culture. (Bredella 2002: 14).

The literary range of postcolonial experience is apt to promote various forms of multicultural learning in German schools – especially in classes with distinct patchwork identities. The increasing conviction that such a promotion of mutual understanding and empathy can largely be attributed to the converging interests of academic discourse and classroom discourse (Raddatz 2010: 147).

So according to Raddatz and following the ideas of Bredella, key parameters of postcolonial discourse such as identity and alienation, empathy and ethnocentrism are apt to trigger cognitive and affective learning processes. As Eisenmann points out, it is especially for adolescents and their crossing the threshold between childhood and adulthood that the postcolonial discourse about individual and collective processes of understanding is vital in overcoming traditional role schemata (Eisenmann 2015: 225).

In this vein, facilitating the development of transcultural awareness has often been associated with the teaching of texts of people from other cultures, often drawing from the field of children´s and young adult literature so as to even emphasise its pedagogic potential. Here, the vital role of the text corpus becomes obvious: postcolonial literature or "new literatures in English" which accentuates the recentness of their histories, or 'world literatures' which defines their 'global' nature and amplifies the geographic spread of colonialism, past and present (Mullaney 2010: 3f).

The underlying thought is based on at least two assumptions revolving around the idea of understanding otherness. I am deliberately summarizing them very poignantly:

a) It may seem that a kind of 'magic formula' for intercultural competence lies in the careful selection of the right text, which is likely to be found in the ever-growing corpus of postcolonial literature – if only we search well enough. Hence, the interest in questions of text selection has become more prominent in recent years. Questioning the 'old canon' from a didactic perspective does different things than questioning the canon from the perspective of literary studies.

b) Cultural difference is often posited as the starting-point for processes of intercultural learning. Misunderstandings or conflicts displayed in texts labelled as 'postcolonial literature' are supposed to be used as a source for pedagogic reflections. Cultural encounters in culture-clash-scenarios and their resolution or at least attempts for coming to terms with them – are very much in the centre of teaching.

While the goal of understanding 'other cultures' seems a perfectly reasonable procedure in literature and language teaching, there are good reasons to doubt whether the very idea of understanding 'other cultures' itself is conducive to reaching that goal. Considering the alleged 'shortcut' to inter- or transcultural learning via postcolonial literature may lead to more theoretical discussions considering the following questions:

a) The question of the literary canon

The so-called literary canon itself has come under discussion. New texts have apparently become a new rationale and starting-point for questioning the validity of the traditional text canon for the EFL Classroom.

b) Questions of identity formation, empathy, and changing power relations

In line with revisions of the canon, topics have been discussed considering aspects concerned with some of the big issues brought up in the context of 'understanding otherness' (*Didaktik des Fremdverstehens*). In the works of Lothar Bredella and others following his approach towards teaching literature and culture, the concept of empathy is central and relevant. Changing and coordinating perspectives in order to come to terms with other world views, life situations, human struggles and conflicts is vital. The selection of literature adhering to these concepts may lead to a neglection of other important aspects of literary quality.

c) Questions of teaching methodology

Considering text selection criteria based on a literary canon with postcolonial topics, multicultural settings, cross-cultural encounters and conflicts, the question arises how much this impacts on questions of teaching methodology. There may well be some kind of over-emphasis on postcolonial, intercultural encounters, culture conflict situations and an over-exposure of these 'difficult' topics in a well-meant but possibly counter-productive way.

Keeping these questions in mind it is important to be aware of the possible danger of alleged easy shortcuts or trodden paths – or truisms – about intercultural and transcultural learning with postcolonial literature. Should we in fact blindly follow them?

In recent years, transculturality has emerged as a new approach to culture particularly suited to exploring the hybridity of individual and collective identities and the cultural 'connection between things' in an increasingly globalized world. The 'New Literatures in English' provide a fascinatingly diverse corpus of literary texts. But it is important to keep in mind that they are neither simple expressions of 'those other cultures' conjured up by benign or malign alterity discourses, nor harbingers of a new global monoculture.

4. Pitfalls on the Road to Transcultural Learning?

One of the most important reasons for a close connection between postcolonial literature and transcultural learning as pointed out above might be seen in what has been welcomed as the opening of the canon, the potential of teaching about the changing world and its global interconnections and the alleged chances of changing the pupils' mind sets on their way towards what has been labelled the intercultural speaker or the global citizen.

If we step back and reconsider the role of postcolonial literature in ELT settings, it is particularly the normative framework that needs to be taken into account as a basic precondition for much of the theorizing in this field. Interculturality as an educationalist approach is always embedded within a framework of language policies which becomes manifest in curricular documents. The prescriptive character of any educational framework necessarily has a bearing on the criteria for text selection, the approach and the methodology applied. Given the fact that values, attitudes and beliefs are an important part of intercultural communication, particularly in educational settings, no neutral stance seems possible or desirable when it comes to considering the function of (postcolonial) literature in an EFL classroom.

The Common European Framework (CEFR) as the main tool for foreign language education is very explicit here:

> In an intercultural approach, it is a central objective of language learning to promote the favourable development of the learner´s whole personality and sense of identity in response to the enriching experience of otherness in language and culture. (Council of Europe 2001:1)

Promoting the favourable development of the learner's whole personality may be an extremely challenging task. Teaching and learning in the context of "the enriching experience of otherness" is at the same time a message and a goal for all language teachers with a clear bias for a value-oriented dimension. It is from the perspective of this inevitably normative framework in educational settings that we must be aware of at least two potential pitfalls on the road to transcultural learning via postcolonial literature:

1) The ontological dimension

   Postcolonial literature is supposed to provide opportunities for transcultural learning as much of the research literature in ELT suggests. Plots and storylines with intercultural topics, cross-cultural encounters and various fictions of migration may qualify for the inter- and transcultural classroom. The underlying assumption is that there is some kind of 'innate quality' of this literature – if only for improving one's (inter)cultural competencies. The idea that postcolonial literature provides opportunities for transcultural learning relies on the premise that these texts have a natural advantage over other texts and are more likely to initiate fruitful encounters with otherness – and possibly enriching experiences, as the CEFR suggests. In fact, this ontological dimension of the argument may not only functionalize literature for well-meant pedagogic purposes, but more importantly, it may completely ignore the fact that understanding otherness as an educational goal might sometimes be too naively transferred to the realms of the literary world. As Tobias Döring quite rightly points out,

> *All* readings of *any* book – with the possible exception of one's own diary – involve engagements with otherness, so that all efforts to give 'a meaning to the meaningless' [...] must lead us beyond our established sense of self, entangle us in wider networks and so lead us to confront, experience and remake difference. (Döring 2011: 205, emphases in the original)

Coming to terms with what otherness implies, how it should ideally be introduced into the foreign language classroom and, most importantly, what literature would have to look like in order to satisfy the needs of a transcultural EFL classroom, requires still far more theorizing *and* practical application likewise. Quick answers that seem to easily place any postcolonial literature within a pedagogic scenario might be seen as dubious. Not only should we remain aware of the literariness of postcolonial literature – we must consider that we are here faced with fiction. But the very definition of what otherness entails and how literature may depict, mirror and transport this rather abstract notion will not be limited to national or ethnic aspects of difference alone. Ascribing postcolonial literature the status of a universal remedy for intercultural learning purposes would indicate both a literary and a didactic misunderstanding.

2) Essentialist and reductionist dimensions

Well-meant pedagogical objectives of intercultural understanding may lead to an over-emphasis of texts focusing on culture clash situations and cultural misunderstandings – albeit their potential resolutions – and thus unwillingly reproduce stereotyped notions of cultural difference. Cultural essentialism and reductionist approaches to literature as a mere 'tool' for intercultural learning goals need to be taken seriously as potentially counter-productive forces possibly setting up binary oppositions.

The danger of using postcolonial literature as a quarry for inter- and transcultural learning purposes may not seem so obvious at once and it may be questionable to what extent this may in fact apply. However, the apparent shortcuts in the discourse should not neglect the two fundamental pitfalls inherent in some superficial interpretations of the alleged benefits of postcolonial literature for intercultural learning purposes. We should refrain from notions operating with the vision of an innate quality of postcolonial texts and on re-establishing essentialist readings in the classroom. In order to do so an awareness for one of the main tasks of all didactic efforts needs to be developed: How can we effectively reduce complexity without false or inadequate simplifications? If our aim is to overcome simple binarisms of 'us' and 'them' in postcolonial texts, what does this imply for the selection of literature? Would this have an effect on the criteria or on teaching methodology?

5. Winding Roads and Common Ground: Perspectives for ELT

If there is a lesson to be learnt from the current postcolonial discourse and its interface with literature didactics, it may be the common ground in terminology and the impact on a more differentiated awareness for new directions in academia and in application, in writing, teaching and reflecting the meandering (dis)course itself. A transcultural approach not necessarily replaces intercultural learning, but certainly transforms it, as Schulze-Engler (2011) has pointed out, and, in a similar vein, as Freitag-Hild (2010) has further supported this notion from an ELT perspective. Post-colonial studies have moved towards enlarged and less binary concepts of cultural hybridity turning against simplistic oppositions of 'us' and 'them'. Still, the truism of Cultural Studies – that nations are 'imagined communities' – may not have quite percolated to the level of intercultural learning and teaching (see Volkmann 2012), and the process seems far from 'resolved' in the sense that an easy transfer from postcolonial epistemologies into inter- and transcultural concepts in foreign language education seems to be accomplished.

However, we may tentatively come to the conclusion that – summing up previous research – some notable implications are clearly evolving in the ELT context:

- Decolonizing the mind – particularly by unlearning to view the world through the prism of Western hegemonic discourse – is not merely a matter for literary scholars, philosophers or politicians. It is an eminently important pedagogic task.

- Rather than laying bare 'other' cultures in an essentialist reading of postcolonial literatures and their challenges alongside sometimes exotic, nostalgic or even orientalist concepts of alterity, insights into the complexity of cultural topics are important teaching goals – both at university and school level. Challenging readers to come to terms with cultural difference on various levels is among the most important goals.
- The "unlearning of binarisms and othering" has been judged as an important precondition for the intercultural speaker, certainly also for the new concept of a "global citizen" (Lütge 2015) and should quite generally become an integral part of intercultural learning and teaching. It is not, however, just the process of 'unlearning' entrenched modes of perception and interpersonal discourses, but reading, listening and viewing in a new way. Most importantly, if the 'unlearning' process is not supposed to end in an uncritical and unanalytical approach to cultural learning, we must face the question of how a structured process can be initiated.

In order to support these goals, ELT approaches considering the impact of Postcolonial Studies might be structured along three stages that I have suggested elsewhere (Lütge 2013):

a) Culture-sensitive perception: representations of otherness

   Working on a culture-sensitive perception is an important part of inter- and transcultural teaching. Among other things, the dramatization of cultural and global topics in literature and in films should take into account the constructedness of all literary representation. Possible tasks may include questions like the following:

   - How are intercultural encounters dramatized?
   - What roles do specific nations/ethnicities play in the context of the text?
   - How are members of different ethnic groups depicted?

b) Evaluating cultural images and global views

   Coming to terms with and evaluating the representations put forward in literary text with regard to the depiction of cultural topics requires careful analyses which take into account literary devices and the focalization of attention in different narrative stances. Starting-points for discussions may include questions like:

- How does an author construct perceptions of cultural or global issues?
- Which solutions for global problems are offered? Are they culture-specific?
- Are there stereotypical views about cultural topics? What problems or topics are displayed most prominently? Are they connected with specific cultural backgrounds?
- Which characters are depicted positively/negatively? Can they be ascribed to specific cultural or ethnic groups?

c) Developing cultural and global awareness

Understanding ideological undercurrents and developing an awareness for cultural subtleties is an important goal that may be focused on in the literature classroom. Questions may include examples like the following:

- Are there clichéd views and conventions about the narrative?
- Does the text (or film) follow a specific ideology or a certain – culture-specific – bias?
- What narrative techniques are used to display cultural 'otherness'?
- Is the mode of presentation innovative or conventional?

The agenda for EFL research as informed by the trajectories of Postcolonial Studies must reach across disciplinary methodologies. Coming to terms with the complexity of cultural theories and the necessary simplification for classroom contexts may be one of the extremely difficult challenges to be mastered.

Furthermore, inter- and transculturality and the affordances of cultural learning on the one hand and the current competence discourse in ELT on the other are sometimes judged to be incommensurable discourses themselves. Can questions of identity, hybridity, cultural complexity, intertextuality and developing an understanding or at least awareness of cultural concepts ever be brought in line with issues of competence development, standardization, assessment, educational monitoring, efficiency orientation and testability?

Rather than establishing new dichotomies in ELT, we might in fact take into consideration other concepts such as global citizenship education or more broadly global education in EFL (Byram 2008, Lütge 2014). Rather than focusing on 'otherness', global approaches are more interested in commonalities, thus shifting the perspective away from differences between people, ethnic groups or between majorities and minorities towards an understanding of more comprising categories with transcultural interconnections beyond national lines of demarcation.

It seems high time to eventually broaden the scope of teaching and discus communication between heterogeneous cultures within the realm of postcolonial literature. Such an approach would in fact aim to reject traditional ways based on the paradigms of opposition, difference and conflict rather than cultural dialogues, fusions and translations from the vantage point of the global landscape of modernity.

Using one of Spivak's (1994) words, "how to read" – and teach, as I would like to add – "a culturally different text" will remain one of the big challenges for ELT in the future. The potential of postcolonial theory and postcolonial literature for the EFL classroom is considerable. It should not, however, be superficially and inappropriately functionalized. Rather than looking out for alleged shortcuts between postcolonial literature and transcultural learning we should be aware of the winding road touching upon both discourses – and their various crossovers.

Bibliography

Alter, Grit (2015). *Inter- and Transcultural Learning in the Context of Canadian Young Adult Fiction*. Münster: LIT.

Antor, Heinz (2006). *Multikulturalismus, Interkulturalität und Transkulturalität: Perspektiven für interdisziplinäre Forschung und Lehre.* In: Antor, Heinz (Ed.): Inter- und transkulturelle Studien. Theoretische Grundlagen und interdisziplinäre Praxis. Heidelberg: Winter, 25-39.

Ashcroft, Bill (2011). Reading the Other: Constitutive Transculturality in a Hong Kong Classroom. In: Doff, Sabine / Schulze-Engler, Frank (Eds.). *Beyond 'Other Cultures' – Transcultural Perspectives on Teaching the New Literatures in English.* Trier: WVT, 17-30.

Ashcroft, Bill / Griffiths, Gareth / Tiffin, Helen (2003). *The Empire Writes Back. Theory and Practice in Post-colonial Literatures.* London: Routledge.

Bauman, Zygmunt (2000). *Liquid Modernity*. Cambridge: Polity.

Beck, Ulrich (2008). *Weltrisikogesellschaft.* Frankfurt a. M.: Suhrkamp.

Bhabha, Homi K. (1994). *The Location of Culture.* London: Routledge.

Blell, Gabriele / Doff, Sabine (2014). "It takes more than two for this tango: Moving beyond the self/other-binary in teaching about culture in the global EFL-classroom." *Zeitschrift für Interkulturellen Fremdsprachenunterricht* 19(1), 77-96.

Bredella, Lothar (2010a). *Das Verstehen des Anderen. Kulturwissenschaftliche und Literaturdidaktische Studien.* Tübingen: Narr.

Bredella, Lothar (2010b). Trans- oder Interkulturalität als Bildungsziel des Fremdsprachenlehrens und -lernens? *ForumSprache* 4, 21-41.

Bredella, Lothar (2010c). How to Conceive of Intercultural Understanding. Considering the Tensions Between the Liberal and the Communal Concept of the Self? In: Antor, Heinz / Merkl, Matthias / Stierstorfer, Klaus / Volkmann, Laurenz (Eds.). *From Interculturalism to Transculturalism: Mediating Encounters in Cosmopolitan Contexts.* Heidelberg: Winter, 15-38.

Bredella, Lothar (2002). *Literarisches und interkulturelles Verstehen.* Tübingen: Narr.

Byram, Michael (2008). *From Foreign Language Education to Education for Intercultural Citizenship. Essays and Reflections*. Bristol: Multilingual Matters.

Clifford, James (1992). Travelling Cultures. In: Grossberg et al. (Eds.). *Cultural Studies.* New York: Routledge, 96- 116.

Council of Europe (2001). *Common European Framework of Reference for Languages: Learning, Teaching, Assessment (CEFR).* Strasbourg: Council of Europe.

Delanoy, Werner (2013). From Inter to Trans? Or: Quo Vadis Cultural Learning? In: Eisenmann, Maria / Summer, Theresa (Eds.). *Basic Issues in EFL Teaching and Learning*. Heidelberg: Winter.

Delanoy, Werner / Volkmann, Laurenz (Eds.) (2006). *Cultural Studies in the EFL Classroom.* Heidelberg: Winter.

Derrida, Jacques (1982). Différance. *Margins of Philosophy*. Chicago & London: University of Chicago Press.

Doff, Sabine / Schulze-Engler (2011). Beyond 'Other Cultures': An Introduction. In: Doff, Sabine / Schulze-Engler (Eds.). *Beyond 'Other Cultures' – Transcultural Perspectives on Teaching the New Literatures in English.* Trier: WVT, 1-14.

Döring, Tobias (2011). "A Meaning to the Meaningless". Anita Desai's Baumgartner´s Bombay. In: Doff, Sabine / Schulze-Engler (Eds.). *Beyond 'Other Cultures' – Transcultural Perspectives on Teaching the New Literatures in English.* Trier: WVT, 193-207.

Döring, Tobias (Ed.) (2007). *A History of Postcolonial Literature in 12 ½ Books.* Trier: WVT.

Eisenmann, Maria (2015). Crossovers – Postcolonial Literature and Transcultural Learning. In: Delanoy, Werner / Eisenmann, Maria / Matz, Frauke (Eds.). *Learning with Literature in the EFL Classroom.* Frankfurt a. M.: Lang, 217-236.

Eisenmann, Maria / Grimm, Nancy / Volkmann, Laurenz (2010) (Eds.). *Teaching the New English Cultures & Literatures*. Heidelberg: Winter.

Freitag-Hild, Britta (2010). Theorie, Aufgabentypologie und Unterrichtspraxis inter- und transkultureller Literaturdidaktik. *British Fictions of Migration* im

Fremdsprachenunterricht. *ELCH - Studies in English Literary and Cultural History* 42. Trier: WVT.

Gadamer, Hans-Georg (1997). *Truth and Method.* New York: Continuum.

Korte, Barbara / Sternberg, Claudia (1997) (Eds.). *Many Voices –, Many Cultures. Multicultural British Short Stories.* Stuttgart: Reclam.

Kramsch, Claire (1996). *Context and Culture in Language Teaching.* Oxford: Oxford University Press.

Kristeva, Julia (1991). *Strangers to Ourselves.* New York: Columbia University Press.

Lütge, Christiane (2015). Introduction: Global Eduaction and English Language Teaching. In: Lütge, Christiane. (Ed.). *Global Education: Perspectives for English Language Teaching.* Münster: LIT, 7-16.

Lütge, Christiane (2013). Global (Audio)visions: Teaching Cultural Studies through Film. In: Elsner, Daniela / Helff, Sissy / Viebrock, Britta (Eds.). *Films, Graphic Novels & Visuals. Developing Multiliteracies in Foreign Language Education – An Interdisciplinary Approach.* Münster: LIT, 141-153.

Mullaney, Julie (2010). *Postcolonial Literatures in Context.* London: Continuum.

Raddatz, Volker (2010): 'Gemeinsam sind wir stark.' Synergien von Fachdidsziplin und Fachdidaktik am Beispiel postkolonialer Literatur im Fremdsprachenunterricht. In: Caspari, Daniela / Küster, Lutz (Eds.). *Wege zu interkultureller Kompetenz. Fremdsprachendidaktische Aspekte der Text- und Medienarbeit.* Frankfurt a. M.: Lang, 147-156.

Said, Edward W. (1978). *Orientalism.* New York: Vintage Books.

Schulze-Engler, Frank / Helff, Sissy (2009). Introduction. In: Schulze-Engler, Frank / Helff, Sissy (Eds.). *Transcultural English Studies. Theories, Fictions, Realities.* Amsterdam: Rodopi, 9-19.

Sommer, Roy (2001). *Fictions of Migration – Ein Beitrag zur Theorie und Gattungstypologie des zeitgenössischen interkulturellen Romans in Großbritannien.* Trier: Wissenschaftlicher Verlag.

Spivak, Gayatri C. (1994). How to Read a 'Culturally Different' Book? In: Barker, Francis / Hulme, Peter / Iversen, Margret. *Colonial Discourse/Postcolonial Theory.* Manchester: Manchester University Press, 126-150.

Spivak, Gayatri C. (1990). Questions of Multi-Culturalism. In: Harasym, Sarah (Ed.). *The Post-Colonial Critic: Interviews, Strategies, Dialogues.* New York: Routledge, 59-66.

Thiong'o, Ngũgĩ wa (1986). *Decolonising the Mind.* Harare: Zimbabwe Publishing House.

Volkmann, Laurenz (2015). Literary Literacy and Intercultural Competence: Furthering Student's Knowledge, Skills and Attitudes. In: Delanoy, Werner / Eisenmann, Maria / Matz, Frauke (Eds.). *Learning with Literature in the EFL Classroom.* Frankfurt a. M.: Lang, 49-66.

Volkmann, Laurenz (2012). Intercultural Learning and Postcolonial Studies: "Never the Twain Shall Meet"? In: Eisenmann, Maria / Summer, Theresa (Eds.). *Basic Issues in EFL Teaching and Learning.* Heidelberg: Winter, 169-180.

Welsch, Wolfgang (1999). Transculturality – the Puzzling Form of Cultures Today. In: Featherstone, Mike / Lash, Scott (Eds.). *Spaces of Culture: City, Nation, World.* London: Sage, 194-213.

Authors

Christiane Lütge holds the Chair for Teaching English as a Foreign Language (TEFL) at the University of Munich.

Grit Alter is post-doctoral Researcher and University Assistant at the School of Education at the University of Innsbruck.

Kylie Crane is Junior Professor of Anglophone Literatures and Cultures at the University of Mainz, Germersheim.

Mark Stein holds the Chair of English, Postcolonial, and Media Studies at the University of Münster.

Peter Freese is Professor emeritus of American Studies at the University of Paderborn.

Susanne Reichl is Associate Professor in the Department of English at the University of Vienna.

Werner Delanoy is Associate Professor in the Department of English and American Studies at the University of Klagenfurt.